The Behavior of Pigeons
Posthumous works of Charles Otis Whitman

by Charles Otis Whitman
Edited by Harvey A. Carr

with an introduction by Jackson Chambers

This work contains material that was originally published in 1917.

This publication is within the Public Domain.

*This edition is reprinted for educational purposes
and in accordance with all applicable Federal Laws.*

Introduction Copyright 2017 by Jackson Chambers

Self Reliance Books

Get more historic titles on animal and stock breeding, gardening and old fashioned skills by visiting us at:

http://selfreliancebooks.blogspot.com/

Introduction

I am pleased to present yet another historic title on raising Pigeons.

The work is in the Public Domain and is re-printed here in accordance with Federal Laws.

As with all reprinted books of this age that are intended to perfectly reproduce the original edition, considerable pains and effort had to be undertaken to correct fading and sometimes outright damage to existing proofs of this title. At times, this task is quite monumental, requiring an almost total "rebuilding" of some pages from digital proofs of multiple copies. Despite this, imperfections still sometimes exist in the final proof and may detract from the visual appearance of the text. The original plates in these titles are often moved to the rear of the text to adhere to modern publication standards.

I hope you enjoy reading this book as much as I enjoyed making it available to readers again.

Jackson Chambers

PREFACE.

Under other circumstances the subject-matter of the present volume would have been much increased; it would doubtless have included ample treatises on the voice and on comparative behavior and voice as indices of species relationship and of the direction of evolution in pigeons. If Professor Whitman's term of life had but been extended by the years necessary merely to write up his own completed work, it is probable that this would have sufficed for the production of important treatises on these two last-named subjects. But the condition in which these two divisions of his studies were left has not permitted an extensive presentation by the hands of others. The manuscripts treating of behavior in pigeons were, however, far nearer to a definite and final form. It is chiefly this material that is here organized and made available to others.

Though the present volume deals with behavior—a topic seemingly quite distinct from the subjects of the previous volumes of this work—the reader of the earlier volumes will not fail to find occasional strands of continuity between those and this the last. He will, in some cases, here find orthogenesis applied in the fields of instinct and intelligence and will note here again a limited but possible rôle for natural selection. He will observe that in pigeon behavior and intelligence, origins again seem to reveal themselves as improvements and modifications rather than as chance-wise saltations. Behavior and voice characteristics are noted— though they are rather scantily discussed—to blend, as did nearly all of the characters previously treated, and the studies here recorded on the reproductive cycle furnish illuminating data, not elsewhere available, as to the mechanism by which "overwork at reproduction"—as shown in the second volume—produces "weakened germs." Though all of these elements of continuity are present, they are quite subsidiary in importance to the chief purposes of the volume, which are, to elucidate and interpret the behavior of doves and pigeons.

The completed manuscript, as it comes from the hands of Professor Carr, who has very generously and most conscientiously carried out the work of its preparation, can hardly give an adequate idea of the difficulties of his task. He merits much more than the thanks of all who may profit by this volume. Acknowledgments are made to the Open Court, and Ginn & Co.—publishers respectively of the Monist and of the Biological Lectures—for the privilege of republishing parts of two papers.

OSCAR RIDDLE.

EDITORIAL STATEMENT.

The material upon which this work on behavior is based is to be found, in the main, in 32 manuscripts varying in length from 1 to 40 pages. Professor Whitman's interest in the behavior of pigeons was evidently subordinate to his main tasks of a more biological nature. His work on behavior falls into two distinct periods. The first period includes the years 1895 to 1898. The greater number of the manuscripts bear these dates and consist of numerous short notes and descriptive material with some degree of topical arrangement. In 1897 and 1898 the author delivered lectures at Woods Hole on animal behavior; nearly half of these lectures were devoted to the pigeons. These two lectures were published in 1899, and from a perusal of the manuscripts it is evident that they were based to a large extent upon the studies made during the two preceding years. Soon after the above publication there appeared in the Monist, 1899, a short article on "Myths in Animal Psychology," a part of which again refers to pigeon behavior.

After an interval of 5 years the author's interest in behavior again recurs, and we find a second period of study covering the years 1903 to 1907. The manuscripts bearing these dates consist mainly of very detailed diary notes of the reproductive activities of several species of pigeons, and these, with one exception, were not summarized. From a remark in one manuscript (R 29) it is evident that at this time the author contemplated an extensive and intensive comparative study of the behavior of several species of pigeons. In August 1906 he delivered a lecture on "Examples of pigeon behavior" to a class at Woods Hole. This lecture was not published, and according to a note on the title-page it was delivered extemporaneously. This lecture evidently utilized data gathered during both periods of study.

A copy of Fulton's Book of Pigeons contains many marked passages, and on one of the fly-leaves was found in pencil a list of topics with their page references, evidently for the purpose of copying. As a consequence, the editor has felt at liberty to introduce several of these marked passages into the body of the present text; he has also incorporated those parts of Professor Whitman's two published articles on behavior which pertain primarily to pigeons. This has seemed advisable for two reasons: It brings together in one volume all of the author's material on behavior, and these writings furnish the reader the author's own interpretations and generalizations of the data of the manuscripts.

In organizing this heterogeneous material the editor has followed, in the main, the scheme made evident in various of the author's writings and in his final unpublished lecture. The material is thus grouped around the three main divisions: The Reproductive Cycle, Homing and Other Instincts, and the Relation of Instinct and Intelligence. In each of these divisions, as nearly as possible, the topical arrangement found in the manuscripts has been preserved. The first purpose has been to present a naturalistic account of the behavior of pigeons in Professor

EDITORIAL STATEMENT.

Whitman's own words. In general, each topic is introduced by one or more paragraphs from one of his lectures or writings, or from his best-formulated notes. Further illustrations are then given from other notes, or by condensed excerpts, digests, or tables constructed from records which had not been summarized. The editor has refrained from additional comment, except for the purpose of making the account as smooth as was possible under the circumstances.

It has been thought well to utilize all the collected material. Selection by other hands than by the author himself might twist and perhaps distort his meaning. Although this procedure, in many cases, introduced considerable repetition of the description of the same type of behavior, it possesses the advantage of giving the reader all of the material for reference, and an appreciation of the care, the detail, and the completeness of the observations upon which these studies were based.

In this section on behavior we have followed the procedure of the preceding volumes of adding at the end of each topic the folder designation from which the material was taken. Such symbols as R 33, B 2b, C 7/17, SS 10, etc., mean that the material to which they are attached can be found in manuscripts contained in folders thus designated by the author. In these cases the text represents approximately the author's own words. The reader must bear in mind, however, that in many cases these manuscripts contain "notes" of the roughest sort. We have deemed it advisable to publish the material in its original form whenever possible, and as a consequence only grammatical and rhetorical alterations of the more obvious sort have been attempted.

For the fuller illustration of many topics, we have grouped together, in a running fashion, numerous statements selected from various parts of a diary record, and these quotations have been designated as "excerpts." At times this procedure has not been possible and we have summarized the pertinent data of a record in our own words and characterized it at the end as a digest or summary. In the construction of the five tables of statistical data we have been compelled to gather the material from so many divers sources that the use of any folder designation for each item was impossible. In these tables, and elsewhere, species and genera are often referred to by their popular names; but the names they bear in zoological classification have been added at such points and intervals as to leave no doubt as to the identity of the form under consideration. In the previous volumes of this work this feature is adequately treated.

Besides those editorial comments necessary to secure a continuity of account of the material, we have added at the end of several chapters a brief summary of the various facts and principles developed, and in Chapter IX we have attempted a summary and analysis of the data of the previous eight chapters, which deal with the reproductive cycle. In the main the reader will have no difficulty in distinguishing between the author's material and those parts representing the words of the editor. In order to avoid any ambiguity, however, the two materials have been printed with different type.

EDITORIAL STATEMENT.

The entire task of compiling and editing Chapter X, Voice and Instinct in Pigeon Hybridization and Phylogeny, has been performed by Dr. Wallace Craig and Dr. Oscar Riddle. From the manuscripts and materials reviewed by them a number of excerpts have also been taken and utilized, under proper designations, in some of the other chapters. Dr. Craig, while studying pigeon behavior under the author's direction, made a practice of taking notes of his remarks during their conferences. From this material he has selected those observations closely related to the topics under discussion. This material has been inserted in the form of footnotes with the designation of "conv."

Any editorial criticism, evaluation, or interpretation of the results has been steadily avoided as far as possible. The single wish and hope actuating our labors has been to present this material to the reader in a serviceable form and to leave to him the final task of criticism and evaluation. Any evaluation of the material at the present time must consider the date of these manuscripts. The work began twenty-four years ago, two years before the appearance of Thorndike's monograph on "Animal Intelligence," which publication is generally regarded as the first experimental contribution to the subject of comparative psychology. Whitman's work was thus begun shortly after the appearance of the initial works of such authors as Romanes, Lubbock, and Lloyd Morgan.

I wish to express my appreciation of the courtesies extended me by the Station for Experimental Evolution of the Carnegie Institution of Washington, which have made this labor possible. Acknowledgments are also gratefully rendered to Dr. Riddle for his stimulating interest and suggestive help in the task.

HARVEY A. CARR.

UNIVERSITY OF CHICAGO, *January 1919.*

TABLE OF CONTENTS.

	PAGE
PREFACE, by OSCAR RIDDLE	iii
EDITORIAL STATEMENT, by HARVEY A. CARR	v–vii
CHAPTER I. The Mating Period	3–14
The Breeding Season	4
Prolongation of Breeding Season in Wild Pigeons	5
Length of Mating Period	6
Initiation of the Cycle	7
Manner of Display	10
Striking or Stamping	11
Charging and Driving	12
Periodicity of the Disposition to Fight	13
Jealousy	14
CHAPTER II. The Mating Period (continued)	15–26
Behavior in Uniting	15
Behavior of the Bronze-Wing	15
Comparative Behavior	17
The "Jumping Over" Phenomenon	18
Billing and "Feeding" by the Male in Mating Behavior	18
The Quest for a Nest	20
Nest-Building	21
On the Method of Nest-Building	21
On the Purpose of Nest-Building	22
Nest-Call	23
The Purpose of the Nest-Call	23
The Nature of the Nest-Call	23
The Nest-Call of the Male Bronze-Wing	24
Ground-Call of the Male Bronze-Wing	25
Nest-Call of the Female Bronze-Wing	25
Nest-Call and Mating Instinct in the Young	25
CHAPTER III. The Pairing of Pigeons	27–40
Influence of Behavior	27
Influence of Voice	28
Influence of Social Environment	28
Pairing of Females	28
Pairing of Males	35
Promiscuous Tendencies	36
Unusual Proclivities	37
A Special Case—not Aberrant Mentality	38
CHAPTER IV. The Incubation Period	41–52
Length of the Period	41
Number of Eggs	43
Time of Laying	43
Behavior in Laying	48
Time of Hatching	50
Method of Hatching	52
Increased Interest at Hatching	52
CHAPTER V. Incubation Behavior	53–62
Early Incubation	53
Typical Incubation Records	54
Roosting Habits	55
Alternation	56
Initiative in Interchange	57
Defective Alternation	58
Copulation	59
Nest-Building	59
Neatness in Nest	60
Influence of Temperature	61
Hiding on the Nest	61
Voice	61
Nest-Call	61
Alighting, or Short-note Call	62

TABLE OF CONTENTS.

PAGE

CHAPTER VI. Feeding and Care of the Young 63–71
  General Nature of the Activities 63
  Feeding of Young 65
  Anomalous Feeding Behavior 67
  Transference of Young to Foster Parents 68
  Voice 69
    Food-Call of Young 69
    Food-Call of Adult Bronze-Wing 69
    Feeding-Call of Bronze-Wing 70
    Resistance to Intruders 70
    Note of Alarm of Bronze-Wing 71
    Flock Whistle of Young Bronze-Wing 71

CHAPTER VII. Defective Cycles 73–86
  Bronze-Wing 73
    First Cycle 73
    Second Cycle 74
    Third Cycle 75
    Fourth Cycle 75
  Geopelia Humeralis 76
  Passenger-Pigeon Male and Ring-Dove Female 76
    First Cycle 76
    Second Cycle 77
    Third Cycle 78
  Crested-Pigeon Male and Ring-Dove Female 79
    First Cycle 79
    Second Cycle 81
  Blond Ring Male and White Ring Female 81
  Hybrid Male and Mourning-Dove Male 83
  Leucosarcia picata 83
  Mourning-Dove Male and White-Ring Female 83
  Homer Male and Hybrid Female 84
  Ectopistes 84
  Miscellaneous 84

CHAPTER VIII. The Genetic Standpoint in the Study of Instinct 87–91
  Genealogical History Neglected 87
  The Incubation Instinct 87
  A Few General Statements 90

CHAPTER IX. Reproductive Cycle—Summary and Analysis 93–110
  Descriptive Summary 93
  Species Differences 96
  Sex Differences 97
  Mating Preferences 98
  Fidelity of Pairing 101
  Functional Inter-Relationship of Activities 101
    Feeding 101
    Incubation 102
    Nesting 105
    Sexual Activities 106
    Egg-Laying 108
  Miscellaneous 109

CHAPTER X. Voice and Instinct in Pigeon Hybridization and Phylogeny 111–123
  On Species Relationships in Pigeons 112
  Voice and Instincts in Hybrids from Crosses of Species and Genera 113
    Hybrid between a Male *St. alba-risoria* and Female *Spil. suratensis* 113
    Male Hybrid between a Male Blond Ring and a Female Japanese Ring 114
    The Voice of Ring-Doves 114
  Voice and Instincts in Hybrids from Crosses of Families and Subfamilies 115
    Male Hybrid between Male Common Pigeon and Female Japanese Turtle 115
    Hybrid between a Male *Zenaidura carolinensis* and Female *St. risoria* 116
    Hybrid between a Male *Ectopistes* and a Female Ring-Dove 118
    Instincts in *Ectopistes* Ring-Dove Hybrids 118
  Voice and Behavior in Certain Wild Species 119
    Voice and Sexual Behavior of *Ectopistes* 119
    Voice of the Mourning-Dove (*Zenaidura carolinensis*) 121
    Voice of *Zenaida* 121
    Voice and Behavior of the White-Winged Pigeon (*Melopelia leucoptera*) 122
  Summary 123

TABLE OF CONTENTS.

	PAGE
CHAPTER XI. The Homing Instinct	125–136
General Principles	125
Illustrative Material	128
Memory	128
Orientation	132
Home Instinct	132
Lack of Intelligence	134
Summary	135
CHAPTER XII. Other Instincts	137–148
Tumbling and Pouting	137
The Instinct of Pouting	138
The Instinct of Tumbling	138
Sociability	140
Fighting	141
Fear	144
Food	144
Bathing	145
Instinctive Preferences	145
Appreciation of Height	146
Sleep	146
Modification of Instinct	146
Illustrations of Variation of Habits and Instincts—Induced and Spontaneous	147
Domestication of African Guinea-Pigeon	147
Summary	148
CHAPTER XIII. Habit, Instinct, and Intelligence	149–161
Habit of Place or Position	151
Recognition of Individuals	154
Imitation	156
Effects of Experience	156
Instinct and Intelligence	158
Experiment with Pigeons	159
The Step from Instinct to Intelligence	159

THE BEHAVIOR OF PIGEONS

POSTHUMOUS WORKS OF CHARLES OTIS WHITMAN

EDITED BY
HARVEY A. CARR, Ph.D.

VOLUME III

CHAPTER I.

THE MATING PERIOD.

The mating period refers to that part of the activities of the reproductive cycle which begins with courting and copulation and ends with the laying of the first egg. It embraces such activities as courting, copulating, and the hunting, acceptance, and construction of the nest. In the majority of cases its duration is six or seven days. The quest for a nesting-place begins one or two days after the initiation of the cycle and extends over a period of two to three days. The final acceptance of the nest-site is indicated by the beginning of nest-building. The construction of the nest continues for the rest of the period and may extend for several days into the incubation period. Copulation occurs intermittently throughout the entire mating period. These statements are based upon a very detailed record of the bronze-wing pigeon,[1] which covers a number of cycles. Excerpts from this record are herewith given in sufficient fullness to establish the above conclusions.[2]

First Cycle—Dec. 10, 1905. The male goes to the nest-box and calls. He attempts copulation. On the 13th copulation was successful. It was attempted on the previous days, but there was no certainty of its completion. On the 14th the nest was accepted and there was some nest-building. The 15th and 16th were occupied with nest-building and copulation, and the first egg was laid on the 16th.

Second Cycle.—On Jan. 1, 1906, the male was ready to begin a new cycle and kept attempting to entice the female. The young bird died on the 7th. Courting and attempts at copulation occurred on the 8th, and the first successful copulations were noted on the 9th. The quest for a nest was begun on the 10th, and this activity, interspersed with copulations, continued until the 13th. Nest-building was noted on the 13th and the 14th. The 15th and the 16th were occupied with nest-building in the forenoon and copulations in the afternoon. The first egg was laid on the afternoon of the 16th.

Third Cycle.—On Jan. 23, both birds were courting, but there was no contact. On the 25th they were interested in courting and copulation. Courting was continued without contact on the next day, when the egg was deserted. The quest for a nest was begun on the 27th, and the nest was accepted on the 30th. Nest-building began at once and successful copulations were noted. No records were made for Jan. 31 and Feb. 1. Nest-building was noted on the 2d, and the egg was laid on the day following.

Fourth Cycle.—Courting and attempted copulation by the male were begun on Feb. 21. The young died on the following morning, and the day was occupied by courting, copulation, and hunting for a nest. The quest for a nest was continued throughout the 23d and 24th, and the final acceptance of the nest was noted on the 25th. Nest-building was recorded on the 26th and the egg was laid on the 28th.

---

[1] The author remarked to one of his students (W. C.) that the bronze-wing pigeons (*Phaps, Ocyphaps*), coming from the Southern Hemisphere, at first bred in Chicago in winter, but that they gradually changed their cycles until they bred in summer.—EDITOR.

[2] In this volume the largest print represents the words of the editor. The author's material has been printed in a medium-sized type. The small type has been used for the tables, notes, and other incidental matter. With this typographical distinction the reader will be enabled to identify the manuscript material.

4 BEHAVIOR OF PIGEONS.

Fifth Cycle.—The pair was separated on March 16. They were brought together during the mornings of bright days in order to secure photographic records of their mating behavior. Both were ready to mate and copulated whenever brought together. On Apr. 26 they were paired again and courting began immediately. Copulations and acceptance of the nest were recorded on the 28th; and on May 3 the first egg was laid. (Excerpts from R 33.)

THE BREEDING SEASON.

The manuscripts contain but few statements as to the normal breeding-season for the various species of pigeons. Table 1 has been compiled from the various

TABLE 1.—*The breeding season.*

Species.	Time of first egg of season.	Time of last egg of season.
Passenger (*Ectopistes*)		8/29/96
" "	3/17/97	8/28/97
" "	7/14/98	8/ 7/98
" "	2/24/99	
Geopelia humeralis	1/13/06 (kept in house)	3/10/06
Bronze-wing (*Phaps*)	12/16/05 (kept in house)	5/16/06
White-face (*L. picata*)	4/11/07	6/ 2/07
Fantail (common pigeon)		9/22/98
Crested (*Ocyphaps*)	7/25/96	
" "	2/ 4/97	5/22/97
" "	2/23/98	
Mourning-dove (*Zenaidura*)	3/24/97	8/ 4/97
" "		8/ 8/98
" "	4/26/97	8/18/97
" "	3/15/98	7/30/98
" "	4/ 3/99	7/29/99
" "	4/13/00	7/12/00
Band-tail (*C. fasciata*)	2/11/03	
Wood-pigeon (*C. palumbus*)	1/ 8/01	
Satinette (common pigeon)	3/22/98	
Common pigeon	2/28/97	8/12/97
European turtle (*T. turtur*)	5/31/97	6/ 2/97
Blond rings (*St. risoria*)	3/12/95	12/23/95
" "	5/12/96	12/25/96
" "	2/ 8/96	
" "	1/28/97	6/ 4/97
" "	1/ 1/97	4/21/97
" "	3/ 5/97	6/ 8/97
" "	1/26/06	
Zenaidura ♂ × white ring ♀	1/ 8/97	3/10/97
" "	4/19/97	5/ 1/97
" "	6/16/98	
White fantail ♂ × ring-dove ♀	1/ 2/97	8/ 2/97
Common ♂ × ring-dove ♀	5/ 3/96	12/22/96
"	1/23/97	8/22/97
Jap. tumbler ♂ × ring ♀	7/23/97	12/15/97
"	1/20/98	2/21/98
Common ♂ × blond ring ♀	1/12/98	
Archangel ♂ × blond ring ♀	2/18/97	8/31/97
Ectopistes ♂ × ring ♀	2/24/97	6/29/97
Ectopistes ♂ × bl.-wh. ring hyb. ♀	1/26/97	8/15/97
"	3/24/98	
Homer ♂ × blond ring ♀	3/11/97	5/ 2/97
"	3/24/97	6/28/97
"	6/ 5/97	8/ 5/97
Common ♂ × Jap. turtle ♀	9/ 6/97	12/20/97
Hyb. ring ♂ × homer ♀	6/16/97	12/18/97
"	1/ 9/98	2/12/98
Blond ring ♂ × white ring ♀	11/27/96	
Red ring [1] ♂ × blond ring ♀	12/20/00 (kept in house)	8/30/01

[1] Most of the species listed here, besides several others, have been drawn in color; these illustrations are given in Volumes I and II of these works.—EDITOR.

THE MATING PERIOD. 5

breeding-records, giving the dates for the first and last eggs for the year. Too much reliance may not be placed upon these data. Frequently the birds were not together early in the year, being mated late in the season, and as a consequence the date of the first egg is often not a true index of the beginning of the season. In some cases the records state that the birds were kept in the house, and this special care may have accentuated, in some pairs, the early development of the breeding impulse. As to the location of the birds, within or out of doors, there is no indication in many of the records. Frequently the pairs were separated and remated during the season for experimental purposes and, from the manuscripts dealing with behavior, no clue can be obtained as to the normal end of the season.[1] Further, experimental control and quasi-domestication (see following topic) may profoundly influence the duration of the season. Besides the table referred to above, the following comment is given:

During 1898 not an egg was laid by the passenger-pigeons until July 14. One was laid on July 15, and the remaining pairs soon became active. Why they began so late I do not know. They were brought to Woods Hole, May 25, and should have begun to lay in April at the latest. Possibly I fed them too much corn or too much in general. I ceased giving them corn about the end of June and lessened the amount of seed given. I do not know whether the laying was brought about by the change, but think it probable. In the season of 1899 the first egg from these birds was laid on Feb. 24, and the second on Mar. 1. Perhaps the late and small work of the previous year led to an earlier activity this year. The birds have been in the pen outside all winter, and it is the coldest winter experienced here for many years.

A mourning-dove × ring-dove pair (*Zen. 5-C*) failed to fertilize eggs after August, the end of the regular season for the mourning-dove. Eggs were laid September 5 and 7, after the mourning-dove ceases normally to coo or care for eggs. (R 19, R 11.)

"Fancy pigeons generally show an inclination to mate together some time in the month of February; but much depends upon the temperature, as in very severe weather they will sometimes show no signs of doing so until March, whilst if it be mild some birds, if allowed, would go to nest in January."[2]

PROLONGATION OF BREEDING SEASON IN WILD PIGEONS.[3]

A pair consisting of a mourning-dove and a ring-dove[4] was mated in April 1899. Three sets of eggs were produced and incubated by the end of August. Four sets of eggs were laid between Sept. 8 and Dec. 23, but all failed of development. The male continued to sit faithfully until the first week in November, but after that time he lost interest and performed his incubation duties very irregularly. It is noted that "this pair, although remarkably successful in fertilizing and hatching during the normal season, failed after August, *i.e.*, at the end of the regular season for the mourning-dove."

Another similar pair was also mated in April of the same year. Six young were raised by Nov. 1. A pair of eggs was laid on Nov. 15 and 17 and these were successfully incubated by the male up to Dec. 17, when they were removed. Another set of eggs was produced on Dec. 23 and 25 and the male exchanged faithfully until the removal of the eggs on

---

[1] A large number of complete and reliable data on this topic may be found in Volume II. The designations of pairs of birds—*e.g.*, *Zen. 5-C*—which are often appended in this volume, will enable those who care to do so to make further examination of the entire breeding record, as this is given in the previous volume.—EDITOR.

[2] Fulton and Lumley's Book of Pigeons, London, 1895, p. 35.

[3] For a further reference to this phenomenon, see wood-pigeon, Vol. II, table 87.—EDITOR.

[4] In these designations the name of the male is written first, that of the female last. The same order is used in referring to hybrids.—EDITOR.

2

6 BEHAVIOR OF PIGEONS.

Jan. 6, 1900. The male sat faithfully in October 1900, but two succeeding sets in November and December received no attention from him. In 1901 the sitting continued until December. It is noted that "the mourning-dove normally ceases to coo or care for eggs after Sept. 1. This late and regular sitting is remarkable, showing that the normal period can be prolonged as a result of domestication. Notice that this 'prolongation' is in a case where the male is unusually successful in fertilizing the ring-dove's eggs." (Excerpts from R 11.)

LENGTH OF MATING PERIOD.

The mating period[1] has a duration of 5 to 9 days; in the majority of cases its duration is 6 or 7 days. Apparently, no species differences exist. The average time for all cases after May is slightly less than that for the extremely early part of the season, but the difference is so slight that no confident assertion can be made. Table 2, giving exact data for several species, has been compiled from the various

TABLE 2.—*Length of mating period.*

Species.	Date of first egg.	Length of period.
Bronze-wing	12/16/05	6 days after mating.
"	1/16/06	8 days after first courting.
"	2/ 3/06	8 days after desertion of eggs.
"	2/28/06	6 days after death of young.
"	5/ 3/06	8 days after pairing.
Geopelia humeralis	1/31/06	8 days after breaking eggs.
" "	2/31/06	10 days after breaking eggs.
" "	3/ 8/06	7 days after desertion of eggs.
" "	4/15/06	7 days after death of young.
Blond ring ♂ × white ring ♀	4/ 9/96	6 days after mating.
Band tail	2/11/03	9 days after beginning nest.
Fantail	8/19/96	6 days after removal of egg.
"	9/22/96	7 days after ceasing incubation.
Zenaidura	4/21/97	9 days after mating.
"	4/26/97	5 days after breaking egg.
"	5/27/97	9 days after leaving young.
"	7/14/97	17 days after breaking egg.
"	4/ 9/98	7 days after breaking egg.
"	4/22/98	9 days ca. after breaking egg.
"	7/ 3/98	7 days after removal of young.
Zenaidura ♂ × white ring ♀	1/ 8/97	7 days after first copulation.
"	3/ 7/97	6 days after removal of egg.
"	3/18/97	6 days after removal of egg.
"	4/19/97	7 days after mating.
"	6/16/98	6 days after removal of eggs.
"	6/26/98	6 days after removal of eggs.
Zenaidura ♂ × blond ring ♀	11/25/99	8 days ca. after removal of eggs.
"	12/21/96	6 days after removal of eggs.
Zenaidura ♂ × ring dove ♀	12/23/99	6 days after removal of eggs.
Ectopistes	7/29/96	9 days after pairing.
"	8/29/96	6 days after first billing.
"	3/17/97	6 days after first courting.
"	4/ 4/97	8 days after removal of egg.
"	4/22/97	5 days after removal of egg.
"	4/28/97	5 days after removal of egg.
"	5/23/97	5 days after first courting.
"	5/30/97	7 days after removal of egg.
"	6/24/97	12 days after hatching of young.
"	8/16/97	7 days after pairing.
"	7/20/98	7 days after removal of egg.
"	7/27/98	7 days after removal of egg.
"	7/25/98	6 days after breaking egg.
"	7/31/98	6 days after removal of egg.
"	8/ 7/98	7 days after removal of egg.

[1] That is, the portion of each reproductive cycle during which copulation occurs.

THE MATING PERIOD. 7

records. The length of this period for females of various kinds, and variously mated, was given the following tests:

On Oct. 16, 1897, I removed the eggs from the following four pairs: (1) a male common dove and a female Japanese turtle; (2) a male archangel and a female ring-dove; (3) a male hybrid between a common pigeon and a ring-dove and a female black Japanese tumbler; (4) a male ring-dove and a female homer. On Oct. 23, or *7 days* after the removal, all of the four females laid again. Thus a Japanese turtle-dove (*Turtur orientalis*) a ring-dove (*Streptopelia risoria*), a tumbler (*Columba gyrans*), and a homer (*Columba tabellaria*) all took the same time.

On June 10, 1898, the eggs were removed from four pairs which had laid between June 1 and 5. The four pairs were: (1) a male mourning-dove and a female white ring-dove; (2) a male mourning-dove and a female ring-dove; (3) a male hybrid and a female ring-dove; (4) a male mourning-dove and a female ring-dove. A second set of eggs was produced by each of these four pairs in *six days* after the removal of the eggs. The first egg in each case was laid at about the same hour ($3^h 16^m$ to $5^h 05^m$) in the afternoon of June 16; and the second egg at also about the same hour ($7^h 50^m$ to $8^h 05^m$) in the morning of June 18, after an interval of one day and two nights. The conditions of temperature and food were here the same for all. The time required for producing new eggs is sometimes only 5 days, but in colder weather it is sometimes 7 or 8 days.[1]

On June 20 I removed the eggs from the following pairs: (1) a male mourning-dove and a female white ring-dove; (2) a male hybrid and a female ring-dove; (3) a male mourning-dove and a female blond-white hybrid; (4) two blond-white hybrids. These had laid between June 16 and June 19. Eggs were produced in three cases on June 26, *six days* after the removal. In the fourth case, the female persisted in sitting for several days after the removal, and the first egg was dropped on July 2, after a 12-day interval.

A pair of European turtle-doves (*Turtur turtur*) laid eggs on June 3 and 5 and the young were removed on June 26. The first egg of the succeeding cycle was laid on July 2, or *six days* after the removal of the young. (Summarized from R 19.)

Fulton, in his Book of Pigeons, p. 37, states that:

"Most pigeons[2] lay in from 8 to 16 days after being mated, some being what are called much 'freer breeders' than others. If a hen does not lay within three weeks of mating she should be separated from the cock for about 8 days and then returned to him, which will usually produce eggs."

INITIATION OF THE CYCLE.

The male usually takes the initiative in beginning the cycle, and the female may succumb to his advances at once or she may resist for some time. The female may also take the initiative and make advances, the male in the meantime being on the defensive. Either bird may thus remain in a state of readiness for a considerable period of time. If a pair, when ready, are prevented from mating by being separated, both birds may remain in a state of readiness for a month or longer. The primary sexual impulse seems to arise relatively automatically, and the succeeding activities of the cycle must normally await the reciprocal sexual activities of the two birds. Since the primary impulse may arise at different times in a pair of birds, this ability for either to remain in a state of readiness for some time is the means by which the two series of activities become synchronized with each other.

---

[1] After breaking up a nest the birds will often start a new cycle of copulations within half an hour.—EDITOR.

[2] Common or "fancy" pigeons are referred to here. The several species concerned in the preceding paragraphs and studied by the author, are more popularly known as "doves" of various kinds.—EDITOR.

8   BEHAVIOR OF PIGEONS.

The hypothesis that the sexual impulse arises relatively automatically with each bird does not imply that the two birds do not stimulate each other to any extent. While synchronization is normally effected, yet exceptions occur and the cycle may progress with one bird lagging a few days behind the other. Neither will a bird *always* remain in the first stage of readiness until the succeeding activities of the cycle are released by the reciprocal activity of the mate. Occasionally the cycle may progress to completion without the coöperation of a partner. These statements are illustrated by the following excerpts from the manuscripts.

A pair of *Geopelia humeralis* were put together on Dec. 23, 1905. On Dec. 26 it was noted that the male had every day shown some interest in nesting, but that the female did not seem to be ready. On Jan. 9, 1906, it was noted that the male had kept up his endeavors to interest his mate in a nest, but that so far she had remained indifferent. The first egg was laid on Jan. 21. Allowing 7 to 8 days as the normal time between the beginning of mating and the laying of the first egg, there was a period of about 3 weeks in which the female remained indifferent to the advances of the male. In the third cycle for this pair the female resisted the male's attentions for several days, while in the second and fourth cycles both birds seemed to be ready simultaneously.

In a bronze-wing pair the male took the initiative in all five cycles. The period of feminine resistance varied from 1 to 7 days. On the last cycle the pair was separated on March 16, 1906, just as they were beginning a new cycle. After a separation of 15 days they were brought together for a short time and courting began immediately, both birds seeming to be ready to continue the cycle. They were tested from time to time up to April 28, and both exhibited some interest in mating. They were now left together permanently and the new cycle started at once. Both birds thus remained in a state of more or less readiness for a period of 45 days.

A male mourning-dove (*Zen. 3*) was paired with a white ring-dove (*W 1*) on December 20. The female was eager to mate, and tried all possible ways to ingratiate herself in the favor of the male. He refused to have anything to do with her until 12 days later. On this date (Jan. 1), the female advanced to within a few inches and began billing her wings, bowing, cooing, and casting amorous glances. He soon began to be attracted, billed his wing, and showed that he was yielding. When she touched his head with her beak he repelled her by pecking because of fear. After these maneuvers were continued for 15 or 20 minutes he finally had the courage to take her beak in his, and thereupon the consummation followed quickly. I am quite certain that this was the first time that a union had taken place. On Jan. 5, *W 1* is still doing most of the courting. She is wonderfully persistent, taking no discouragement from any rebuff. On Jan. 20 I saw the male courting the female for the first time. This pairing was never successful. Although unions occurred, the eggs did not develop for lack of fertilization, and the male took no part in incubation. After $3\frac{1}{2}$ months (of trial) he was given another female.

A young male fantail was paired on Aug. 13 with an impure fantail female which had previously mated and had been incubating eggs with another female. Two days later this female took the initiative and attempted to mate with the male. He was quite bashful at first, and although pleased with the advances, appeared to fear to let her come very near. He fought her off the stand and would not let her remain a moment in the cot. During the day he became more enamoured and by degrees suffered her to approach him, but always retreated at the moment she offered her beak, or else attacked her as if not yet quite sure that she could be trusted. This behavior continued throughout the day. On the following day, they were both coquetting and billing, and seemingly fully mated.

THE MATING PERIOD. 9

Three days later (Aug. 19) the first egg was laid, but the male did not begin to assume his duties of incubation until two days after the second egg was dropped.

The female of a blond and white ring-dove pair was nearly ready to lay and was inclined to mate. The blond male was savage and would not tolerate her presence; I was therefore forced to keep her in a small cage within his cage. On the following day he was still intolerant, but began to yield a little; he went to the box and called. She at once responded, went to him, tried to take the nest, and began cooing in her turn. The male endured this for a time and then drove her off. He next went to the opposite nest-box and repeated the same behavior with her. The white ring was patient and took all his abuse, and by night the blond finally became reconciled to her and condescended to sit beside her. (Excerpts from R 29, R 33, C 7/7, C 7/33, C 7/15.)

That females may take the initiative in mating is also evident from the fact that two females may mate and complete the cycle of nest-building, production of eggs, and incubation. (See topic on Pairing of two females, Chapter III.)

The completion of the cycle without the stimulus of a mate is illustrated by the following references: "Indeed a young and rank hen (domestic pigeon) will often lay, like a fowl, whether she be mated or not."[1]

A male hybrid (mourning-dove $\times$?) was paired with a California mourning-dove which was supposed to be a female, but which turned out to be a male also. The hybrid attempted courting during an entire month, but his advances were repelled. He then began the course of incubation on the floor of the cage. I soon saw by his behavior,— i.e., his refusal to move and threatening to peck at me—that he was actually engaged in sitting, although he as yet had no mate and no eggs. This cock had never been mated, and I was surprised to find him sitting with all earnestness, and that too on the floor, instead of in the nest-box. He went on sitting in this way night and day for a week, when I placed a couple of eggs in his nest-box and placed him upon them. He at once took possession and continued his incubation faithfully night and day for a week, when I placed the two birds in another pen outside of the house in the hope of securing a mating. (Excerpts from C 7/48.)

The lack of a proper synchronization of the two cycles of activities in a pair of birds is illustrated by the following note. For a more detailed account, the reader is referred to the record of pair X-W 1 in Chapter VII. The female W 1 had been with another female and had started on her cycle. When paired later with the male (X) she was nearly ready to lay. She at once made advances, but he was intolerant and resisted. He first began sexual advances about the time the first egg was dropped, and continued these for four or five days, while the female had passed through her sexual period and was engaged in the work of incubation. Only at the end of his sexual period did the male first take part in incubation; this was three days late.

This male (X) was evidently not in the spirit of sitting, and the presence of the egg did not stimulate him to the act. The decisive stimulus for such an act is thus not external but internal—probably a feeling which comes over a male *periodically*, and which he will manifest perhaps only if the external stimulus is also present. He has no impulse to sit. He is ready for making a nest and to accept a mate, but he requres *time to*

---

[1] Fulton, *op. cit.*, p. 35.

10   BEHAVIOR OF PIGEONS.

generate the impulse to sit. This impulse naturally follows the period of sexual activity, and he was still in the latter period.

In a brief note under the heading of "Sexual periodicity," it is remarked that "this (sexual periodicity) is apparent especially in Australian pigeons—speckled-necks, geopelias, crested pigeons, etc. It is also marked in *Ectopistes*. The wood-pigeon and mourning-dove are good examples."[1]   (R 20, C 7/15.)

MANNER OF DISPLAY.

The crested pigeon (*Ocyphaps*) has a very striking mode of display. The tail is raised and spread, and at the same time the wings are lifted just enough to show the whole surface. The bird bows and coos and strikes its feet, and all these movements are rhythmically combined in a very effective way. I noticed one of the *Geopelia humeralis* also performing by quite the same combination of movements. One of the *Geopelia striata* has exhibited itself in the same way, and with a peculiar coo. It is remarkable that two genera so different as *Ocyphaps* and *Geopelia* should have the same peculiar manners.

Darwin had a red tumbler which had a coo like the "laughter," and "the habit, to a degree which I never saw equalled in any other pigeon, of often walking with its wings raised and arched in an elegant manner." (See Darwin, Animals and Plants, I, Chapter V, p. 198.) I have seen this in a white fantail and in a black tumbler (Japanese), and also in a white and crested male dove-cote pigeon. It is quite common behavior. It is done usually when a male sees a female—or a male—whose attention he wishes to attract.

In giving the "coo" to the female, the male *G. humeralis* bows and follows the female *with the tail raised to about 45 degrees or a little more, or nearly vertical, and spread,* so as to show it to the best advantage. He uses it in the same way when trying to drive another cock. So the same behavior serves at least two purposes—one to frighten and the other to display.

I saw this display first in the male bronze-wing. This male was on the ground; the female was on the step-ladder looking down, as if about to fly down to the male. He noted this and began to display as if to attract her. He faced her, held his head on a line with his body, raised the wings without spreading or only a very little; raised his tail a little and held it spread; and meanwhile he stood actually on tip-toes and lifted first one and then the other foot, and so raised one side of the body and then the other in a way to exhibit his iridescence in different lights. This performance is remarkable—so well adapted to the end it serves. As the male wags his whole body slowly from side to side, he moves his head and neck back and forth from side to side. The lifting of the foot with the side raised, and then the other foot and side, right and left alternately, is done with an exquisite lightness of foot, as if the bird were overflowing with delight at the approach or the prospect of approach of his mate. I have seen this done by three males within a week or two, and by one of them several times.

A male mourning-dove (11) walks slowly and grandly along the perch, displaying himself to the female. She does not at once respond. He is anxious to mate, and shows no disposition to be aggressive, or to force her in any way. He sits at a little distance, watches her, now and then wags his wing at her, preens his feathers, inviting her to him. When he walks back and forth he raises the feathers of his back and rump, swells up his neck, and makes himself generally attractive. In strutting the wings droop a little, the primaries being held a little lower and not quite so tightly closed as ordinarily. The feathers of the back project backwards, rising above the level of the wing-feathers. The male sometimes flies to a point nearer the female, and as he alights *strikes* his feet against the perch, spreads his tail, and raises his wings a little, so as to show them and the tail at the

---

[1] For sexual periodicity in man, see Loisel, Comptes Rendus, Oct. 29, 1900.

THE MATING PERIOD.   11

same time. This combination of movements is often seen in male domestic doves. I noticed that when the female came to his call in the box the male winked (half closing and opening his eye-lids) and smiled (slightly opening his beak), expanding the lower mandibles so that we could almost see into his mouth. The California mourning-dove male performed in all these ways toward me when I answered his call.[1]   (R 20, R 17, R 29, E 28, Em 7.)

STRIKING OR STAMPING.

A male *G. humeralis* is mated with a blond ring-dove. This pair is kept in a pen in the library. The male has just flown up from the floor to the perch beside the female. As he alighted he arched his neck proudly and gave the perch several quick strokes with his feet; I think both feet were used in alternation. The strokes could be heard very distinctly. The mourning-dove behaves in the same way when he alights beside his mate and sometimes he does this when both are on the floor. He runs up alongside his mate and gives these strokes as if in a burst of joy to be with her. The crested pigeon and the geopelias do this also.

A male mourning-dove flies from his perch to the nest-box and then back again near to his mate; each time, as he alights, he lifts each foot once, one after the other, and strikes it against the perch so as to make quite a loud thump, or rather two thumps in quick succession. It is done so quickly that it is difficult to see the movement, although the sound is quite marked. The crested pigeon strikes his feet in quick succession when spreading and cooing before his mate. I think the ground-dove of Florida does something of this kind, but I have only an indistinct recollection of it. *G. humeralis* does the same. *Leucosarcia* stamps once with each foot, one after the other, and holds its head down and its tail raised when it threatens to attack. This is sometimes repeated two or three times, the bird watching its antagonist to see if it shows signs of fear. If it does not take the hint, this may be followed up by a raising of a wing as if to strike. In presenting the wing, the bird moves sidewise up close to his antagonist before striking just like the crested pigeon. The stamping, the lowering of the head, and the raising of the tail seem here to be a modified form of the display of the crested pigeon.

A male *G. humeralis* began early in the morning to parade on the perch before the female; his performance settled into a repetition of jumping from one perch to the other, then stamping with his feet as he straightened up, and presenting always his beak to the female.

The stamping behavior of a mourning-dove (3) was observed. Each time that this male alighted on the perch he *struck his feet against the perch*; one foot being made to strike after the other. The two strokes were quickly made and were loud enough to be heard quite distinctly. At the moment of alighting he "swelled up" a little, held his tail somewhat expanded, and raised his head with an expression of pride in his appearance. The male mourning-dove No. 11 also *strikes* his feet against the perch as he alights, spreads his tail and raises his wings a little, so as to show them and the tail at the same time.

The behavior of the white-faced pigeons (*Leucosarcia*) in mounting reminds one strongly of the bronze-wing (*Phaps*) and of *Geopelia*; it is, in fact, essentially the same. The male white-face usually flew to a wide shelf (12 inches) 5 or 6 feet from the floor. He then struck his feet a few times in rapid succession against the shelf, so that one could hear the thumps plainly across the yard, even at many yards distance. When the male flew up and the female was already on the shelf the latter would straighten up and strike her feet on the shelf; then turn her back with the tail held down, the head up, and the tail spread just a little; then walk off, wheel around, and run up to him—stamping her feet. The male then would offer his beak, she would accept, and be fed with a few shakes,

---

[1] Further material on this and the following topic may be found in Chapter X.

BEHAVIOR OF PIGEONS.

then he would press his neck over hers, and, if she inclined, would mount. After waiting for a few moments on her back, he would dismount with a slap of his wings over his back. As he struck the shelf after dismounting he opened his mouth and gave a squawk somewhat like the bronze-wing, and would strut away from her. The pair would then bow, approach, strike their feet on the shelf, and repeat the mounting, often several times without a single union. (R 20, R 29, C 7/7, Em 7, Sh 8/13.)

CHARGING AND DRIVING.

The charging and driving of the female occurs when other males are present, as is noted in the subsequent topic on "Jealousy." The same activity occurs during the mating period in connection with courting, the quest for a nest-place, and in nest-building. It may also occur occasionally even during the incubation period. The purpose of the act is to force the female to the nest.

A male bronze-wing began to *charge* at the female, driving her quite vigorously. He evidently recognized her as his mate, but for some reason not clear he *charged* at her as if displeased at something. As soon as the birds were put together in the same cage the male began to *charge* the female, though they soon began their love-making and for two hours they kept up hugging, etc. The male began by charging, clucking all the time as he drove the female. It was more evident now that he wanted to start the female off *for a nest-place.* (Excerpts from fifth cycle, R 33.)

On January 13 and 14, 1906, the male bronze-wing was again seen driving the female. He would charge at her with his wings lowered a little and his back and feathers elevated, emitting a short cluck so rapidly as to leave nearly no interval between them. The notes and manner appear petulant. (From second cycle, R 28.)

The following description, covering the period from Jan. 29 to Feb. 2, 1906, refers to a pair of bronze-wings while seeking and building a nest (during the third cycle). On Jan. 29 the male is anxious to build a nest. The birds have been uneasy for 3 or 4 days, running along the side of the pen next to the window, as if they desired to get out. They have been in the nest-box several times, but have not yet decided to accept it and begin work. The male just now took to driving the female, charging at her, and giving her a spiteful peck, as if for some reason displeased with her. I then saw him do what I have not before noticed. He first charged at her; then lowered his head until his beak *touched and rested on the floor,* and with tail raised and slightly spread and wings a little raised, he gave plainly two little coos, in doing which he opened his beak at each note *without once lifting his beak.* The beak opens but little. The notes sounded like oo-oo, with a very short but distinct separation between the syllables—the first shorter, the second somewhat fuller and longer. This could be called the "driving coo," and is analogous to the cooing of a domestic pigeon. I later heard this oo-oo or cu-coo several times from two other males. It is, in fact, not a frequent behavior, but it occurs with all males in connection with charging and driving, whether for a nest or because the male is jealous of the presence of another bird.

On Jan. 30, the male is driving the female again. He gives the "short cluck" as he charges at her and walks about after her. The cluck is repeated slowly, except when he rushes at her, when it runs off hurriedly as a bubbling sound as before described. While following her up in this way, he sometimes resorts to the "driving coo." He has just given this twice. This time I feel sure that there are three notes and that the male is driving the female to find a nest as quickly as possible.

The notes sound sharper than yesterday, more as if beginning with *C* and could be represented thus *coo-coo-coo,* the second and third notes being shorter and closer together.

THE MATING PERIOD. 13

On Jan. 31 the male is again driving the female. He seems quite excited, holds his head high, the feathers of his forehead loosened so as to stand apart and out straight. The female tries all the while to get out of the cage in the direction of the window. The call described above certainly has three syllables, the second and third partially linked together.

On Feb. 2 the female has been sitting on the nest calling for straw and the male has been at work. The female left the nest and came to eat when I put food in their cage. The male at once became excited and began to drive her. He gave the cluck—the short petulant note described above, and followed it with the quicker rattling note as he charged and pecked at her. She seemed to understand his displeasure and returned to the nest without food. He then quieted and, after helping himself to the new food, returned to carrying straw. This shows what the driving clucks, the charging, and the coos mean. They mean, in this case, "go to the nest!"

The following case of charging occurred during the incubation period of the second cycle of the bronze-wing pair; it occurred about four hours after the second egg was laid. It was not connected with the initiation of a new cycle, as this did not begin until 5 days later. On Jan. 18 the male took his turn at nesting the egg; when he came off about 2 p. m., he charged at the female and even pecked her rather roughly twice. She soon went to the nest. (R 28.)

PERIODICITY OF THE DISPOSITION TO FIGHT.

The disposition to fight comes on in all pigeons at the time of mating and choosing a nesting-place. While fixing on a nesting-place, the male of a pair of homers (*C. tabellaria*) was pugnacious, fighting off other males whenever they came near. The disposition to fight and drive other doves away from the neighborhood of the nest becomes strong as soon as nest-building begins, and it is still stronger when the eggs are laid and after hatching. My young male passenger-pigeon (*Ectopistes*) while mated with a blond ring-dove bristled up, raised his wings, and scolded fiercely at the crested pigeons in the adjoining pen as soon as the first egg was laid. The wood-pigeons (*C. palumbus*) have been cooing and courting for at least 2 weeks, and the male drives off the 3 or 4 others of his *own* species from the nest. He seems to care little for the presence of birds of another species. A pair of white-faced pigeons (*Leucosarcia picata*) became savage, during the nesting period, towards the others of their own species, and I had to remove all of them; other species, however, were left with this pair. (R 4, R 11, Sh 8/13.)

In pigeons, as in many other birds, this disposition to resist enemies shows itself as soon as a place for a nest is found. While showing a passionate fondness for each other, both male and female become quarrelsome towards their neighbors. The white-winged pigeon (*Melopelia leucoptera*) of the West Indies and the southern border of the United States is one of the most interesting pigeons I have observed in this respect. At the approach of an intruder the birds show their displeasure in both tone and behavior. The tail is jerked up and down spitefully, the feathers of the back are raised, as a threatening dog "bristles up"; the neck is shortened by drawing the head somewhat below the level of the raised feathers, and the whole figure and actions are as fierce as the bird can make them. To the fierce look, the erect feathers, and the ill-tempered jerks of the tail there is added, moreover, a decidedly spiteful note of warning. If these manifestations are not sufficient, the birds jump toward the offender, and if that fails to cause retreat, the wings are raised and the matter is settled by vigorous blows.

The pugnacious mood is periodical, recurring with each reproductive cycle, and subsiding like a fever when its course is run. The birds behave as if from intelligent motive, but every need is anticipated blindly, for the young pair, without experience, example, or tradition, behave like the parents.

14 BEHAVIOR OF PIGEONS.

It seems to me that this mood or disposition,[1] although in some ways appearing to be independent of the disposition to cover the eggs, can best be understood as having developed in connection with the latter. It has primarily the same meaning—protection to the eggs—but the safety of the eggs and young depends upon the safety of the nest, and this accounts for the extension of this period to cover all three stages, building, sitting, and rearing.[2]

JEALOUSY.

The males of mourning-doves display as much jealousy as the common doves and the ring-doves, driving their wives at the approach of other doves. I have been amused at seeing a male guard his mate. In one instance I had placed a small cage with ring-doves within the larger mourning-dove pen. The male mourning-dove would drive his mate away from the cage to the farther end of the pen, then he would run back to the cage and peck at the ring-doves, and then back to his mate, billing her most affectionately. This behavior he kept up from day to day. Such behavior is a proof of his making a most decided distinction between his "mate"—a ring-dove—and other ring-doves.

In the case of a pair of homers I noted that just as soon as the nest-place was settled they both began to spend some time on the nest every day; copulations were then frequent (about a week before laying). A little later the male began to follow the female jealously and closely if other males were about. This male became so anxious to guard his mate that he would not, in many cases, stop to fight off a strange male, not even from his own stand; instead, however, he kept his eye constantly on his mate, paying no heed to another male, except to drive his mate out of reach of the latter.

The female bronze-wing, of a pair just beginning to build a nest, came to the floor at a time when several geopelias were strutting about in the adjoining cage; the male bronze-wing, for this or some other reason, tried to drive the female away. In doing this he drooped his wings a little, raised the feathers of the back, and charged at her, uttering a rapid note—a "cluck" rolled off rapidly. The charge was made several times and reminded me of similar charges that I have seen made by *Geopelia* males.

When a male dove sees another male in the act of soliciting or mounting his mate, he appears to understand instantly what the purpose is, and often makes frantic efforts to intercept the act, giving the danger signal in the loudest and most excited form and flying directly at the offending bird.[3] (R 20, R 4, R 33, R 7.)

---

[1] This disposition to fight is further described near end of Chapter VI; see topic "Resistance to intruders".—ED.

[2] Woods Hole Biological Lectures, p. 326.

[3] If one male sees another male copulating, he immediately flies to knock him off. It is surprising the distance at which the bird will recognize this. If two birds make ready to copulate on the barn, a male which is on the roof of the house will immediately spy them and fly to prevent it. It is not that the intruder wishes definitely to take the place of the first male. His chief aim seems to be to knock the first male off. He then generally struts about and coos to the female, but only in a very general way. I have seen female birds act similarly, but the female's object of spite seems to be the other female, whom she attacks, pecking her head. Espinas says that even dogs do not seem to know when other dogs are copulating, and do not show jealousy. The birds certainly seem to understand what is going on. I think Espinas is wrong in regard to dogs. Dogs seem very peaceable in the matter, yet they seem to know what is going on. You commonly see half a dozen males after one female. Among pigeons, a bird sees and knows what is being done just as surely as you or I do. (Conv. 7/2/10, W. C.)

CHAPTER II.

THE MATING PERIOD (continued).

BEHAVIOR IN UNITING.

BEHAVIOR OF THE BRONZE-WING.

Preceding a sexual union in the bronze-wings (*Phaps chalcoptera*) the male begins bowing and at each bow touches the floor with his beak strongly enough to be heard distinctly at each tap. This bowing is solicitation and the female, if inclined, generally responds with bows in the same way, although not so energetically as the male. Then hugging or "necking," as we may call it, begins, each bird trying to get the upper hold with the neck so as to bear down upon the back of the neck of the other. In this play the male generally proves the stronger and the female submits to being held until he mounts. He holds her until he has moved sidewise up to a position which enables him to mount before she could well escape, even if she were disposed to do so.

The male of this species,[1] unlike other species I am acquainted with, does not dismount immediately on completing contact, but resumes his position on the back of the female, lowers his head, and utters a short cluck-like note several times, as he prepares himself for a jump with a single slap of the wings. The wings are lifted just a little and, as he suddenly springs, his wings are thrown up in such a way as to come together with a vigorous slap. When he lands on the floor he immediately lowers his tail and wings until their tips touch the floor, raises and arches his neck, and rushes with a strutting movement of his legs and with wide-open beak up to the female, or, in this rush, he may partly encircle her. She bows and so does he until their beaks have touched the floor several times; in some cases she then puts her beak into his, and they go through with movements similar to those performed by other species as a prelude to copulating.

The courting is all done on the ground. The male bows to the ground and the female answers in the same fashion. Sometimes the male jumps at the female, emitting a quick succession of threatening notes that roll off with the rapidity of a rolling *r*-sound. She retreats and he follows with several jumps, sometimes stopping to bow his head and to lift his tail and wings for a moment in display; he then rushes on after her.

The male mounts by a jump, then slowly takes his position. If the female does not respond to suit him he stands nearly still and slowly drops his wings until the tips nearly touch the ground, when he suddenly brings his wings together with a slap over his back as he jumps off, and at the same time emits an explosive grunt, arching his head and neck and strutting away with tail spread and trailing on the ground. Then he may return bowing, and hugging may begin on the part of both; but the male is the stronger and soon the female submits to another mount carried out in the same way; or perhaps the sexual union will take place, when the same vigorous slap of the wings is made and the male emits his grunt with beak wide open. This grunt is given as a sort of hearty growl by the wood-pigeon, and is accompanied by arching neck, contracting pupil of the eye, and two or three stamps with the feet on the perch.

I see again (1906) in the bronze-wings what I several times observed during the previous year. When the male has amorous propensities he bows before the female, touching the floor with his beak each time; this is followed by raising the head to nearly the height of usual carriage, or even a little higher. The male keeps on bowing and the female

---

[1] This paragraph and the five following ones were not written at the same time. They are given here in the order in which they were written.—EDITOR.

16 BEHAVIOR OF PIGEONS.

responds in like manner, if disposed to accept his advances. In his bowing the male slightly expands the wings, so that the feathers are arranged to sit to best taste. The tail is held at the usual height and width; but the rump feathers, including the upper tail-coverts, are raised, as they are when the bird is on the ground and bristles up (raises wings, etc.) to threaten an intruder. Then hugging begins, and if the male prevails, as he usually does, he bears down on the back of the neck of the female, moves up sidewise, halts a moment, then mounts neatly with an even hop of both legs. On the female's back he again halts all motion for 3 or 4 seconds, holding his neck very low, just over that of the female; while steadily holding his position he then gives a series of three or four or more guttural chuckles or muffled clucks or notes, beginning very low and rising gradually in each successive note until, with a much louder and explosive final note, he gives the dismounting jump and simultaneously a quick snap-like clash of the wings over the back. As he lands, he lowers his wings to his sides so that the tips touch the floor, and with spread tail also sweeping the floor, he rushes or circles with high-arched neck and wide-open mouth around the female. If the female prevails, as she did twice within a few minutes in the present instance, she goes through the same performance, only with every act reduced in energy and life. The male mounted four times on the particular occasion described here, but without reaching a sexual union in either case. This play is often carried on for rather long periods.

On the day following the behavior that has just been described I saw the male mount and carry the sexual act to conclusion. When the contact between male and female is effected, the male, unlike most or all other species, does not instantly dismount as contact is ended, but resumes his position on the back of the female, and then begins with the copulation notes previously described, finishing up with the leap, wing-clash, open-beak, strut, etc. This is a most theatrical performance. The male proceeds as if he foresaw and calculated each item with a view to closing the act with a grand climax. He is silent for a moment to make sure his feet are in place; he lowers his head to the front where it is ready for the final jump; he then prepares for a crescendo of chuckles, beginning the series with an inaudible one (seen in movement of throat), then a chuckle that is just barely audible, then one stronger, then another stronger still, and then the grand explosion, in which the chuckle expresses all the vim the bird can master, and which is cut short with an impetuous *w-h-e-w*, just as he springs with a sudden and loud clash of the wings to the floor, where the orgasm becomes complete, as expressed in pose, dress of feathers, sparkling of eyes, open mouth, and proud parade with trailing wings and tail. The male's recovery of position on the back of female is peculiar to this species, so far as I know.[1] Immediately after this copulation the hugging was renewed, and the male mounted and went through with all the usual performances, except that of contact. Then hugging began again, and the female was mounted with the usual behavior; then the male tried it again, but without contact.

At a still later date I was able to learn that when the male bronze-wing has mounted he makes the clucks slow and low as he reaches back and moves his tail from side to side until union is made; and that he then recovers his position and begins a "series" of clucks— one inaudible, a second just barely audible, a third a little stronger, a fourth and fifth increasing in force, a sixth and seventh close together, with an explosive seventh as he dismounts. There were seven clucks increasing in *force* and in *rapidity* to the last of the series.

After four unsuccessful cycles a pair (*I*) of bronze-winged pigeons were separated for 15 days in the hope of inducing regular work. After this period they were

---

[1] The male of *Geopelia humeralis* never recovers this position, but slips off the female the moment the union is effected, alighting on the perch, then bristling up and driving the female, as if angry with her.

THE MATING PERIOD. **17**

brought together on bright mornings in order to secure photographs of their mating behavior. This behavior is described in the following additional records:

As soon as the pair was put together the male began to *charge* at the female, driving her vigorously. He evidently recognized her as his mate, but for some reasons not clear he charged at her as if displeased at something. The male later resumed these charges at the female, but they soon began their love-making, and for *two hours* kept up hugging, mounting, jumping, and strutting with mouth open, etc. The female often mounted the male; sometimes she came up to the male in a number of mounts, but towards the end the male was not so easily held by the neck, seemingly getting impatient of such play on the part of the female. On a later occasion the pair was active for an hour and then began to show less earnestness. The male began by charging, clucking all the time as he drove the female. It was more evident now that he wanted to start the female off *for a nesting-place.* The male carried through one copulation, but mounted many times besides, and the female succeeded in mounting only twice; of the two the male was plainly more active, and also less submissive to efforts of his mate to mount. The female, nevertheless, kept up her efforts, fruitless as most of them were. Her behavior is that of the male; it is merely *less energetic.*

COMPARATIVE BEHAVIOR.[1]

The behavior of the geopelias in uniting offers one or two unique and distinctive features, but it is of greater interest for the several points of likeness which these birds share with the bronze-wings. The male of *Geopelia humeralis* (and other geopelias) mounts several times, clucking slowly each time until, with a sudden spring and a vigorous striking together of the wings over the back, he jumps off; he walks away slowly with tail spread, and after a few jumps he returns and takes the female's beak once or twice, mounts again, etc.; he continues this until the female is thoroughly aroused and ready to respond. After copulating, however, he shortens his neck and bristles up as if angry and drives the female away. *G. cuneata* does the same.

A female *G. humeralis* mated with a ring-dove does not flee from him after a union as she does from a mate of her own species. Her difference of action is due to different behavior on the part of the male. The male ring-dove allows himself, after a union, to be fondled by the female, and she expresses her joy by so doing. The male *Geopelia*, on the contrary, bristles up in a most savage manner and repels her love and drives her off, acting as if his pleasure had turned to displeasure and nausea.

The same slapping together of the wings over the back which is exhibited by these geopelias has already been noted as a common feature in the bronze-wing pigeon. It is, however, not so regularly seen in the bronze-wing; the male often jumps off with only a flirt of the wings and struts around the female. The bronze-wing also rarely takes the beak of the female (he does sometimes), but he often opens wide his beak as he approaches her. In pressing his neck over that of the female the bronze-wing acts much as *Ectopistes* does.

The behavior of bronze-wings in mating shows, therefore, some decided affinities with the geopelias. Most marked is the similarly repeated mounting of the female by the male; the lowering of the male's head over that of the female; the giving of a short note and the repetition of it while the male gradually lowers his wings preparatory to raising them and striking them together over his back as he jumps to the ground. A part of the behavior after jumping off is also similar in the two forms—the raising of the head, with arched neck stretched; the tail dragging on the floor; the strutting off and circling around the female; and at the same time offering the wide-open beak to the female. (R 28, R 33, R 17, R 1.)

---

[1] Further material on this topic may be found in Chapter X.

BEHAVIOR OF PIGEONS.

THE "JUMPING OVER" PHENOMENON.

This aspect of the mating behavior is nowhere mentioned in the manuscripts, although Professor Whitman had commented on it in conversation with his students and associates. The following account has been given by Dr. Riddle, who has since studied and analyzed this bit of behavior in terms of *degree* of sexuality in pigeons.

If one follows closely the mating behavior of many pairs of presumably normal doves it will be found that, in addition to the "mounting" by the male which is followed by a consummation of the copulation, both male and female doves occasionally exhibit quite definite motor activities of a similar or related sexual nature. The erotic male, for example, will sometimes *jump quickly over* the back of the female. In many such cases there is no attempt whatever to take the copulating position, but it seems to be the reaction normal to a male in a state of submaximal sex-stimulation; perhaps the reaction is associated with a weakly stimulated consort as well, for the latter usually thereafter stoops more intently, or otherwise invites the promised union with more ardor than before. The male, too, most commonly concludes his "jumping over" with a completed copulation.

It will be found, moreover, that an occasional female will *sometimes* mount the male. Possibly it is a sexually unresponsive male, with a lagging response, that is thus humiliated; but so far as the writer has observed, it is also *usually* a female that is *tubercular* that thus discounts the prerogatives of the male. In our experience, however, we have not yet seen a female "jump over" the *male*. This latter reaction seems, among the pure forms under consideration, to be a more distinctly masculine reaction than is that involved in the mounting which precedes copulation. And this, we shall see in a moment, is true once more among *hybrid* females when these are mated with each other. There it has been shown that *masculine* females will "jump over" other females when the latter assume strongly *feminine* attitudes.

The study of the sex-behavior of *hybrid* females has been developed into a method of arranging a group of sisters—proceeding from a sex-controlled mating[1]—in a quantitative series of more and less "masculine" females. Concerning this situation we will, however, make only a short statement here. It has been found that females from a mating so arranged as to produce nearly all males from the stronger germs of the spring and early summer, and nearly all females from the eggs of late summer and autumn, are not equally feminine, as measured by their copulatory and "jumping-over" behavior. The first females of the season, and from the relatively stronger germs generally, function more often as males in copulating with their sisters hatched later in the season from weaker germs. These same females, from stronger germs, also readily and often show the "jumping-over" reaction, whilst this reaction has never been seen in many of the otherwise most feminine females; and it has been very infrequently seen in any of the more feminine ones.

BILLING AND "FEEDING" BY THE MALE IN MATING BEHAVIOR.

There is a widespread custom among pigeons to precede the sexual act by what is known as billing.[2] In this act the male presents an open beak into which the female inserts her own. This process is of longer or shorter duration, and varies greatly for the different species. During this process there is evidence for a regurgitation, by the male, of a small amount of food into the beak of the female,

---

[1] These matings are described in Volume II.

[2] This process is well known in the various varieties of domestic pigeons. The phenomenon is also referred to in the materials cited in Chapter X.

THE MATING PERIOD. 19

carried out in much the same way as both parents feed their young. This part of the activity of billing may also be spoken of as "feeding." That billing is not universal among pigeons, though it occurs in widely different groups, is indicated by the several observations which follow:

Bandtail pigeons (*Columba fasciata*) approach each other by the usual method of billing the wing, but the female does not insert the beak, and the male does not offer her an opportunity. The preliminary movements are slow in these birds. The male mounts without offering the beak and slowly takes his position, while the female as slowly aids by raising her wings to support him. The male then finally pitches back rather suddenly and dismounts after a flash contact. As he alights beside her he raises his head and *points his beak upward* for a moment in the expression of his pleasure.

I have seen a male mourning-dove (*Zenaidura carolinensis*) take the beak of his mate in his mouth and give one or two quite quick and vigorous shakes. This bird then mounted and finished the act in a moment's time—much quicker than in any other species known to me except the small ground-doves of Florida. The rapidity of the mourning-dove's movements in these acts was in striking contrast to that of the passenger-pigeon (*Ectopistes*). The mourning-dove rapidly bills his wing, shakes his feathers, and offers his open beak, gives a few jerks when it is accepted, and then finishes in the usual way.

The male of *Geopelia humeralis* mounts, jumps off, takes the female's beak once or twice, mounts again, etc., until the female is thoroughly aroused and ready to respond. The male of the bronze-wing seems rather rarely to take the beak of the female, but often opens wide his beak as he approaches her. (Sh 30/13, C 7/7, R 28, R 33.)

The male sometimes feeds the female during the billing activity. This phenomenon was recorded three times in the bronze-wing records. We shall quote the references and then give the detailed circumstances under which the act occurred:

The female was sitting on the ladder 3 feet from the ground. The male was 5 or 6 feet away on the ground. He bowed and called; she flew down, ran up to him, and put her beak in his. The male fed her with an up-and-down shake; after billing from one side of his beak the female shifted to the other side. On the following day the male called the female from the ladder. He opened his beak and she inserted her beak, first on one side and then on the other. He apparently fed her; at least he went through the motions of doing so.

On Jan. 5, at 2 p. m., I saw the male walk off on the perch and fly to the floor, where he then began bowing profusely; the female put her beak in his mouth, and the male gave a few very vigorous shakes, during which the rattling of the contents of his crop could be heard. The female after accepting this feeding from the male at once returned to the nest.

At 7^h 30^m a. m. on Jan. 26 this female bronze-wing was on the floor. The male bowed and the female ran to him and the two began hugging. The female soon reached out her beak to that of the male, feeling about as if she wanted to be fed. Then the male opened his beak and received that of the female, and fed her with a few shakes. Hugging by the male occurred for a moment. The female again at once reached out her beak to be fed, and the male again fed her with a few strong shakes. This was repeated for a third time, and shortly afterward, without any coitus, the female went to the nest. (R 28, R 33.)

The circumstances under which the first of these "feedings" occurred are not definitely stated, except that the act was connected with their courting. Judging from the context, this case probably occurred during the incubation period, and

20 BEHAVIOR OF PIGEONS.

hence it was connected with the premature beginning of the next cycle. The description was given under the caption "The male feeds the female."

The second case occurred during the latter part of the first cycle. The male had finished prematurely his incubation period on January 1, 1906, while the last egg was hatched on January 4. In the meantime the male participated in the incubation perfunctorily and half-heartedly and spent much time in attempting to entice the female to a new cycle. When the eggs were hatched the male did not feed the young nor take his turn in covering them. The female was thus forced to do double duty in both feeding and covering the young. The young birds died for lack of proper care, and a new cycle was started immediately on January 8. The feeding occurred on the 5th, the day after the second egg was hatched. The motive of the female's behavior in accepting food could well be hunger and not sexuality, for she had been doing double duty in nesting and feeding for several days, and she did not respond to the sexual advances of her mate until three days after the event in question. Since the male normally participates in the feeding of the young, one might suspect that this act of feeding his mate represented the onset of this normal impulse. This interpretation is improbable, however, because the male's conduct was not normal. He had finished his incubation period and had started on a new cycle four days previously. Under these conditions the feeding impulse does not develop, and, moreover, he gave no sign of this tendency in his behavior towards the young. The act seems rather to be connected with his sex behavior.

The third case of feeding occurred on January 26, *i.e.*, on the tenth day of the incubation period of the second cycle, and 7 to 8 days before the eggs were due to hatch. Both birds had been engaged in courting and attempts at copulation for three days previously, and the eggs were definitely deserted; the third cycle started on the day the act occurred. The act was thus connected neither with hunger nor with the impulse to feed the young; it occurred in the midst of their courting activities, so that in both birds this behavior was undoubtedly in some way connected with their sexual activities.

During the fifth cycle of this pair it was noted in connection with the detailed description of their uniting behavior that "there was no *feeding*[1] this time." This cycle was begun after a lapse of about 40 days.

THE QUEST FOR A NEST.

When ready to find a place to nest many pigeons may be often seen to raise their wings a little as if to fly, and while the wings are thus raised they are wagged or moved a little and the head is stretched forward. This is common conduct in *Ectopistes* when it is ready to seek a place for a nest. The same behavior has been seen in stock-doves (*C. ænas*), and I have often seen the same in common pigeons. In this state the bird seems uneasy, is ready to fly, but is undecided where to go; it executes a flying movement which is held in restraint, and which is sometimes only a sort of vibration of the wings while closed and held a little loose. At other times the wings are more or less extended, as if for flight.

---

[1] This statement probably means that there was neither billing nor feeding.—EDITOR.

THE MATING PERIOD. 21

It was abundantly evident from the following behavior that a pair of passenger-pigeons was prepared for the second reproductive cycle. They flew several times against the wire of their cage, and seemed to wish to get out in order to find a new place for a nest. The behavior was the same that I had seen in the blond ring-doves (*St. risoria*) at such times. Two days later these passengers were very active, but not yet decided where to place the nest. The male was especially active, taking the lead in the search. He kept alighting on a small tree inclosed in their large pen, and here he would put down his head and call the female. I repeatedly saw this pair flying about in search of a nesting-place. I note, too, that when the male flew back and forth he called to his mate *while on the wing*. These birds stoop as if to fly, and often, before starting, raise and lower the *closed* wings in the rhythm of flight. Here the flying movement is held in check by the knowledge of the bird that the window and wire were not pleasant things to fly against.

A pair of blond-rings (*E*) were very restless this morning and both are now trying to get out of the cage and are evidently intent on finding a place for a nest. These birds stood before the door and kept flying up, as if wishing to have the door opened. They finally went to the old nest and settled down there as a last resort. It is remarkable how strong is the instinct *to place the new nest in a new locality*.

A pair of old bronze-wing birds were two or three days in settling on a nesting-place in the same box formerly used by them. They ran back and forth on the floor as if desiring to get out, and on the next day they tried the box, but were not content. Their contentment was finally fixed, as they could do no better. They were fully decided and at work in the box two days afterwards. The eggs laid here, however, were deserted. On the day following their desertion the birds were both uneasy, running back and forth to get out of the cage; they were evidently hunting for a new nesting-place. On the next day they were beginning to accept the old nest-box again, but they did no real work. A little later these birds again began the hunt for a nesting-place; both ran back and forth to get out of the cage, and when the male went to the nest-box and called, the female flew to the perch and answered. They were not satisfied, however, and soon left the box. Three days later the female was on the nest calling for straw, but the male was running about on the floor trying to get out; apparently he had not yet decided on a place for the nest. An hour later the male began carrying straws and the nest-building was continued industriously thereafter.

A female blond ring that has a crested pigeon for a mate to-day acted like a dove that, after rearing young, is looking for a place at a distance for a new nest.[1] She flew back and forth in a very uneasy manner, trying to get out of her pen into the large room in which it stands. On the following morning the female was driven about by the male, who then seemed uneasy and evidently looking for a place for a new nest. This male tried very hard to get out of the pen and to interest the female, but she appeared comparatively indifferent. (R17, SS4, C7/17, R33, R19.)

NEST-BUILDING.
ON THE METHOD OF NEST-BUILDING.

The details of the activities connected with nest-building, as this was observed in a pair of bronze-wings, may be had from the following record made while nest-making was in progress: The male bronze-wing has just carried a straw, delivering it by jumping onto the female's back and placing it near her beak. A second straw has just been

---

[1] It is natural for the pigeons to take to a new nest for the second brood. This is especially true of the common pigeon. But sometimes a bird, more shiftless and indolent than usual, will lay in the old and filthy nest. Many of the species use two nests. Apparently they want a *clean* nest as well as a new, fresh situation. The male common pigeon, while his mate is sitting, generally seeks another room in the cot for his roost; and when it is time for the second brood he leads the female there; other pigeons have been driven away, and the place is ready for her to nest. Probably the common ring-dove uses two nests naturally; and so do many other species. (Conv. 6/24/08, W. C.)

delivered in the same way and now again a third in the same manner. When the male approaches the nest, the female continues her calls but bows each time and waves her closed wings slowly up and down as if welcoming her mate. The female has turned in her nest so that she faces in the opposite direction, and the male jumps on her back in delivering. She has again turned, so that she now faces him as he arrives with her tail at the corner of the cage; in this position he delivers without mounting, but he tries to side up to her so that his head may point in the same direction as hers. In other words, he seeks to deliver from above and behind, but omits the mounting, owing to the awkward or unfavorable position which he can not well meet by mounting.

On the following day I find that the male is still taking hay to the nest. Yesterday I noted one case in which the female changed her position, so as to have her tail at the corner of the cage and her head at the opposite side, so that she faced the male as he arrived. I have just seen the taking of this position repeated and the male make two deliveries. In the first instance he jumped onto her back and turned, placing his body parallel with hers, and then placed the straw under her breast. In the second case he jumped on her and stood at nearly right angles and placed the straw under her wing; the female here turned her head to take the straw. The male's behavior in jumping onto the back of the female is very probably a necessity in nature, since the male bird would usually not find it possible to deliver otherwise; besides, his taking this position serves to test the strength of the nest and of its support, and helps to keep the straws in place and well pressed together.

I now note that when the male flies to the perch he stands still for a few seconds, about 3 to 5 seconds, as if to see that there is no danger of discovery before he visits his mate. Wild birds generally are cautious in this way; if they were otherwise their nests would be easily discovered by enemies. I have found that the male passenger-pigeon also delivers his straw or twig by mounting on the back of the female and placing it in front of her in the place most convenient for her to receive it.

All pigeons, so far as I know, carry but *one straw* at a time; the sparrow, on the other hand, loads itself up with as many pieces as it can hold in its mouth, and thus saves trips to the nest. The sparrow's method is the more economical—less wasteful of time and energy. What an interesting step—for a bird to learn to take many instead of one at a time. In this simple difference of method we see a wide difference in intelligence. It is not supposable that the step could have been first taken by the sparrow as a mere accident (without the aid of the intelligence above that of pigeons), and then confirmed as a general habit through natural selection of the individuals who were lucky enough to adopt it. The first impulse to pick up several straws instead of one implies greater intelligence, and this superiority would be favored in the struggle for existence, in a thousand different ways, of which that here considered is but one.

The pigeon often shows great stupidity in gathering straw. If it happens to pick up a stray straw on the side of the nest, instead of turning right around and delivering it, the bird will often first fly off with it, as if in search of a new straw, and then fly back and give it to its mate. I have often seen such performances. If the pigeon drops a straw in flight to the nest it never stops to pick it up, but goes off again to find another. If a sparrow drops a part of its load of straw it will often try, while still holding fast to what remains, to catch it in mid-air, and will follow it to the ground if need be to recover it. Here again the sparrow displays intelligence quite above that of the pigeon.

On the Purpose of Nest-building.

The following instance throws some light on the nest-building instinct: A pair of young common pigeons only 30 days old were kept in a pen in my library. They occupied a small nest-box with a nicely saucer-shaped nest. In this nest-box they were hatched and

THE MATING PERIOD. 23

reared. The box was kept on the floor of the pen. To-day I removed the box from the pen, leaving only the hard floor for the birds to rest upon. This afternoon I noticed that they were trying to rest on the floor in the place where the box had been. They found the floor did not afford them the comfortable bed which they had had in their old nest, and they showed by uneasy actions that they realized that their bed had not the proper shape. One of the two young then began the nest-making movements with its feet and legs, as if to work out a more comfortable place. The act was repeated several times under my eye at a distance of only 2 feet, so that I could see plainly that the motions were exactly those of an adult bird in preparing a nest.

In this case we see one of the more essential combinations of actions involved in nest making performed by a young bird that has certainly never learned the trick from old birds. The bird doubtless remembered its easy nest, and sought to make its bed a nest-like concavity. It is *instinct* and *intelligence*, for having just a while before enjoyed something better, the bird was not satisfied with a plain hard floor. The discomfort would probably not have been felt had the bird been accustomed from the first to such a surface. The cause of the action may have been of the same nature as that which stimulates the old bird in nest-making. *The purpose of the bird is to make her place easier*, and she does not think of the need of a hollow bed to hold eggs. The two needs—her present comfort and the future need of the eggs—are identical and are satisfied by the one act. The future purpose is not in the bird's mind, but it is this need that the observer usually thinks of, wholly forgetting the need that the bird thinks of. (R 33, SS 4, R 7.)

NEST-CALL.[1]

THE PURPOSE OF THE NEST-CALL.

The nest-call is given very frequently by both birds throughout the entire mating period. It may be given from either the nest, the floor, or on the wing. The purpose of the call is evident from the following disconnected excerpts gathered from various records. The call also occurs throughout the incubation period. (See Voice, Chapter V.)

A pair of bronze-wings were beginning to prepare for a nest, the male taking the lead in going to the nest-box and calling. The female took her place in the nest and called for the male to bring straw. The female was in the nest and calling, while the male was on the floor looking for straws. The many calls of the male evidently indicate that he has a sexual inclination. The male calls the female to a new nest-making, absolutely indifferent to the young. The male calls to the nest much during the forenoon and some in the afternoon. The male began calling in the nest-box in the very early morning, before there was daylight. The male goes to the nest-box and calls. The female sat in the nest-box and called for straws. During the afternoon, and especially in the morning, the male spends considerable time in the nest calling for the female to come to the nest-box and renew the cycle.

THE NATURE OF THE NEST-CALL.

The nature of the nest-call is illustrated by the following excerpts taken from several different manuscripts:

When on the nest the male bronze-wing gives calls which are rather loud and strong—like a groan of a cat, a deep moaning sound. The male's call is stronger and a little longer than that of the female. His call is nearly a second long. The female's call has a vibration which I can not detect in that of the male; his call is a deep, full, moan-like sound. The male makes a distinct nod of the head with each call. The male gave two

---

[1] Much material on this topic is given in Chapter X.

24   BEHAVIOR OF PIGEONS.

calls, nodding his head strongly with each call as usual. This call sounds a little like the groan of a cat that is cornered and threatened with a stick—a groan, a growl of despair, as the animal seems to realize there is no escape and lies down and faces you. The female's call has a distinct vibration in it, and there is always a slight opening of the beak as it is made. The male's nest-call is 1 second long, and about 2 calls are given in 5 seconds; this was the usual rate, but it was sometimes slowed up to 2 in 6 to 7 seconds. The interval between calls was thus sometimes 3 seconds or longer. These calls were answered by the female from her cage, but her calls were not as loud and full as those of the male. The male went to his nest-box and began calling at the rate of about 12 times in 60 seconds. The male wags his wings slowly as he calls and also bows with each call. The wings are moved outward and upward and returned to the side of the body, sometimes 6 to 7 times in 5 seconds. There are usually 3 to 4 wags of the wings for each call; these are larger or smaller according to the earnestness of the bird and his call. If the female calls and walks forward and the male sees her trying to reach him, he becomes more animated in calls and movements of the wings. The nest-call of the bronze-wing is a single note, homologous with the nest-growl of common pigeons. It is a monotone and like a low groan; it is clear and hollow, like the sound from blowing in the mouth of an empty bottle. The male is on the floor calling at the rate of 9 times in 30 seconds; his calls appear to be a whole *second* in duration. In delivering, he bows his head so that the back of his head is about on a level with his beak, and his beak is turned vertically downward. The male is in the nest, and the female is on the floor; he is calling leisurely, at the rate of 17 times a minute. He usually bows with each call, although the female scarcely moves her head. The female called twice in answer and flew to the perch; the male then quickened his calls to about 3 in 5 seconds, each call being nearly a second in length.

The nest-call of the male *Geopelia humeralis* is the single note of the bronze-wing broken up into rapidly repeated short notes: it is a string of notes run off consecutively.

The call of the male *Ectopistes* is a succession of short notes, and sometimes a louder and more prolonged call, corresponding to the coo-call of doves. The female's call is less loud than that of the male; her call is a very crude one as compared with that of ringdoves. It is a rather hoarse, low sound, impossible to describe. It is a simple squawk, somewhat as if produced by a bird that has lost control of her organs of voice or that has never learned to use them. The male makes a similar call, but louder and more explosive. The male passenger flew back and forth, calling his mate *while on the wing*. This behavior was noted a second time.

The male white-faced pigeon (*Leucosarcia picata*) calls his young with the same call and at the same rate as he calls his mate; it is also the same call that he uses after his mate has laid an egg. He gives two calls a second, and, posting himself on a perch or a shelf, he keeps up this monotonous call by the hour. The calls are evenly run off, the bird holding himself in one position. The call is loud and clear, and sounds like a short whistle, the breath being expelled in a short forcible puff. I know of no other pigeon with such a voice. Still, one can say that it is the pigeon *oo, whistled twice each second*. The sound is not like *oo* vocalized, but whistled across the mouth of a bottle; *i.e.*, the lips are held as if to give the vocal *oo*, but the air is first put into vibration when expelled through the lips.

The Nest-call of the Male Bronze-wing.

The nest-call of the male bronze-wing has then about the same *length* as the "perch call," but the latter is accompanied by a bowing of the head, which means that the effort is stronger than in the former, this position being one that conduces to rather deeper and stronger sound. I notice, however, that a slight nodding of the head does accompany the nest-call. The bowing done in connection with the nest-call is greater the louder the call, *i.e.*, when the male exerts himself most earnestly he strengthens his call with the

THE MATING PERIOD. 25

bowing. He may keep on with the calling for some time without any bowing movement. When the female comes to the nest he keeps on calling with his head held low, so that no bowing is required. The nest-call is accompanied, not by any appreciable bowing of the head, but by a slow and even up-and-down movement of the wings. This latter is a shoulder movement, the wings being lifted from the sides of the body and wagged up and down simultaneously; or, if in a shorter arc, they are moved out and in. If the female comes near the nest the action is quickened and the calls are more frequent; then, too, the head is held lower and the tail a little higher. The "wing-movements" are those of the *young* when appealing to the old birds for more food.

GROUND-CALL OF THE MALE BRONZE-WING.

In order to get records of the time occupied by the ground-call of the male bronze-wing I placed the two members of a pair in different rooms of my home. The male was placed in a rear room and the female was in a front room. The female answered the calls of the male. His calls were loud and strong and were given with a full neck and a slow bow. My various counts were as follows: 11 calls in 30 seconds; 21 calls in 60 seconds; 10 calls in 30 seconds; and 20 calls in 60 seconds. This gives about 3 seconds for a call, 1 second of which is the duration of the call and 2 seconds is the interval between calls.

NEST-CALL OF THE FEMALE BRONZE-WING.

The rate and duration of the nest-call of the female bronze-wing was recorded for two particular females. In the first case the female had been on the nest for an hour. She was then calling, and her consort was on the floor looking for straws. I found that she sometimes gives a single call at intervals of 5, 10, 15, or more seconds; and that she will then begin to call at shorter intervals, for example, two or three times in 5 seconds, 8 times in 16 seconds, 4 times in 8 seconds, then skipping over intervals of 5, 10, or more seconds. She repeats the call continuously, when the male goes to the nest, at the rate of about 7 times in 10 seconds. Each note is three-fourths of a second in length. It is a single note, a moderately prolonged monotone, with a little vibration in it that is sometimes quite noticeable.

In the second individual the call was a little less than a second in length. It was repeated frequently while the male was away hunting for straws. The call has a distinct vibration in this female, and it is often a little husky and jarring. The female calls at about the rate of 2 in 4 to 5 seconds or 3 in 7 seconds. Sometimes this goes on for half a minute without particular pause. Sometimes the interval between the calls is only a second, then a second and a fraction, varying from 1 to 2 seconds. The *interruptions* are from 5 to 30 or more seconds. Some series gave:

Rate.	Interruptions.	Rate.	Interruptions.
3 in 5 seconds...	15 seconds.	5 in 10 seconds....	30 seconds.
8 in 20 seconds...	5 seconds.	4 in 8 seconds....	10 seconds.
3 in 5 seconds...	5 seconds.	4 in 10 seconds....	9 seconds.
6 in 10 seconds...	8 seconds.	3 in 6 seconds....	10 seconds.
11 in 30 seconds...	10 seconds.	5 in 10 seconds....	8 seconds.
10 in 20 seconds...	20 seconds.	6 in 18 seconds....	9 seconds.
12 in 30 seconds...	10 seconds.	7 in 15 seconds....	5 seconds.
8 in 20 seconds...	12 seconds.		

NEST-CALL AND MATING INSTINCT IN THE YOUNG.

The young of a pair of bronze-wings had been removed to the adjoining half of the cage on the day a first egg was laid. Shortly afterward one of the young, presumably the male, went into his nest-box and began to call and to wave his wings slowly up and down, precisely like an adult male calling the female to the nest. The voice of the young is not yet mature and is a little broken, but the call is delivered in the correct manner. At that time this young bird was only 9 weeks and 1 day old.

Another instance of the giving of the nest-call by a very immature bird was as follows: A young passenger-pigeon, only 59 days old, was standing on the perch in his pen in my library. I let a pair of ring-doves free in the room. These very tame doves flew about in delight. When they alighted in front of the pen containing the young passenger the latter promptly raised his tail and bowed his head, giving the call-note of the parent species perfectly. This occurred 5 weeks and 3 days after it had been taken from its parents, and since its parents had been kept in the back yard the young passenger certainly could not have made the note in imitation. When he was about 2 weeks old he must have heard his parents thus call in preparing for a second nest, but this was the last time the old birds gave the call, for they molted soon afterward and made no more calls for nesting. The young passenger repeated this call again on the following day. (R 28, R 33, R 29, SS 4, Sh 8/13.)

CHAPTER III.
THE PAIRING OF PIGEONS.

Pigeons normally pair with the opposite sex of their own species, and these matings are popularly supposed to represent a high degree of fidelity. Their fidelity is, however, by no means absolute, and they may mate with individuals of their own sex and with members of a different species. On occasion they may attempt to gratify the sexual passion by other means. Descriptive of such anomalous behavior, this chapter contains material bearing upon the question of species, sex, and individual recognition, and the basis of species and individual preferences.

INFLUENCE OF BEHAVIOR.

That birds of the same species usually mate together is a matter of the commonest observation. It is, however, a very interesting fact that among pigeons the sexes are not able to distinguish their opposites by sight. The male, for example, does not know what the female sex is; he will just as quickly mate with a male as with a female, provided the opportunity is given. But these birds have a way of finding out the sex of their associates. If, for example, two male ring-doves are put together and both are disposed to mate, they will begin to pull each other's ears or feathers; each will shake the other, and by and by, as this continues, one or the other will get a little angry. This display of temper is not proper behavior for the female sex; it will be resented by the other bird and a fight will result, in which one or the other eventually drives the other off. If a female is put with the male the latter behaves in precisely the same manner as before. He first gives her a few shakes and she becomes very submissive—the proper behavior for the female. When the female does not appear to resent or return the shakes, but walks away, the male follows her.

It is very instructive to watch this behavior between two birds of different species. As an example, let us take the situation presented by mating a common pigeon and a ring-dove. The common pigeon is very much the larger; and if we try to mate a male ring-dove with a female common pigeon the small male will approach this large female very cautiously. If she is disposed to mate with him she will retreat; that gives him courage, and he begins to coo. She dresses her feathers and struts and makes no resistance to the domineering behavior of the male, and the mating is soon completed. If the female is indifferent or averse to mating, she may give the male a peck if he comes too near, and that usually puts an end to his efforts to mate; he becomes frightened and does not pay her any further attentions. It is therefore necessary to know beforehand, if possible, whether the birds are disposed to mate. If the female common pigeon is disposed to mate before the birds are brought together the mating can be readily accomplished.

In another cross-mating a male hybrid ring-dove was paired with a California mourning-dove which was supposed to be a female. The hybrid was eager to attract the mourning-dove, but the latter showed not the slightest interest in him. No progress was made in 2 weeks, though the male hybrid persisted in courting. After 2 months they became entirely friendly with each other. I then thought the match was to be a success, but, to my surprise, a little later I saw the supposed female trying to mount the male. It was soon learned that this supposed female was a male. I then placed this same California mourning-dove with another male mourning-dove. The two began to coo face to face; each offered the beak and tried to mount the other. Soon they returned to striking each other, and otherwise making it evident that both were males.

28   BEHAVIOR OF PIGEONS.

These mourning-doves, then, like ring-doves, do not know the differences between the sexes until they meet and exchange salutations. The male's place is to coo and strut, while the female retreats, bowing and showing herself off if she happens to be disposed. If she does not retreat, the male tests her by pecking and claiming his mastership. The behavior is the only guide they have in selecting a mate of the right sex. This may seem incredible, but it is certain.[1]   (SS 10, C 7/48.)

INFLUENCE OF VOICE.

Fulton, on page 38 of the work already cited, states in regard to the influence of voice:

"One more caution must be added in regard to mating the birds. It frequently happens that, on account of proved sterling qualities, it is desired to breed from an old pigeon as long as fertile eggs can be obtained from him; and this can only be done by matching him with a very young hen. Such a pair will frequently breed well; and we have had fine, strong young ones from an old barb over 10 years of age which had won many prizes. But it is in such cases particularly needful to avoid having in the same loft a lively young cock *with a strong voice*, for if this is the case the young hen will frequently leave her eggs to reach and pair with the young bird, even though he be already mated, and thus all the owner's plans are liable to be frustrated."

INFLUENCE OF SOCIAL ENVIRONMENT.

If a bird of one species is hatched and reared by a wholly different species, it is very apt when fully grown to prefer to mate with the species under which it has been reared. For example, a male passenger-pigeon that was reared by ring-doves and had remained with that species was ever ready, when fully grown, to mate with any ring-dove, but could never be induced to mate with one of his own species. I kept him away from ring-doves a whole season, in order to see what could be accomplished in the way of getting him mated finally with his own species, but he would never make any advances to the females, and whenever a ring-dove was seen or heard in the yard he was at once attentive.[2]   (SS 10.)

It may be remarked by the editor that the discovery of this principle furnishes the key to Professor Whitman's success in hybridizing the various species of pigeons. A novel and important principle of behavior is here involved. The range of stimuli to which an instinctive tendency will respond may be modified by habits acquired long before the first expression of the instinct. The first expression of a delayed instinctive tendency may thus be in part a function of all that the organism has previously acquired.

PAIRING OF FEMALES.

That behavior is of prime importance in sex recognition is apparent from the fact that females sometimes pair with each other. It is not always easy to distinguish the sexes on the basis of any observation of morphological features. Such distinctions are best made in terms of behavior during the breeding cycle. For this reason it happened that, in his breeding experiments, the author occasionally

---

[1] Does a pigeon distinguish males from females in general, or does he know the female only in his own mate? The male pigeon usually knows the sex of each bird in the flock, and is always ready to play up to the females. When a new bird comes to the flock he does not seem to be so sure of its sex at first; but he tests it by display behavior. If the newcomer proves to be a male, he then pays less attention to it. It is wonderful how quickly one pigeon can tell whether he is looked upon with favor and liking by another. It seems as if the expression of the eye tells at once that the bird likes or does not.

I have noticed that some males are less successful than others in securing mates. Of two given males it will generally be observed that different females prefer the same one. And this is usually the more active male. An exceptionally strong male may even entice a female away from her mate, especially if he defeats her mate in fight. The female is more inclined to thus desert her former mate for a victorious male at the time the female is ready to start a mating cycle than at other times. At any other time she would pay no attention to the strange male. (Conv. 7/2/10/ W. C.)

[2] Illustrative material may be found in Chapter X.

THE PAIRING OF PIGEONS. 29

mated two birds on the supposition that they were male and female, and the mistake was not discovered until the latter part of a reproductive cycle. Sometimes more or less spontaneous mating of females may occur. "Two females, one an ordinary domestic dove and the other an impure fantail, settled in a cot and both laid in one nest and exchanged with each other as if male and female."

It is probable that females *W1* and *W2*, for which complete records are given in Chapter VII, constitute another case in point. These two female white rings (*St. alba*) had been purchased in November, 1895, and had been mated on the supposition that they were male and female. The record shows that they had long been together. *W2* laid two eggs before being mated with the male *X*. *W1* laid her first egg two days after being mated with *X*, but he did not respond at once and it was noted in the record that there were probably no unions and it is unlikely that the egg had any chance of being fertilized. Since the two females laid at practically the same time (one day apart), it is very probable that they had united and stimulated each other to the production of eggs.

An extended account of the behavior of two pairs of female blond ring-doves (pair *D*, and pair *E*) will be given. These two matings present most of the phenomena that are to be met with in such matings of female with female. To aid the reader in grasping the intricacies of the detailed account of "pair *D*," the following brief synopsis of events is appended by the editor:

A first egg was laid during the afternoon of January 24, though the act was not observed. No account of the previous mating activities is given. The second egg was laid at 9 a. m. on the 26th, and this act was observed and described. At this time and during the rest of the day the alleged male persistently tried to take the nest and perform his regular incubation duties. On the next day he failed to exhibit normal masculine behavior, *i.e.*, he did not incubate the eggs during the day and sit on the perch at night; he did, however, behave normally thereafter until February 8, a period of 11 days. On the 8th and 9th his behavior was regular, with the single exception that he tried to obtain the nest late in the evening, when he should have been on the perch for the night. A second set of eggs was laid February 27 and 29, and this bird did not begin to exhibit masculine incubation behavior until March 3, when he attempted to assume incubation duties late in the afternoon. On the 5th this alleged male was discovered *laying an egg* at 10 a. m.; and 4 eggs were found in the nest, so that the third egg was probably laid on the afternoon of the 3d, when he attempted to take the nest from the female. The account is given as it was written—the bird which was thought to be a male is referred to as a male.[1]

For some time before this egg was laid on Jan. 26 the male of "pair *D*" kept getting into the nest-box[2] and trying to get possession of the nest. After driving him away several times and finding that he was determined to continue his efforts, I gave him a

---

[1] The two birds of this pair hatched together in the same nest—were full sisters—as is shown by reference to table 174, Volume II. It is there noted that the "second egg of the clutch was smaller than the first"; this is a reversal of the more usual size-relations of the eggs. In view of later work on sex it seems not improbable that the "supposed male" described here was hatched from an egg which was less definitely "female" than was the more feminine mate.—O. R.

[2] This nest-box was about 8 inches long, 6 inches wide, and 5 inches deep.

30   BEHAVIOR OF PIGEONS.

cuff that frightened him and put a stop to his returning to the nest. He then went to an empty box on the other side of the cage and settled down as if he were over the eggs. After an hour or so the female came off the nest, and I then had to go and drive him out of his empty box. He flew over to the nest, but remembered his cuff and seemed to anticipate another. I stepped back so as to relieve him from any anxiety, and was surprised to see him deliberately forsake his nest and eggs and walk back to the empty box, into which he at once jumped and then settled down as if performing his duty. I drove him out several times with the same result. I then put the female back and she at once went on the nest. The male, again dislodged from his box, went to the nest and fairly induced the female to leave. He remained only a few moments after she left and then walked back to sit in his empty box. Again I placed the female back and left her there and the male in his box. During most of the afternoon I was away and could not observe what occurred. On returning at 6 p. m. I found the female on the nest and the male sitting on the edge of the box immediately over her. This seemed again unaccountable, for in the parental pair the male never sat near the nest. To sit right over the mate, without regard to consequences, was a departure from usual neatness and good breeding that surprised me. I carefully removed him to a perch, where he at length remained.

Why did this male behave thus in regard to sitting? Evidently he felt the impulse to sit in the morning at the usual time. But it happened that the second egg was about to be laid and the female would not leave. He followed his impulse, and when I taught him by rough usage that he could not sit on the nest just then, he sought to satisfy his wish by sitting in an empty box. Having sat an hour or so there, he became accustomed to the place, and persisted in leaving the eggs before his eyes and going back to sit on nothing but the dry dung with which the box was partly filled. For a male dove that had never before seen an egg, or had any experience in nesting, this strong desire to sit—and to sit on nothing rather than not at all—is very remarkable. It would seem that the whole organization is ready to sit. The male and female advance from one stage to another together; they mate, and the actions of the male stimulate the female to the production of eggs, and her actions carry him along, so that at the proper time both take part in finding a nesting-place and in building the nest. They coöperate in building the nest, and when the eggs are laid the male is all prepared to perform his new duties and to renounce, for a time, his sexual pleasures.

At the end of the period of incubation (two weeks), and a week or more in care of the young, the pair renew the cycle of events. The young are fed by both parents until the female is about ready to lay again, then the male continues the work alone and the young begin to help themselves. As soon as the time of hatching arrives, the previous young begin to learn that they are no longer wanted, and if they do not leave the male takes them in hand and drives them without mercy. All this is to the end that the new comers may be safe in their nest from attacks by their elder brother and sister when the parents are away. The bird has no idea of what its actions mean, for its actions are according to *feelings*, which follow each other in regular *serial* order, making the same round each time.

On Jan. 28, the second day of sitting, the male began his duties by again returning to the empty box; this was done a few moments after the female came off the eggs. I then covered the box so that the male could not get into it, and left him to see what he would do. He went to the box and tried every way to get into it; failing, he went to the nest and sat a moment, but was not satisfied, and soon returned to his box, flying over it and around it in vain endeavors to get into it. He seemed desperate in his efforts. Again he returned to the nest, but did not stop to sit down, but got up on the edge of the box and dressed his feathers a few moments, quite free from any fear; he then again tried to enter his empty box. Seeing that it was hopeless to try to get him to cover the eggs in the nest, I filled a pasteboard box—just large enough to fit in the empty box—with hay, put the

THE PAIRING OF PIGEONS. **31**

eggs into it, and placed all inside the empty box. The male went at once to the eggs, but remained only a few moments, and then came down to his mate.

I then tried the female to see if she would accept the eggs in the new place. She looked at the eggs with an inquisitive air, but decided to leave them. I then returned the eggs to the first nest and there she at once covered them. But very soon the male came to her and got into the box beside her; this she took as an invitation to leave, which she did. But the male, as before, stopped only a moment, then went to his box and began to work at forming a nest in the hay which I had left there. I then again returned the female to the nest. She was unwilling to enter the box, but I placed her inside and held my hand so as to prevent her getting out. She moved about carefully, noticing the eggs, and finally decided to cover them. The male went on working at his nest. At $8^h 50^m$ the female left the eggs, and at $8^h 55^m$ I transferred the eggs to the nest of the male, placing them under him. He drew back a little from my hand but did not leave the nest. Soon after I left him, however, he came off and flew down to the floor of the cage with his mate. At $9^h 05^m$ I placed the female back on the nest and gave her the eggs; the male went to his nest again, and continued to fashion his nest. At $9^h 10^m$ I placed one egg under him, leaving one with the female. Both remained quiet, the male working to complete the shaping of his nest, turning round now and then, and placing now this straw, now that. At $9^h 15^m$ the male left his box and went to the female's. She resigned, but he did not stop but went back to his own nest. I then gave both eggs to the female in her own nest, which she again accepted. At $9^h 30^m$ I again gave both eggs to the male, taking the female off her nest. But he soon left them. I next transferred the paper box containing the eggs from the box of the male to that of the female, and she accepted the new box and nest here, although a moment before she had refused them in the box of the male. This shows how strongly the "place" of the nest acts on these doves.

The male soon returned, claiming the box, nest, and eggs. The female retired and the male remained a few moments, then ($9^h 45^m$) went to his empty box; but he now missed the straw and did not feel as if things were right. Still he persevered, and entering the empty box he began to call vigorously for his mate, as if inviting her to make a new nest. This was the first time that he had so called, and it may be taken as an indication that he is forgetting his business of sitting and thinking of a new nest. At $10^h 15^m$ he is still calling. I give him some strands of hay, which he uses. At $10^h 30^m$ he flies over to the female, and she retires at $10^h 34^m$. The male remains 5 minutes, then goes back to his box, and then to the floor to eat. At $10^h 45^m$ the male returned to the female's nest, but did not really settle down to cover the eggs, and soon left for his box. I then covered his box so he could not get inside. He then went back and the female again retired ($10^h 49^m$); he stopped only a moment, then went to his own box and began to call, although he could not enter, and had only a naked flat surface to stand on. Soon after ($10^h 52^m$) the female went back to the eggs of her own accord. I was then absent until $11^h 35^m$, at which time I found the male beside the female on the nest; she retired, leaving him in possession; but he almost immediately flew down to the floor of the cage with the female, picked up a straw and went back, did not stop to sit, but returned to the floor just as the female picked up a straw. She carried this to the nest and then took her place on the eggs; again she was visited by the male and retired as before.

The male was on the nest at $11^h 43^m$ but again deserted at $11^h 45^m$. The female carried another straw at $11^h 47^m$ and took her place. The male returned at $11^h 48^m$ and the female retired and brought straws. The male goes off at $11^h 50^m$, prompted by the presence of other doves near his box. The female notices that he is off, and goes back, but has not time to take her place before the male returns; she again retires, but he flies back again to his box ($11^h 58^m$) to drive off the other doves which are in a box close to his and separated only by a wire netting. I then put up a screen so that he could not see the doves in the

32   BEHAVIOR OF PIGEONS.

neighboring box. But he did not sit properly, moved about, and flew off at 12 o'clock. A moment later the female returned of her own accord, but was immediately followed by the male, and she again retired without entering the nest. The male entered and beckoned with his wings and by calls for the female. At 12^h 15^m the male left the nest again, went to his box, and called the female. She went back to her nest, only to be followed by the male and again to retire, leaving him at the nest. This happened several times between 12^h 15^m and 12^h 30^m. The male went off at 12^h 35^m, went to his own box, and called the female. She returned to the nest of her own accord at 12^h 46^m, while the male was still calling on his box. Between 1 and 1^h 50^m I was away. At 1^h 50^m both birds were on the floor, but the female went at once to her nest and was followed by the male. She left the nest and he went off to his box, calling her as usual. A moment later she went to the nest and at 1^h 55^m he returned; she promptly left the nest to him. At 2 the male abandoned the nest and she returned to it. At 2^h 10^m she left for a moment and then returned while he remained on the floor. At 2^h 12^m the male carried a straw and took the nest from her again. At 2^h 13^m he flew to his box and she returned of her own accord; the male in the meantime was calling. At 3 she came off and both were on the floor; she at once went to the nest. I was absent from 3 to 6 p. m. At 6 p. m. the male was sitting on the edge of the box over the female. I placed him on his perch beside the box and he remained.

At 8^h 30^m a. m. on Jan. 29, the third day of sitting, the male took his place on the nest and remained there quite contentedly. He behaved normally in every way but came off at 9 o'clock and remained for 15 minutes, both doves then spending the time together on the floor of the cage. At 9^h 15^m he returned to the nest; he came off for a few moments at 10^h 50^m and then went back. He now seems to be in a normal mood. The male has behaved properly all day, except for his long stay away from the eggs in the morning. When night came he did not perch over his mate, but took a place at the opposite side of the cage. Thus *regularity* in behavior sets all points right; in other words, normal conduct in one particular is correlated with normal conduct in other respects.

On Jan. 30 the male was found on the nest at 7^h 30^m a. m. He came off at 7^h 45^m and the female went on. He returned with a straw at 7^h 50^m and she resigned her place to him. All went normally for nine days thereafter, or until the night of Feb. 8, just before the day on which the young would begin to hatch. The male went to the nest and tried very hard to crowd out the female and obtain possession. Having failed in one attempt, he left the nest for a few moments, but again returned and struggled to work his way in. Again he failed to get possession and soon retired to his perch, as it was fast getting dark; but he tried yet a third time before giving it up. On the next night he again behaved in the same way.[1]

The second set of eggs was laid on Feb. 27 and 29. The male took his place on the nest beside the female for the first time on the evening of Mar. 3, having kept the perch regularly up to that time. He left the nest, however, at 8^h 40^m p. m. of this date and took the perch. Probably my going to the nest stimulated him to retire; at any rate, he did so just after I had left the nest.

On Mar. 5, at 10^h 05^m a. m., I found the supposed male laying an egg; and, just after the egg was dropped, the bird stood up so that I could see under her, and I was astonished to find 4 eggs. The second pair of eggs were not measured, but they were fully as large as the first. *It is now clear that "pair D" represents two females,* and this explains the fact that the two birds have behaved towards each other now as male, and again as female. I could not understand this before. It explains further why the supposed male has never done much crowing.

---

[1] Since this pair, as determined later, consists of two females, the eggs necessarily did not hatch. The failure to hatch, however, would arouse no suspicion as to the state of affairs. Incubation was imperfect during the first stages, and failures under these circumstances are not uncommon.—EDITOR.

THE PAIRING OF PIGEONS. 33

The second pair of blond ring females was known as "pair *E*" and their behavior was described as follows: This pair of blond rings has behaved in a remarkable way in preparation for egg-laying. On Feb. 2 the female began to remain over-night on the nest. I expected she would lay, but she kept on sitting on the nest for four nights and for much of each day. Her wings did not droop at any time as they usually do when eggs are about to be laid.

A very remarkable change was made on Feb. 8, for the male took the nest for the night and the female took the perch perfectly contented. The male remained on the nest as if to the manner born. It is certainly very strange, this sitting on an empty nest so long, and then the male usurping the functions of the female in night-work.

On the following morning the male came off the nest quite early, at about 7 o'clock or a little before, and the female went on soon after. At $8^h 30^m$ I found the male on the nest again, and apparently acting just as if he was in charge of the eggs. At $9^h 10^m$ he came off, and the female went on soon after. They thus continued to exchange with each other during the day. At night, at about 5 o'clock, I saw the male go to the nest, and saw the female retire to her perch without making any objection. They continued this, he sitting at night, and both during the day. On the night of Feb. 12, *both* sat on the nest during the early evening, but the female took her place on the perch at $8^h 45^m$. Both sat on the nest during the nights of the 14th, 15th, and 16th.

On Feb. 23, these birds were still sitting on the empty nest, regularly exchanging during the day and both sitting at night. But I now notice that both are at times less devoted to the nest, *i.e.*, they come off occasionally to eat, and do not hasten back with the usual anxiety; still, I have not noticed any long stay away from the nest. The same conduct occurred on the two following days.

During the night of Feb. 25 and 26, *both birds sat on the nest as usual, but both came off in the morning, and remained off.* They have bestowed the usual attentions on each other preparatory to nesting. They have shown some desire to fly from the cage, but have not shown any long-continued restlessness. They have now evidently finished up the course of sitting without ever having produced an egg, paying the same constant attention to an empty nest that they would have given to eggs. Evidently the instinct to sit does not depend upon the presence or production of eggs, but runs its course and comes to an end without any stimulus from without. The sexual passion rises and the work of making a new nest begins. The period of incubation, if we can so call it, may be said to have begun on Feb. 8, and to have continued until this date (Feb. 26) or 2 weeks and 4 days. But I am mistaken in thinking the nest to be fully abandoned. I now find both birds on the nest at night as usual.

On Feb. 27 both are off the nest and very restless, trying to get out of the cage. At night I find both have left the nest and gone to the opposite side of the cage to perch in the old place where they used to roost before making a nest. We can now be sure that the nest is finally abandoned and will not be occupied again unless for a second round of incubation. The period of incubation would thus be 2 weeks and 5 days in this case, the last day being a broken and desultory one.

On Feb. 28 these birds were very restless in the morning; both tried to get out of the cage and were evidently intent on finding a place for the nest. On the next day they devoted some time to a box opposite to the old nest which contained no straw. On the day following I covered the box so that they could not get into it. They tried it, and failing, were extremely restless and desirous of getting out of the cage. They stood before the door and kept flying up as if wishing to have the door opened.

After trying first the covered box, and then to get into my room, this pair went, on Mar. 3, to the old nest and soon settled down there as a last resort. It is remarkable how strong the instinct is *to place the new nest in a new locality.* The white rings (*St. alba*)

34 BEHAVIOR OF PIGEONS.

showed no such instinct, in at least one instance, though they might have done so had they not been ready to lay immediately, *i.e.*, without any interruption in incubation.

On March 5, between 3 and 5 p. m., one of these doves laid an egg. *The supposed male had possession of it* when found, and the other (supposed female) sat on the nest close beside. Is the supposed male a female? And have we thus another pair of females, *mating, nesting, copulating,* and *incubating,* as if male and female? The two doves are devoted to each other, and their behavior is that of male and female. The supposed male acts as a male, except that he crows very little and does not have the full sonorous voice of the known males. Which dove laid the egg I am as yet unable to say. On Mar. 7, a second egg was laid at $7^h 10^m$ a. m. *Both doves are females.* Their age at the time of the second egg was 6 months and 20 days. (R 19, C 7/17.)

In continuing Professor Whitman's work, Dr. Riddle has studied with some detail this pairing phenomenon between two females and has given the following summary account of his observations:

The continued isolation of two female doves is usually sufficient to induce their mating with each other. Many of the phenomena of a normal pairing will be exhibited by such unnatural pairs. Copulation, nest-building, egg-laying, incubation, and feeding of young, all follow in the usual order. In working with hybrids between *T. orientalis* and *St. alba*— sex-controlled material produced by Professor Whitman—I have been able to carry considerably further the analysis of this conduct, obtaining the following significant results:

(1) One or both members of a pair of females may function as the male in copulation, and one may so function much more frequently than the other.

(2) The amount of this predominance in mounting is dependent upon the *relative masculinity* of the females of the pair.

(3) A bird predominantly masculine in one mating will show predominantly feminine behavior in another mating with an exceedingly masculine female.

(4) This relative masculinity rests upon a physical and physiological basis imposed upon these birds by the conditions which affect their own sex-determination.

The several features involved in the sex-control are treated elsewhere (see Volume II of these works). A complete account, by the present writer, of the relative masculinity and femininity of female and male birds respectively will appear in a volume now in course of preparation.

In our more recent studies of the detailed behavior of the members of pairs of the same sex, some data have accumulated which touch the question of the relation which "energy" and "aggressiveness" bear to sex.

In the main, Professor Whitman's conclusion that the male is the more energetic and aggressive finds confirmation here; furthermore, the more "aggressive" females studied in the new lines of work have proved, in most cases, to be the more masculine in their sex behavior; *i.e.*, they have more often taken the part of the male in copulation. There seem, however, to be some instances where this simple rule does not hold. Certainly there are cases where the "larger" bird is not the more masculine; likewise, more "eager" birds which are not more masculine. The exceptions to the above rule, though possibly of importance, can be treated adequately only in connection with our own forthcoming work.

One may ask, How completely will the more masculine of a pair of females assume the duties and behavior of a male? In reply it can be said, first of all, that *both try to be females;* and that it is chiefly where two simultaneous feminine behaviors are precluded by the nature of the activity, as in billing or copulating, that the testing struggle comes.

If two such females differentiate themselves in the matter of "display" I have not noted it; though I have not definitely, consistently, or preparedly looked for it. The more masculine female has more often been the "jealous" driving one. I have failed to note different rôles taken in "nest-building."

In sexual "billing" the more masculine bird usually, but not invariably, receives the bill of her consort. Sometimes, however, in the rather tense sharp contest on this much-indulged detail, the more feminine female is induced or forced to yield her open mouth; in which event she is more often induced to follow this by mounting than when the billing contest terminates differently. She may, however, play the part of the male in the "billing" and yet function as a female in the succeeding copulation. In general, the one that usually "bills" as a male also "jumps over" and mounts, as a male. Important here too is our finding that such a masculine member of the pair is usually *a day or more behind her mate in egg-laying, and may not lay at all!*

It is evident, therefore, that those females which mount as males much more than do their consorts are rather *consistently masculine* towards these consorts. But, as stated above, where quite free and unopposed their activities are those of females. This fact must not be disregarded. Whether a pair of females maintain this sort of differentiation during the incubation period is a matter not yet tested; in fact, this may not prove easy to decide since most female doves seem willing to go to the nest by day whenever the eggs are left uncovered; and both, or either, will sometimes sit at night in cases where both have laid eggs. This matter certainly needs further investigation.

PAIRING OF MALES.

Males have also been known to mate. Two of my male passenger-pigeons mated with each other, notwithstanding they were in a pen where there were several unmated females desirous of mating. (C 7/48.)

Dr. Riddle has noted the same phenomenon and has furnished the following account of the behavior:

The mating of male with male has been seen to occur among certain doves. That is to say, two males may pair, cease to drive or fight each other, mutually defend a nest, and either or both actively, and with apparent completeness, take the part of a female in copulation. Thus mated they may go through the whole of the breeding cycle of copulation, nest-building, feeding, and rearing of foster young. The few cases of such matings that I have thus far observed present, however, widely varying degrees of completeness of the mating. Only a single pair of (young) blond ring-doves has been seen to carry out the entire program stated above.

The male birds thus far known actively to take the part of a female in the sexual act are blond rings (*St. risoria*), white rings (*St. alba*), and hybrids between the Japanese turtle-dove (*T. orientalis*) and the white rings. Among these forms matings are more easily secured if *young* males are used. The latter statement can now be made confidently, though the first mating observed was between two *orientalis-alba* hybrids whose age was 4 or 5 years. The fact that one of these birds seemed actively to function as a female, in a copulation which I chanced to see, led me to make several matings with a view to a study of this situation. I had already learned that the sisters of these same hybrids, of all ages, can be made to mate with each other under certain conditions. A number of pairs of mature males were isolated; some of these were observed for several months, but no real matings resulted from any of these cases. Even the pair of birds which was first seen to copulate, in a pen where there were only male birds, fought and drove each other when isolated from the group. Between these two birds very few matings were later observed which could give any reason to believe that one was really and actively functioning as a female; both birds of course occasionally attempted the part of the male in copulation, but to the end fierce fighting was the rule of the day in this cage as it was in the others.

36 BEHAVIOR OF PIGEONS.

Early in 1913, however, two young (4 to 8 months) ring-doves were obtained from a dealer who thought them to be a male and a female. These birds, kept apart from other doves, mated with each other within a month and proved to be two males. One of these males during a whole season frequently and actively functioned as a female, though more often attempting to copulate as male. It is doubtful, however, whether the *other* blond ring ever *actively* functioned as a female in a complete copulation; usually he flew, or slipped, from the perch soon after the mate mounted him. This pair incubated eggs and reared young.

Other pairings were obtained between young *orientalis-alba* hybrids, but in both successful cases the birds soon passed into a fighting, driving stage. In one of these cases either male would sometimes actively function as a female. Two other pairs were obtained, the first consisting of a pure white ring male and a pure blond ring male; both were very young. Both birds were seen actively to take the part of females. The second pair was formed by the union of two very young birds. One was a white ring and the other was an *orientalis-alba* hybrid. This mating has now been continued for more than 3 months.

The following data concern the incubation behavior of two male blond ring-doves. These birds have now incubated and reared two nests of young. In incubating the first lot it was not noted whether the more masculine or the more feminine of the pair nested mostly at night; it is known only that the more feminine one was on the nest during two nights of the incubation period. During the incubation of the second lot, however, more complete records were made. Here the more masculine male was on the nest during 9 nights and the more feminine male nested during 5 nights. For 2 nights there was no record. In considering these data it is probably well to note that the more masculine of this pair was nearest ready to incubate when eggs were given, and that the unnaturally functioning male was late in getting ready (third night) for incubation; an unnaturally functioning female is similarly delayed one or more days in the delivery of her eggs.

The difference in masculinity of these two birds lies not so much in any difference in their willingness to mount as in the fact that the one has almost uniformly refused to take the part of the female in a completed copulation, whereas the other has readily done so. This latter bird also has a wider space between the pubic bones and so was at first taken, by a dealer and by myself, for a female.

PROMISCUOUS TENDENCIES.

The author has noted the phenomenon of "stolen matings" in numerous breeding records, but without any discussion of it. Examples may be found in manuscripts BB 9, G 19, and G 20. Naturally these matings will be found only among those birds which were allowed their freedom, *i.e.*, the common or domestic pigeons. The female of a pair, during the mating period, will accept matings from other males as well as from her own mate. These illicit copulations on the part of a *paired* female were observed, but no statement was made as to whether the offending male was free or paired. Probably this promiscuous tendency characterized the male also. In one manuscript (C 7/7) we find the case of a male mourning-dove who regarded the author as his mate. This bird was twice confined with white ring females and refused to pair with them, although both were very eager to do so. This male, however, did not exhibit any hestitation in gratifying his sexual impulses at every opportunity. The important fact to be noted is that though *fidelity* is the rule, yet exceptions do occur; some tendency to *promiscuity* does exist. It is impossible to state whether this promiscuous tendency is

THE PAIRING OF PIGEONS.

universal or limited to the domestic varieties.[1] In this connection one might suggest the possibility that the promiscuous tendency is somewhat universal and deep-seated, while the marked degree of fidelity characteristic of pigeons is a product of their division of labor in nest-building, incubation, and feeding of young. This division of labor of necessity keeps the two birds together and somewhat isolated from others of their kind and thus reduces the opportunities for illicit matings. In other words, pigeons might be promiscuous like fowls if, like these, the males were so constituted as to take no share in mating activities other than copulation.

Fulton, in his work previously cited, states:

"For although pigeons as a rule pair with great fidelity, exceptions are by no means rare; and cases have been known in which a cock has mated with two hens, and even assisted both in hatching and rearing their young; while we once possessed a cock which, though he never aided them in family duties, regularly paired with no less than *five* hens. This case being so very remarkable we took particular notice of it, and can vouch for the truth of what we state. To the naturalist such instances are particularly interesting, as showing that, under some instances, pigeons might possibly become gregarious, like poultry."

UNUSUAL PROCLIVITIES.

The old bronze-wing birds were beginning to prepare for a nest, the male taking the lead in going to the nest-box and calling. The male gradually became more earnest and more attentive towards the female. Not satisfied with her coolness, the male frequently mounted the *young* of the previous cycle (these young birds were 7 to 8 weeks old at the time).

The male bronze-wing was again anxious to copulate and renew the cycle, while the female was still taking care of the young. In response to the call of the female on the nest, the male raised his feathers a little and let his wings hang loosely at his side; he then wheeled about and gave a jump onto the corner of the seed-pan, stood there a moment, dropped his abdominal feathers, and fixed those about the anal opening as they are placed preparatory to sexual union. He turned again without going further and hopped off. Three times in succession he repeated this performance. The female's call set him off. I have seen him behave in this way two or three times before during the last few days. There was another call from the female and similar behavior over the corner of the seed-dish resulted. Before mounting, the male lowers his head and acts as if pressing down on the dish just as he does with his mate; then he gives a quick jump— both feet at once— halts on the edge, fixes his feathers, dismounts, quickly remounts, etc. When the female came down to the seed-dish the male attempted to mount her.

I once had a mourning-dove which I kept in my room during the winter. He became well acquainted with me and was quite tame. There were some other mourning-doves in the room and I expected that he would of course pick out one of them and mate. But when the mating season came, in March, he began to show an interest in *me!* Every time I came into the room he would jump into the nest-box, raise his tail and spread it somewhat, put his head down low, and begin to give the nest-call, looking at me and vibrating his wings very slowly as if inviting me to come. If I approached the nest he would be still more active and seem very much delighted. His little eyes would twinkle and he would turn around and look at me in the most loving and inviting way. He kept on in this way for a week or two and I finally had to break him of it by simply keeping out of his sight. At the time he was very anxious to mate and finally accepted one of his own kind:

---

[1] Dr. Riddle reports an instance of a hybrid blond-white ring-dove male being paired simultaneously with two females, one a white-blond hybrid the other a Senegal turtle-dove.

4

BEHAVIOR OF PIGEONS.

A fuller account of the history and mating proclivities of this same male, which was probably partly raised "by hand," is found in the following: A male mourning-dove (*Zen. 3*) was obtained when a few months old. He was mated $2\frac{1}{2}$ months later (Dec. 20, 1896) with a white ring-dove (*W1*). The male regarded *me* as his mate and drove other doves away from his nest-box. I had to cease going to his call in order to turn his attention away from me to *W1*, who was eager to mate and tried all possible ways to ingratiate herself in his favor. On Jan. 5, 1897, this male is still as fond as ever of me, and often tries to call me to the nest-box; if I go to him he looks happy and delighted and frequently drives his mate out of the nest if she answers to his calls. On Jan. 20 he flew to the nest-box and began calling me. Whenever I go near him he struts around and appears to welcome me as a mate, for he usually goes to the nest-box and drives his white mate off if she intrudes. On Jan. 27 this male still flies to the nest-box when he sees me come into the room, and he often calls me long and persistently. I now keep away from him. On Feb. 10, he still flies to the nest-box every time I enter the room; he then sits on the nest-box calling me. On Mar. 7, he still drives his would-be mate if she approaches him when I am near; he drives her and calls to me. This mourning-dove, on Apr. 7, still continues to call me, although I no longer answer him. He was finally mated with another bird. (R 33, C 7/7, SS 10.)

A SPECIAL CASE—NOT ABERRANT MENTALITY.

This story, which is taken from the Mental Evolution of Animals (p. 173) by Mr. Romanes, has been thought worthy of translation into German by Karl Gross in his *Spiele der Thiere*. The case was reported to Mr. Romanes by a lady, and is given in her own words:

"A white fantail pigeon lived with his family in a pigeon-house in our stable-yard. He and his wife had been brought originally from Sussex, and had lived, respected and admired, to see their children of the third generation, when he suddenly became the victim of the infatuation I am about to describe.

"No eccentricity whatever was remarked in his conduct until one day I chanced to pick up somewhere in the garden a ginger-beer bottle of the ordinary brownstone description. I flung it into the yard, where it fell immediately below the pigeon-house. That instant down flew *pater familias* and to my no small astonishment commenced a series of genuflections, evidently doing homage to the bottle. He strutted round and round it, bowing and scraping and cooing, and performing the most ludicrous antics I ever beheld on the part of an enamoured pigeon. Nor did he cease these performances until we removed the bottle; and, which proved that this singular aberration of instinct had become a fixed delusion, whenever the bottle was thrown or placed in the yard—no matter whether it lay horizontally or was placed upright—the same ridiculous scene was enacted; at that moment the pigeon came flying down with quite as great alacrity as when his peas were thrown out for his dinner, to continue his antics as long as the bottle remained there. Sometimes this would go on for hours, the other members of his family treating his movements with the most contemptuous indifference and taking no notice whatever of the bottle. At last it became the regular amusement with which we entertained our visitors to see this erratic pigeon making love to the interesting object of his affections, and it was an entertainment which never failed, throughout that summer at least. Before next summer came around, he was no more."

Mr. Romanes remarks:

"It is thus evident that the pigeon was affected with some strong and persistent *monomania* with regard to this particular object. Although it is well known that insanity is not an uncommon thing among animals, this is the only case I have met with of a conspicuous derangement of the instinctive as distinguished from the rational faculties—unless we so regard the exhibitions of erotomania, infanticide, mania, etc., which occur in animals perhaps more frequently than they do in man."

This pigeon, whose behavior has given it so wide fame as a case of deranged instinct, was undoubtedly a perfectly normal bird; and had Mr. Romanes been familiar with the antics of male pigeons, he would have found nothing in the performances to indicate

THE PAIRING OF PIGEONS. **39**

insanity. I have seen a white fantail play in the same way to his shadow on the floor, and when his shadow fell on a crust of bread he at once adopted the bread as the object of his affection, and went through all the performances described by the lady, even to repeating the behavior for several days afterward when I placed the same piece of bread on the floor of his pen. If one is looking for insanity in pigeons, let him first know the normal range of sanity and pay little heed to stories of inexperienced observers who are apt to overlook circumstances essential to a correct understanding of what they report.

It is not improbable that the lady's amusing pigeon at first took the bottle for a living intruder upon his ground and flew down to it for the purpose of driving it off. Finding it at rest, if his shadow fell upon it, or if his image was even faintly reflected from its surface, he would readily mistake it for a female pigeon, and after once getting this idea and performing before it, the bottle would be remembered and the same emotions excited the next time it was presented. The only value this suggestion can have is that it is based on a similar case. The lady's observations were not complete at the critical moment, *i. e.*, at the time of the *first* performance, and it is too late to mend the failure.[1]

---

[1] Whitman, Myths in Animal Psychology, Monist, 1899, pp. 528–530.

CHAPTER IV.

THE INCUBATION PERIOD.

By the incubation period we refer to that part of the reproductive cycle which extends from the appearance of the first egg until hatching is completed. Some species may begin to sit on the nest before the appearance of the eggs, while in other cases incubation may be delayed until the advent of the second egg. Incubation, in a sense, exists for a week or so after hatching, as the young are at first covered almost as carefully as were the eggs. Our use of the term, however, may be justified as a means of classifying and describing the various activities of the reproductive cycle. The present chapter is concerned primarily with various statistical data rather than with behavior proper.

LENGTH OF THE PERIOD.

The time of incubation varies considerably in the different species. The shortest incubation period that I have known anything about is that of the wild passenger-pigeon, which is only 12½ days; while that of the common pigeon is 17 to 19 days, and that of the ring-doves or turtle-doves is 14 to 16 days. (SS 10.)

T. H. Newman (Avic. Mag., May, 1908, 217–218) gives the incubation period of *T. pictaturus* (Madagascar turtle-dove) as 12 days (reckoned from the date of the second egg). I find these birds have a longer period, and furthermore, it is incorrect to start the period with the second egg, as development begins in the passage through the uterus before the egg is laid. (R 18.)

Fulton (*op. cit.*, p. 39) says:

"The period of sitting among (fancy) pigeons is 18 days, reckoned from the day on which the second egg is laid, for one day intervenes between the first and second egg being produced. Sometimes, if the parent birds sit very close, the young are hatched on the seventeenth day in summer weather; not infrequently, however, the period of hatching is delayed to the nineteenth or twentieth day."

Table 3 has been compiled from the records. Besides differences of species it is to be noted that the period for the second egg is generally shorter than that for the first egg. This fact is probably a result, in part, of the irregularity of early incubation. Until the arrival of the second egg, incubation is intermittent and sometimes lacking (see subsequent topic "Early Incubation," Chapter V). This shortening of the time for the second egg secures a greater equality of the two birds in feeding. This fact is important in that the stronger and better-developed young is likely to monopolize the attention of the parents in feeding (see topic "Feeding of Young," Chapter VI). There is some slight indication in the table that the period tends to decrease with the advance of summer.

In this table we have given the data for the pure species[1] only, not hybrids. When two species with different incubation periods are crossed, the resultant period approaches a mean, with the female exercising a preponderant influence, Given two species *A* and *B*, with incubation periods of 12 and 19 days respectively,

---

[1] Domestic pigeons and the ring-doves are, however, included.

TABLE 3.—*The length of the incubation period.*

Species.	First egg.		Second egg.	
	Date.	Time.	Date.	Time.
		days. hours.		*days. hours.*
Zenaidura	5/11/97	14 22	5/13/97	15 0 ca.
"	6/11/97	14 20 ca.	6/12/97	14 2 ca.
"	7/29/97	14 21 ca.	7/30/97	14 0
"	9/ 2/97	14 12–13	9/ 3/97	14 2 to 4
"	5/ 8/98	15 12 ca.	....	....
"	6/18/98	15 12 ca.	6/19/98	14 20 to 23
"	7/18/98	14 12 ca.	7/19/98	14 0 ca.
"	8/15/98	15 12 ca.	8/16/98	14 12 ca.
"	6/13/99	15 12 ca.	....	....
"	8/13/99	15 ca.	8/14/99	14 0 ca.
"	5/18/00	15 12 to 14	5/19/00	14 20 ca.
"	6/26/00	15 12 ca.	6/26/00	14 few hours.
Fantails.........	9/ 7/96	18 20 ca.	9/ 8/96	17 17 ca.
L. picata........	4/30/07	18 20 ca.	....	....
"	....	....	6/21/07	18 12 ca.
G. humeralis.....	5/13/06	16 12 to 14	5/15/06	15 0
St. humilis......	9/14/00	13 12 to 14	9/15/00	12 21
St. risoria.......	9/13/00	14 0	9/15/00	14 0
Satinette........	4/10/98	18 15 to 16	4/10/98	16 22 to 23
P. chalcoptera....	1/ 3/06	17 12 ca.	1/ 4/06	16 18 to 20
"	3/18/06	17 20 to 21	....	....
"	6/ 2/06	16 12 ca.	6/ 3/06	15 18 ca.
Ectopistes.......	8/11/96	13 ca.	....	....
"	5/11/97	13 ca.....	....	....
"	6/12/97	12 12 to 13	....	....
"	7/25/98	12 18 to 20[1]	....	....
"	8/ 2/98	12 20 ca.	....	....
"	8/ 8/98	12 ca.	....	....
"	8/11/98	12 12 ca.	....	....
"	8/ 9/98	14 to 15 [2]	....	....
"	8/ 4/97	12 1 ca.	....	....
"	9/ 4/97	12 12 to 18	....	....
"	8/28/97	12 12 to 18	....	....
Ring-doves......	3/28/95	15 18 to 20	3/28/95	13 20 ca.
"	4/30/95	14 15 to 17	....	....
"	5/28/95	14 12 ca.	5/29/95	13 20 ca.
"	7/ 4/95	15 12 to 14	7/ 5/95	14 20 to 22
"	8/ 9/95	14 12 to 13	8/10/95	14 5
"	10/31/95	15 20 ca.	10/31/95	15 5 to 6
"	1/ 6/96	15 8 to 12	1/ 6/96	14 3⅞
Common pigeons	3/20/97	19 16⅝	3/20/97	17 13
"	5/ 2/97	17 22 ca.	5/ 3/97	16 14½
"	6/ 2/97	18 20 to 21	6/ 2/97	16 13 to 14
"	8/29/97	18 12 ca.	8/29/97	16 18 ca.
"	3/16/98	18 12 ca.	3/16/98	16 12 ca.

[1] Probably. [2] Incubation was intermittent, not steady.

TABLE 3.—*Probable length of the incubation period—summary.*

	First egg.	Second egg.
	days.	*days.*
Common pigeons....	18½ to 19⅝	16½ to 17½
Fantails............	18⅚	17⅔
L. picata............	18⅚	18½
Satinette............	18⅔	17
P. chalcoptera.......	17⅚	16¾
G. humeralis.........	16½	15+
Ring-doves..........	14½ to 15½	14 to 14⅞
Zenaidura...........	14½ to 15½	14⅛ to 14⅞
St. risoria...........	14	14
St. humilis..........	13½	12⅞
Ectopistes...........	12½	....

THE INCUBATION PERIOD. 43

the mating of a male *A* with a female *B* will produce eggs which will incubate in approximately 18 days, while the resultant period of a male *B* with a female *A* will be perhaps 13 or 14 days. These values are given merely for illustrative purposes. For the data, and the discussion of the phenomenon, the reader is referred to Chapter XV, Volume II.

NUMBER OF EGGS.

Most species lay two eggs; there are some, quite a number, that lay a single egg. Even those that normally lay two eggs sometimes lay but one, so that we do not need any "mutation" to get a species that lays one. I find my white-faced, or Wonga-Wonga, pigeons (*L. picata*) produce only one egg. At least this has been found several times in succession (possibly two eggs were laid in a few cases). The passenger-pigeons (*Ectopistes*) laid one egg in each of 23 cycles recorded.

The editor finds the following list, and references to the literature, of one-egg-laying species:

The following pigeons lay but 1 egg: *Dodo, Calœnas, Ectopistes, Didunculus, Goura,* yellow-billed pigeon, bandtail pigeon, and some species of *Carpophaga* and *Columba.* Generally 2 eggs are laid and in exceptional cases 3 (E. Evans, Birds, The Cambridge Nat. Hist., Vol. IX, 1899, p. 328). Darwin states (Animals and Plants, II, p. 190) that *Ectopistes* invariably lays 2 eggs in America, but only 1 in Lord Derby's menagerie. The same fact is also asserted of the white-crowned pigeon. Le Souef (Emu, II, 1903, pp. 139–159) recorded *Ptilopus ewingi* (rose-crowned fruit-pigeon) and *Myristicivora spilochroa* (nutmeg pigeon) as pigeons that lay but 1 egg. He also found, in one case, but a single egg from *Lophophaps leucogaster* (white-bellied plumed pigeon), but was uncertain as to the normal number. (SS 10, Sh 8/13, SS 4, R 19.)

Among the records for two-egg-laying species a single egg was noted in 8 cycles. These were found in the following pairs: *Geopelia humeralis,* passenger-ring-dove, mourning-dove-white ring, blond ring, homer, a pair of hybrids, and twice in a pair of mourning-doves.

Sometimes eggs may be lacking entirely, although the birds may unite, build a nest, give the preliminary symptoms of egg-laying, and continue with the incubation of an empty nest. This phenomenon occurred in the second cycle of a crested and ring-dove pair and in 2 cycles of another rather similar pair. For further details the reader is referred to the records given in Chapter VII, on "Defective Cycles."

TIME OF LAYING.

The first egg is dropped in the afternoon. Table 4 gives the data for 180 eggs, and there is no exception to the rule; it applies to *Ectopistes* and *L. picata,* which produce but 1 egg in a clutch, as well as to those pairs that occasionally failed to lay a second egg. The recorded times range from $3^h 30^m$ to $6^h 50^m$, a period of approximately 3 hours. Dividing the afternoon into the two periods of before and after 5 o'clock, we find that 68 eggs were laid in the first period and 69 in the second. The more usual laying time for the first egg is thus around 5 p. m.

The time of the second egg depends upon the species, and to a slight extent upon the season. Some species invariably lay in the morning, while others

44 BEHAVIOR OF PIGEONS.

normally lay in the afternoon. The morning period ranges from $6^h 30^m$ to $10^h 30^m$. The period of greatest activity occurs around $8^h 45^m$ a. m., as 54 eggs were dropped before this time and 56 were laid in the second half of the period.

The time of laying of both eggs is influenced by the length of day. It is twice recorded that the first egg seems to be laid earlier, and the second later, in the short days of cold weather than in the long days of summer. This generalization is not readily apparent from an inspection of the table, though the following summary of the data establishes its validity: Of all the first eggs dropped during the six months with the shortest days, 64 per cent were laid before 5 p. m., while 58 per cent were laid after that time during the six months with long days. During the three winter months, 71 per cent were laid before 5 p. m., while in the three summer months 54 per cent were dropped after that time. Of all the second eggs laid in the forenoon during the six months with short days, 91 per cent were laid in the second half of the period, while 57 per cent were laid in the first half of the period during the long days. In the three winter months 100 per cent were laid late, while 65 per cent were laid early during the three summer months. The time of laying is thus influenced to some extent by the length of the day, or by the season. When the egg is dropped in the afternoon, the time is hastened by the early approach of darkness in the winter, while for the morning period the time is delayed by the shortness of the day. This double effect of short days thus increases the interval between the two eggs, and one can notice in the table that the interval for any species tends to decrease with the approach of summer.

The time for the second egg, and possibly for the first egg, varies with the species. The fantails, satinettes, homers, common and crested pigeons lay the first egg rather late in the afternoon and the second somewhat earlier two days later, giving an interval of slightly less than two days. *Zenaidura* has one of the shortest intervals, laying the second egg early in the morning. The blond rings and white rings lay both eggs early, while the bronze-wing, on the contrary, is a late layer. The geopelias lay the first egg early in the afternoon and the second one late in the morning, giving them one of the longest intervals among those species that drop the second egg in the forenoon.

The eggs may also be dropped prematurely, or the time may be delayed beyond the normal period. These facts are evident from the following observations:

The female of a pair of blond rings, after preparing a nest, took her place on the perch at night and dropped an egg probably in the early morning, but the time is uncertain. I discovered a broken egg on the floor of the cage under the perch where it had probably been dropped during the night. A female white ring mated to a mourning-dove laid a soft-shelled egg from the perch in the afternoon. The female of a pair of mourning-doves dropped an egg on the floor from the perch during the night. A female homer mated with a hybrid laid her first egg normally, in the afternoon, but the second egg was dropped too early, at $11^h 40^m$ a. m., two days later.[1]

---

[1] The normal period of the homer is approximately 2 days, and the author remarks that "I have never known of such a case before. I can not account for the early appearance of the second egg. The weather was unusually warm."

THE INCUBATION PERIOD.

TABLE 4.—*Time of laying.*

Species.	Date of first egg.	Date of second egg.	Interval.
			da. hrs. min.
Bronze-wing	12/16/05, 5 to 6 p.m.	12/18/05, 10^h15^m a.m.	1 16 ca.
"	1/16/06, 5 to 6 p.m.	1/18/06, 10 05 a.m.	1 16 ca.
"	2/ 3/06, 5^h10^m p.m.	2/ 5/06, 9 55 a.m.	1 16 45
"	2/28/06, 5 to 6 p.m.	3/ 2/06, 9 42 a.m.	1 16 ca.
"	5/ 3/06, ... p.m.	5/ 5/06, 10 05 a.m.	....
Geopelia humeralis	1/22/06, 4 p.m. ca.	1/24/06, 9 55 a.m.	1 17 ca.
"	1/31/06, 4 p.m. ca.	2/ 2/06, 10 35 a.m.	1 18 ca.
"	2/13/06, ... p.m.	2/15/06, 9 00 a.m.	....
"	3/ 8/06, ... p.m.	3/10/06, 8 58 a.m.	....

Species.[1]	Date of first egg.	Species.[1]	Date of first egg.
Ectopistes	7/29/96, 4 p.m. ca.	*Ectopistes*	7/15/98, ... p.m.
"	8/29/96, 4 to 5 p.m.	"	7/25/98, ... p.m.
"	3/17/97, 4^h52^m p.m.	"	7/31/98, ... p.m.
"	4/ 3/97, ... p.m.	"	8/ 7/98, ... p.m.
"	4/22/97, 6^h25^m p.m.	"	8/22/97, ... p.m.
"	4/28/97, 5 25 p.m.	"	8/28/97, 5^h44^m p.m.
"	5/23/97, 5 10 p.m.	"	8/15/97, 6 00 p.m.
"	5/30/97, 5 to 6 p.m.		
"	6/24/97, 5 p.m. ca.	White-face (*L. picata*)	4/11/07, ... p.m.
"	8/16/97, ... p.m.	"	5/21/07, 3^h40^m p.m.
"	7/12/98, ... p.m.	"	6/ 2/07, 5 p.m.

Species.	Date of first egg.	Date of second egg	Interval.
			da. hr. min.
Zenaidura	3/24/97, 6^h07^m p.m.	....	....
"	4/26/97, 5 05 p.m.	4/28/97, 7 to 9 a.m.	1 14 to 16
"	5/27/97, 5 to 6 p.m.	5/29/97, 6^h35^m a.m.	1 12 to 13
"	7/14/97, 4^h51^m p.m.	7/16/97, ... a.m.	....
"	8/18/97, 4 to 5 p.m.	8/20/97, 7 to 8^h30^m a.m.	1 14 to $16\frac{1}{2}$
"	4/ 2/98, 5 to 6 p.m.	No second egg.	....
"	4/ 9/98, 4 to 5 p.m.	4/11/98, ... a.m.	....
"	6/ 2/98, 4 to 5 p.m.	6/ 4/98, 7 to 8^h30^m a.m.	1 14 to $16\frac{1}{2}$
European turtle	5/31/97, 5^h10^m p.m.	6/ 2/97, 8^h12^m a.m.	1 15 2
Blond rings	3/12/95, 4 to 6 p.m.	3/14/95, 8 to 9 a.m.	1 14 to 17
"	4/15/95, 4 to 5 p.m.	4/17/95, 8^h38^m a.m.	1 $15\frac{1}{2}$ to $16\frac{1}{2}$
"	5/13/95, 5^h30^m p.m.	5/15/95, 8 15 a.m. ca.	1 14 45 ca.
"	6/18/95, 4 46 p.m.	6/20/95, 8 30 a.m. ca.	1 15 44 ca.
"	7/25/95, 4 35 p.m.	7/27/95, 7 36 a.m.	1 15
"	10/15/95, 4 to 6 p.m.	10/17/95, 8 to 9 a.m.	1 14 to 17
"	12/21/95; 3^h30^m to 5^h30^m p.m.	12/23/95, 9^h20^m a.m.	1 16 to 18
"	1/28/97, 5 12 p.m.	1/30/97, 9 51 a.m.	1 16 51
"	3/ 4/97, 4 54 p.m.	3/ 6/97, 9 42 a.m.	1 16 44
"	3/27/97, 5 05 p.m.	3/29/97, 8 56 a.m.	1 15 51
"	4/27/97, 5 01 p.m.	4/29/97, 9 08 a.m.	1 16 7
"	6/ 2/97, 4 43 p.m.	6/ 4/97, 7 to 8^h30^m a.m.	1 14 15
"	5/12/96, 4 50 p.m.	....	....
"	12/23/96, 3 58 p.m.	12/25/96, 9^h18^m a.m.	1 17 20
"	3/ 5/97, 4 43 p.m.	3/ 7/97, 8 51 a.m.	1 16 48
"	3/14/97, 4 27 p.m.	3/16/97, 8 55 a.m.	1 16 28
"	3/27/97, 4 45 p.m.	3/29/97, 8 37 a.m.	1 15 52
"	4/ 9/97, 5 00 p.m.	4/11/97, 8 to 9 a.m.	1 15 to 16
"	6/ 6/97, 4 27 p.m.	6/ 8/97, 8^h12^m a.m.	1 15 45
"	11/29/96, 3 45 p.m.	....	....
"	12/23/96, 3 45 p.m.	12/25/96, 9 15 a.m.	1 17 30
"	....	1/17/97, 9 45 a.m.	....
"	1/ 1/97, 3 53 p.m.	1/ 3/97, 9 55 a.m.	1 18 2
"	3/ 6/97, 5 03 p.m.	3/ 8/97, 9 45 a.m.	1 16 42
"	4/19/97, 5 31 p.m.	4/21/97, 9 15 a.m.	1 15 44
Common pigeon	2/28/97, 5 15 p.m.	3/ 2/97, 5 30 p.m.	2 0 15
"	4/14/97, 5 to 5^h40^m p.m.	4/16/97, 4 35 p.m.	1 23 to $23\frac{1}{2}$
"	5/14/97, ... p.m.	5/16/97, ... p.m.	....
"	8/10/97, ... p.m.	8/12/97, ... p.m.	....

[1] These species lay but a single egg in each clutch.

BEHAVIOR OF PIGEONS.

TABLE 4.—*Time of laying*—Continued.

Species	Date of first egg.	Date of second egg.	Interval.		
			da.	hr.	min.
Hyb. ring ♂ × homer ♀	6/16/97, ... p.m...........	6/18/97, ... p.m..........	....		
"	6/28/97, ... p.m...........	6/30/97, ... p.m..........	....		
"	7/13/97, 6 p.m...............	7/15/97, ... p.m..........	....		
"	7/29/97, 5 to 6 p.m..........	7/31/97, before 6 p.m........	2 ca.		
"	8/12/97, ... p.m...........	8/14/97, ... p.m..........	....		
"	8/29/97, 5ʰ37ᵐ p.m..........	8/31/97, ... p.m..........	....		
"	10/ 7/97, 5 20 p.m..........	10/ 9/97, ... p.m..........	....		
"	10/23/96, ... p.m..........	10/25/97, ... p.m..........	....		
"	12/16/97, ... p.m..........	12/18/97, ... p.m..........	....		
"	1/ 9/98, ... p.m...........	1/11/98, ... p.m..........	....		
"	2/10/98, 6ʰ15ᵐ p.m..........	2/12/98, 2ʰ55ᵐ p.m.........	1	20	40
Crested (*Ocyphaps*)	3/ 1/97, 4 to 6 p.m..........	3/ 3/97, 4 47 p.m..........	2 ca.		
"	3/18/97, 4ʰ55ᵐ p.m..........	3/20/97, 5 18 p.m..........	2	0	23
"	7/25/96, 5 45 p.m...........	7/27/96, 4 37 p.m..........	1	22	52
"	3/10/97, 4 to 6 p.m..........	3/12/97, 4 35 p.m..........	2 ca.		
"	4/ 3/97, 5 to 6 p.m..........	4/ 5/97, 5 44 p.m..........	2 ca.		
"	4/16/97, 4ʰ56ᵐ p.m..........	4/18/97, 5 39 p.m..........	2	0	43
"	5/20/97, 5 43 p.m...........	5/22/97, 5 38 p.m..........	1	23	55
"	4/ 8/97, 4 32 p.m...........	4/10/97, 5 33 p.m..........	2	1	1
"	5/15/97, 6 05 p.m...........	5/17/97, 5 55 p.m..........	1	23	50
Zenaidura ♂ × white ring ♀	4/19/97, 4 to 6 p.m..........	4/21/97, 8 to 9 a.m.........	1	14 to 17	
"	4/29/97, 4ʰ05ᵐ p.m..........	5/ 1/97, 8ʰ10ᵐ a.m.........	1	16	5
"	6/16/98, 5 05 p.m...........	6/18/98, 8 05 a.m..........	1	17	
Blond hyb. ♂ × white ring ♀	5/ 1/97, 3 57 p.m...........	5/ 3/97, 7 25 a.m..........	1	15	33
"	5/10/97, 3 45 p.m...........	5/12/97, 7 15 a.m..........	1	15	30
"	6/ 5/97, 4 15 p.m...........	6/ 7/97, 7 26 a.m..........	1	15	11
"	3/23/98, 4 11 p.m...........	3/25/98, 7 50 a.m..........	1	15	39
White-bl. ♂ × blond-wh. hyb. ♀ .	5/ 9/97, 4 10 p.m...........	5/11/97, 7 58 a.m..........	1	15	48
"	6/11/97, 5 17 p.m...........	6/13/97, 8 39 a.m..........	1	15	22
"	4/30/97, 4 05 p.m...........	5/ 2/97, 7 50 a.m..........	1	15	45
Ectopistes ♂ × bl.-wh. hyb. ♀	3/ 1/97, 4 to 6 p.m..........	3/ 3/97, 9 48 a.m..........	1	16 to 17	
"	3/13/97, 5ʰ10ᵐ p.m..........	3/15/97, 9 02 a.m..........	1	15	52
"	3/27/97, 4 50 p.m...........	3/29/97, 9 07 a.m..........	1	16	17
"	4/ 9/97, 5 02 p.m...........	4/11/97, 8 to 9 a.m.........	1	15 to 16	
"	4/18/97, 4 42 p.m...........	4/20/97, 8ʰ25ᵐ a.m.........	1	15	43
"	4/30/97, 5 10 p.m...........	5/ 2/97, 9 14 a.m..........	1	16	4
"	5/10/97, 5 37 p.m...........	5/12/97, 9 36 a.m..........	1	15	59
"	6/ 5/97, 4 05 p.m...........	6/ 7/97, 6 21 a.m..........	1	14	16
"	8/13/97, 5 48 p.m...........	8/15/97, 8 37 a.m..........	1	14	49
"	4/ 4/98, 3 20 p.m...........	4/ 6/98, 7 40 a.m..........	1	16	20
"	4/15/98, 4ʰ30ᵐ to 5ʰ30ᵐ p.m..	4/17/98, ... a.m..........	....		
Complex bl.-white hyb. ♀	3/22/98, 4 10 p.m...........	3/24/98, 8ʰ23ᵐ a.m.........	1	16	13
Zenaidura ♂ × bl.-wh. hyb. ♀	3/23/98, 4 26 p.m...........	3/25/98, 8 00 a.m..........	1	15	34
Common ♂ × Jap. turtle ♀	9/ 6/97, 5 to 6 p.m..........	9/ 8/97, 10ʰ15ᵐ a.m........	1	16 to 17	
"	10/ 6/97, 5 to 6 p.m..........	10/ 8/97, 10 05 a.m........	1	16 to 17	
"	12/18/97, 3ʰ55ᵐ p.m..........	12/20/97, 10 05 a.m........	1	18	10
"	9/ 6/97, 4 05 p.m...........	9/ 8/97, 9 50 a.m..........	1	17	45
Fantail.	8/19/96, 5 to 6 p.m..........	8/21/96, 1 to 2ʰ30ᵐ p.m.....	1	19 to 20	
Satinette.	3/22/98, 4ʰ05ᵐ p.m..........	3/23/98, 2ʰ30ᵐ to 3ʰ30ᵐ p.m.	1	22½ to 23½	
Zenaidura ♂ × ring-dove ♀	4/10/97, 5 11 p.m...........	4/12/97, 8 39 a.m.	1	15	28
"	4/18/97, 5 06 p.m...........	4/20/97, 8 35 a.m..........	1	15	29
"	4/29/97, 4 50 p.m...........	5/ 1/97, 8 28 a.m..........	1	15	38
"	6/ 2/98, 4 to 5 p.m..........	6/ 4/98, 7 to 8ʰ30ᵐ a.m.....	1	15 ca.	
"	6/16/98, 4ʰ24ᵐ p.m..........	6/18/98, 7ʰ59ᵐ a.m.........	1	15	35
Common ♂ × ring-dove ♀	5/ 3/96, 4 to 6 p.m..........	5/ 5/96, 8 to 9 a.m.........	1	14 to 17	
"	5/23/96, 4 to 6 p.m..........	5/25/96, 8ʰ50ᵐ a.m.........	1	15 to 17	
"	6/19/96, 5 to 6 p.m..........	6/21/96, 9 53 a.m..........	1	16 to 17	
"	7/20/96, 5ʰ30ᵐ p.m..........	7/22/96, 8 45 a.m. ca......	1	15	15 ca.
"	8/ 2/96, 5 30 p.m. ca........	8/ 4/96, 7 to 9 a.m.........	1	14 to 16	
"	8/24/96, 4 to 5 p.m..........	8/26/96, 8 to 9 a.m.........	1	15 to 17	
"	10/11/96, 4ʰ45ᵐ p.m..........	10/13/96, 8ʰ 47ᵐ a.m........	1	16	2 ca.
"	10/31/96, 4 to 5 p.m..........	11/ 2/96, 8 55 a.m.........	1	16 to 17	
"	11/30/96, 4 to 5 p.m..........	12/ 2/96, 9 16 a.m.........	1	16 to 17	
"	12/20/96, 4 to 6 p.m..........	12/22/96, 9 20 a.m.........	1	15½ to 17½	
"	1/23/97, 5ʰ05ᵐ p.m..........	1/25/97, 10 05 a.m.........	1	17	
"	2/26/97, 5 04 p.m...........	2/28/97, 9 28 a.m..........	1	16	24
"	3/19/97, 4 42 p.m...........	3/21/97, 9 16 a.m..........	1	16	34
"	4/17/97, 4 to 6 p.m..........	4/19/97, 7 50 a.m..........	1	14 to 16	
"	5/30/97, 5ʰ08ᵐ p.m..........	6/ 1/97, 7 50 a.m..........	1	14	42
"	6/20/97, 6 21 p.m...........	6/22/97, 8 53 a.m..........	1	14	32

THE INCUBATION PERIOD. 47

TABLE 4.—*Time of laying*—Continued.

Species.	Date of first egg.	Date of second egg.	Interval.
Common ♂ × ring-dove ♀	7/12/97, 5 to 6 p.m...........	7/14/97, 7 to 9 a.m...........	1 13 to 16
"	8/22/97, 4 to 6 p.m...........	Prematurely dropped.	....
Jap. tumbler ♂ × ring-dove ♀	7/23/97, 5ʰ00ᵐ p.m...........	7/25/97, 7 to 9 a.m...........	1 14 to 16
"	8/25/97, 4 to 6 p.m...........	8/27/97, 8 a.m...........	1 14 to 16
"	9/26/97, ... p.m...........	9/28/97, ... a.m...........	....
"	10/21/97, 4ʰ08ᵐ p.m...........	10/23/97, ... a.m...........	....
"	12/13/97, 3 36 p.m...........	12/23/97, 8 to 9 a.m...........	1 16½ to 17½
"	1/20/98, 4 to 6 p.m...........	1/22/98, 7 to 9 a.m...........	1 13 to 17
"	2/19/98, 5 p.m.	2/21/98, ... a.m.	....
Zenaidura ♂ × white ring ♀	1/ 8/97, 4ʰ33ᵐ p.m...........	1/10/97, 9ʰ05ᵐ a.m...........	1 16 32
"		3/10/97, 8 35 a.m...........	
White rings	.... 5 p.m.	.... 8 15 a.m...........	1 15 15
Common ♂ × white ring ♀	4/ 9/96, 4ʰ14ᵐ p.m...........		....
Homer ♂ × blond ring ♀	3/11/97, 4 45 p.m...........	3/13/97, 9 16 a.m...........	1 16 31
"	4/30/97, 5 29 p.m...........	5/ 2/97, 9 10 a.m...........	1 15 41
"	3/24/97, ... p.m...........	No second egg.	....
"	4/ 3/97, 5ʰ02ᵐ p.m...........	4/ 5/97, 9ʰ27ᵐ a.m...........	1 16 25
"	4/17/97, 5 15 p.m...........	4/19/97, 8 52 a.m...........	1 15 37
"	4/30/97, 4 50 p.m...........	5/ 2/97, 7 40 a.m...........	1 14 50
"	6/26/97, 5 05 p.m...........	6/28/97, 7 42 a.m...........	1 14 37
"	6/ 5/97, 4 39 p.m...........	6/ 7/97, 7 55 a.m...........	1 15 16
"	8/13/97, 6 50 p.m...........	8/15/97, 8 45 a.m...........	1 13 55
Zenaidura ♂ × blond ring ♀	6/ 3/98, 4 to 5ʰ30ᵐ p.m......	6/ 5/98, 7 to 8 a.m...........	ca.1 15 (short)
"	6/16/98, 4ʰ18ᵐ p.m...........	6/18/98, 7ʰ50ᵐ a.m...........	1 15 32
Archangel ♂ × blond ring ♀	2/18/97, 4 to 4ʰ30ᵐ p.m......	2/20/97, 9 29 a.m...........	1 17 29?
"	3/14/97, 4ʰ55ᵐ p.m...........	3/16/97, 10 30 a.m...........	1 17 35
"	5/11/97, 5 26 p.m...........	5/13/97, 8 45 a.m...........	1 15 19
"	6/ 6/97, 5 27 p.m...........	6/ 8/97, 8 57 a.m...........	1 15 30
"	6/26/97, 5 37 p.m...........	6/28/97, 9 11 a.m...........	1 15 34
"	8/ 2/97, 5 48 p.m...........	8/ 4/97, 8 37 a.m...........	1 14 49
"	8/29/97, 5 34 p.m...........	8/31/97, 8 50 a.m...........	1 15 16
Common ♂ × blond ring ♀	1/12/98, 4 to 6 p.m...........	1/14/98, 7 to 9 a.m...........	1 13 to 17
Blond hyb. ♂ × blond ring ♀	3/22/98, 4ʰ20ᵐ p.m...........	3/24/98, 8ʰ23ᵐ a.m...........	1 16 18
White fantail ♂ × ring-dove ♀	....	1/ 2/97, 9 48 a.m...........	....
"	2/14/97, 3ʰ30ᵐ to 4ʰ30ᵐ p.m...	2/16/97, 9 10 a.m...........	1 17 ca.
"	4/17/97, 4 58 p.m...........	4/19/97, 7 43 a.m...........	1 14 45
"	5/ 9/97, 4 34 p.m...........	5/11/97, 8 43 a.m...........	1 16 9
"	5/31/97, 5 10 p.m...........	6/ 2/97, 7 42 a.m...........	1 14 32
"	7/31/97, 4 16 p.m...........	8/ 2/97, 7 45 a.m...........	1 15 29
Crested ♂ × ring-dove ♀	....	2/26/97, 8 34 a.m...........	1 15 to 16
"	3/24/97, 5 p.m...........	3/26/97, 8 40 a.m...........	1 15 40
"	4/ 5/97, 4 to 5ʰ10ᵐ p.m......	4/ 7/97, 8 15 a.m...........	1 14 to 15
"	4/17/97, 4ʰ05ᵐ p.m...........	4/19/97, 7 46 a.m...........	1 15 41
"	5/ 1/97, 4 37 p.m...........	5/ 3/97, 8 31 a.m...........	1 15 54
"	5/15/97, 4 35 p.m...........	5/17/97, 7 17 a.m...........	1 14 42
"	6/27/97, 4 34 p.m...........	6/29/97, 7 15 a.m...........	1 14 41

A female ring-dove mated with a common pigeon dropped her second egg at 6ʰ 20ᵐ p. m., only a little more than one day after laying the first. This was due to rough treatment. I found her off the nest and the young hybrid on the egg. I tried to have her return to the nest, but she kept leaving the egg and tried to get away. As she flew from me I tried to catch her, and in the effort my hand struck on her back, forcing her to the ground. The blow was not hard, but it must have jarred her, and within 5 to 10 minutes afterward she dropped the second egg, which had a shell which was still quite thin and which was broken when I discovered it. The female of a pair of blond × white rings laid the second egg between 11 and 12 o'clock but this was a case where the time was evidently delayed on account of moving the doves into the house, and the egg was not laid until the nest was returned to its place in the coop at the rear of the house. This case would not count as normal. (R19, Em 7, C 7/7.)

The time of laying the second egg may occasionally be influenced by the male's incubation activities. He occupies the nest during the day and frequently begins

48 BEHAVIOR OF PIGEONS.

incubation before the arrival of the second egg. He may thus occupy the nest at the usual time and refuse to leave on the demand of the female. (See Early Incubation, Chapter V.)

BEHAVIOR IN LAYING.

A few days before laying the female blond ring shows symptoms which are peculiar and diagnostic. The wings are held loosely and allowed often to drop below the tail. The bird looks as if sick, and moves about heavily and with unusual care. She usually sits in the nest more or less for from 3 to 4 days before laying. The white ring-doves behave in the same way.

At 9 a. m., I watched one of my blond ring-doves lay her second egg. Sitting at my desk, I happened to notice that the bird had taken an attitude as if in the act of laying. On going close to the nest I found that I was not mistaken. The bird was standing with head straight up and the hind end of the body lowered, almost touching the bottom of the nest. She was evidently in some pain and appeared to be struggling to deliver the egg. As the egg came the head was thrown back and turned half way round, with eye-lids closed, in the agony of sharp pain. That it cost pain was evident by a mark of blood on the egg and by the swollen, bloody appearance of the lips of the anus. For some moments after the egg was delivered the bird continued standing, without moving, so that I could see both eggs under her. At length she seemed to recover, put her head down far enough to look at the eggs, put her beak under the new-laid egg with care and fondness, and finally settled down over them, appearing to be somewhat exhausted with the effort. Some 5 weeks after the above observations were made I saw the "supposed male" of this pair lay an egg; it behaved in the same way, except that it did not exhibit any agony, but merely a severe strain.

A crested pigeon mated with a magpie laid her first egg at $4^h 35^m$ to $4^h 37^m$ p. m. She sat upright with tail above her wings. She gave the call-note almost continuously just before laying. She had a hard task to deliver the egg, making repeated efforts, and succeeded only at the end of 2 minutes after her first effort. The egg was not above the usual size for this species.

An *Ectopistes* was observed in laying an egg at $5^h 25^m$ p. m. She moved forward in the nest and held herself in a more or less erect position. When she dropped the egg she lifted her wings a little, just as I saw her do in laying a previous egg. Another *Ectopistes* female stood up for 5 minutes after laying and then sat on the egg. She gave a few low calls shortly before laying.

In laying her second egg a mourning-dove sat up erect, as does the ring-dove, with her tail raised between the ends of her wings. *The small end of the egg came first.* This bird gave a low call several times just before she took a position to lay. This call was the usual call to nest-making.

A female bronze-wing, at $9^h 41^m$ a. m., began to take a position for laying; that is, she stood a little in front of the middle of the nest, so that the coming egg would be placed in the middle. She then raised her head and the fore part of the body and lowered the hind part with the axis of the body inclined at about 45°; she made one or two efforts to drop the egg, then finally lowered the body and laid the egg beside the first so carefully as not to give it any jar. The egg came small end first and was left for a moment standing on this end.[1]

A white dove was observed while laying an egg at $4^h 15^m$ p. m. She gradually raised the fore-body and head, leaning back as if partly supported by the tail. As the egg came

---

[1] "The small end generally comes first, with occasional exceptions. A single exception disproves the idea that form is due to mechanical causes. Form is due to *self-differentiation* of the egg-cell," says W. V. Nathusius (Archiv. f. Entw'mech. d. Organismus, VI, 1898), but the author does not agree.

THE INCUBATION PERIOD. 49

the head was thrown back with a slight jerk, followed by a second jerk as the egg dropped. The whole operation lasted about 30 seconds. The dove then continued standing and closed her eyes as if in sleep for a few moments. After a lapse of a few minutes she lowered herself over the egg and went on sleeping.

At precisely $4^h 50^m$ p. m., the female of a pair of ring-doves laid her first egg. I first noticed the bird sitting upright in the usual position. In the course of half a minute the egg was dropped, and just as it came the head was thrown back and turned momentarily to one side, with an evident strain. After the egg was dropped the bird remained standing over it, barely touching it above with her feathers, for nearly an hour ($4^h 50^m$ to $5^h 45^m$); then she settled down and covered it so that it could no longer be seen. This is the same as I have before described in another female, and I am now sure that it is the usual thing. The bird appeared to go to sleep soon after dropping the egg, and remained quiet most of the time, though closing the eyes only occasionally. The small end of the egg always comes first. I have seen this in several cases.

I saw the second egg laid at $8^h 50^m$ a. m. The female moved about a good deal, preparing her nest and getting ready for oviposition. At length she took the usual position and dropped the egg in not over 15 seconds. As the egg dropped she toppled forward as if she had lost her balance. The head was thrown back and twitched once or twice as the egg passed.

The egg-laying of the crested pigeon was observed. The bird sat upright in the nest and spent 2 to 5 minutes in laying the egg. She made plain efforts, one following the other at little intervals, to relieve herself of the egg. I have seen the same bird lay another egg, and she behaved in the same way. After laying she stood up for about 10 minutes only, then sat down on the egg and went to sleep.

I saw the first and second eggs laid in the case of a pair of blond ring-doves. A crested pigeon laid her second egg at the same time the female blond ring laid her first egg, and I gave my attention mostly to the former. The laying of the second egg by the blond ring was carefully watched. In this latter case the female took the usual position and spent about half a minute in laying. She made several efforts, and the final one caused her to throw her head back and then turn it to one side as if in pain. She stood over the eggs during 8 minutes and then sat down upon them. In case of the first egg she stood 15 minutes before sitting down. The crested pigeon stood for 10 minutes over the second egg before sitting.

The female of a pair of ring-doves laid her first egg at $6^h 05^m$ p. m. The time taken, from the moment when she began to stand upright, was 50 seconds. The bird showed plainly that she made efforts at short intervals, and the final effort was marked by the usual behavior. She stood over the egg 9 minutes, then left the nest to eat; she returned after 3 minutes, looked at the egg, appeared to hesitate about sitting, and after standing 8 minutes came off and went outside. The male went in and sat a moment, but soon left. The female returned a little later and stood beside the egg. She finally took the perch and remained away from the egg all night. The following morning I found the egg warm, showing that one of the birds had been on the nest. But they were sometimes both off at one time and were irregular in sitting.

Another female crested pigeon in laying an egg took the nest a few minutes before 5 p. m. She then gave the call-note, which answers for a "coo," several times. She again gave this same note several times while fixing herself upright for laying and while in the upright position, and only ceased a moment before she was ready to drop the egg, which she did at $5^h 18^m$ p. m.

The female of a pair of mourning-doves laid a first egg at $6^h 07^m$ p. m. In laying she sat about as nearly upright as the ring-dove does, and at the moment of dropping the egg she gave her head a turn to one side with her beak raised, not vertically, but at an angle

50   BEHAVIOR OF PIGEONS.

of about 45°. She spent about a minute in laying and made vigorous efforts at short intervals to expel the egg. As soon as it was dropped she took a standing position over it for about 20 minutes and then flew up to the perch. At about 7 p. m. I found her sitting on the egg.

I expected two females of two pairs of ring-dove females (*L 2* and *GF 1*) mated to crested males to lay for the "first time in life." I found both on their nests at $3^h 50^m$, and kept watch of them in order to get the exact time. Both behaved as if they were just ready to lay. Female *L 2* remained on the nest until $5^h 30^m$, came off for a minute, returned, and came off again in about a minute. She went back almost immediately, but stopped on the edge of the nest-box. Here she sat quietly until $7^h 25^m$, when, frightened by something, probably an owl appearing before the window, she flew to the floor and her mate flew to another corner of the pen. After a few minutes she went back to the edge of the nest-box, where she remained all night, returning to the nest early in the morning. Female *GF 1* came off the nest at $4^h 30^m$, flew to the floor, and then took her place on the perch beside her mate until $5^h 45^m$, when she went to the nest-box and sat quietly until $7^h 50^m$; at this time she got up on the edge of the nest-box and soon after stepped upon the perch close by, where she remained all night, returning to the nest early the following morning.

These two females evidently went through the preliminaries to laying, but they were a little premature in their actions. By experience they will learn to waste less time in fruitless formalities and make less ado over such a small matter as laying an egg. After 10 days there are no eggs from either of these females, but *GF 1* has been busy during the mornings of nearly every day, and to-day her wings droop, showing that she is about ready to try to lay. Female *L 2* has spent less time on the nest, and sometimes seems to have given up nesting for the present. On the following day *GF 1* began to incubate the empty nest, *i.e.*, without having laid, and *L 2* did not lay until 17 days after an egg was expected. The act was not observed. (R 19, SS 4, R 33.)

TIME OF HATCHING.

I have observed one or two interesting things in regard to the time of hatching. I have noted that young birds never hatch, or very rarely, after 3 o'clock in the afternoon; they usually hatch early in the morning. If not early in the morning, then between 10 a. m. and 12 noon. If not within these latter hours there is, as a rule, no hatching between 12 noon and 1 p. m. There may be now and then exceptions, of course, but if the egg does not hatch by 3 p. m. one can be fairly certain that nothing will be done until the next morning. It may be fully time for the bird to hatch, but for some reason the hatching is not completed and the *bird goes to sleep*, apparently rests, and then wakes up very early with the rest of the birds in the morning and concludes the hatch. I have timed this phenomenon and watched so closely that I feel very certain that the bird, before hatching, has his time of resting, and that these times correspond to the times of rest in the old birds. In the middle of the day the birds are always very quiet and resting; the bird in the shell remains quiet also.[1] (SS 10.)

The data of the available records are given in Table 5. These figures support the above statements. Of the 113 cases, only 83 are definite enough to be utilized.

---

[1] The prenatal behavior of the pigeon ought to be studied. The young bird goes to sleep and awakens regularly, and thus it is determined that it shall not hatch out at an improper time. Hatching takes place early in the morning, or sometimes toward noon. It is very rarely, and only in the case of some delay, that a bird hatches out as late as 2 o'clock. I have known a bird to have performed a great part of the work of opening the shell and then go to sleep and wait till the next morning. I suppose they "know the time" by the regular recurrence of their own activities, and by its being the time of greatest activity of the parent birds. The young bird usually first cracks the egg about 24 hours before emerging. It begins to work about 5 a. m. and continues till perhaps 11 a. m., when it takes a noonday rest. The parents rest from about 11 to 1 o'clock. (Conv. 7/20/10, W. C.)

THE INCUBATION PERIOD.

TABLE 5.—*Time of hatching.*

Species.	First egg.	Second egg.
Zenaidura	5/11, 3 p.m.	5/13, before 5ʰ30ᵐ a.m.
"	6/11, 1 to 2 p.m.	6/12, 8ʰ15ᵐ a.m.
"	7/29, 1ʰ20ᵐ p.m.	7/30, 1 to 2 p.m.
"	9/ 2, 6 a.m.	9/ 2, 10ʰ12ᵐ a.m.
"	5/ 8, a.m.	
"	6/18, before 5 a.m.	6/19, 4 to 6 a.m.
"	7/18, 7 a.m. to 2 p.m.	7/19, early a.m.
"	8/15, early a.m.	8/16, early a.m.
"	8/13, p.m.	8/14, before 1 p.m.
"	5/18, a.m.	5/19, early a.m.
"	6/26, early a.m.	6/26, before 1 p.m.
"		7/27, a.m.
Fantail	9/ 7, 1ʰ15ᵐ p.m.	9/ 8, before 7 a.m.
L. picata	4/30, 1 15 p.m.	
"	6/21, before 6 a.m.	
Ectopistes	8/11, before 2 p.m.	
"	5/11, 2 to 3 p.m.	
"	6/12, a.m.	
"	7/25, 1 to 2 p.m.	
"	8/ 2, 1 to 2 p.m.	
"	8/ 8, 2ʰ30ᵐ to 3 p.m.	
"	8/11, before 7 a.m.	
"	8/ 9, after 8ʰ30ᵐ a.m.	
"	8/ 4, before 2ʰ30ᵐ p.m.	
"	9/ 4, before 1 p.m.	
Bronze-wing	1/ 3, 5ʰ30ᵐ to 6ʰ30ᵐ a.m.	1/ 4, 4 to 6 a.m.
"	3/18, 2 to 3 p.m.	
"	6/ 2, early a.m.	6/ 3, early a.m.
G. humeralis	5/13, early a.m.	5/15, a.m.
St. humilis (red ring)	9/14, 5 to 6 a.m.	9/15, 5 to 6 a.m.
St. risoria (blond ring)		9/15
Common pigeon ♂ × ring-dove ♀	6/18, 11 to 12 a.m.	
"	1/ 5, before 6 a.m.	
"		11/17, 12 m.
"		2/ 9, before 6 a.m.
"	4/ 4, 5 to 6 a.m.	
"	7/28, 5 to 6 a.m.	7/29, 5 to 6 a.m.
Ectopistes ♂ × ring-dove ♀	3/16, 8 a.m.	
"		4/12, 6ʰ10ᵐ a.m.
"	4/24, 6ʰ50ᵐ a.m.	
"		5/ 4, 4 to 5 a.m.
"	5/14, 1ʰ50ᵐ p.m.	5/15, 3ʰ41ᵐ p.m.
"		5/29, 4 to 5 a.m.
"	8/19, 6 a.m.	
"	4/ 9, 1 to 2 p.m.	4/11, 6 a.m.
Jap. tumbler ♂ × ring-dove ♀		8/ 8, 1 to 2 p.m.
"	9/10, 5 to 6 a.m.	
"	11/ 6, 1 p.m.	
"	12/30, 7 a.m.	12/30, 6 a.m.
"		2/ 6, a.m.
"	3/ 7, 12 to 1 p.m.	
Archangel ♂ × ring-dove ♀	3/ 6, 11 to 12 a.m.	3/ 7, 5 to 6 a.m.
Ring ♂ × homer ♀	1/27, 9 a.m.	
"		2/28, 3ʰ30ᵐ to 4 a.m.
Ectopistes ♂ × ring hybrid ♀		4/20, 4 to 5 a.m.
"	5/ 1, 5 a.m.	
Fantail ♂ × ring ♀		5/ 4, 7ʰ30ᵐ a.m.
Homer ♂ × ring ♀	3/27, 12 m.	3/28, 5 to 6 a.m.
"	5/16, 5 to 6 a.m.	5/17, 5 to 6 a.m.
"	6/21, 5ʰ30ᵐ a.m.	
"	8/29, 5 to 6 a.m.	
"	9/20, 12ʰ30ᵐ p.m.	
Ring ♂ × homer ♀	1/27, 9 a.m.	
"		2/28, 3ʰ30ᵐ to 4 a.m.
Satinette	4/10, 7 to 8 a.m.	4/10, 1 to 2 p.m.
Common pigeon	3/20, 10ʰ08ᵐ a.m.	3/20, 6ʰ35ᵐ a.m.
"	5/ 2, 3 20 p.m.	5/ 3, 7 08, a.m.
"	6/ 2, 1 40 p.m.	6/ 2, 6 20 a.m.
"	8/29, 5 to 6 a.m.	8/29, 12 to 1 p.m.
"		1/23, 12 m.
"	3/16, 4 to 6 a.m.	3/16, 6 to 7 a.m.
Ring-doves	3/28, 12 to 6 p.m.	3/28, 12 to 6 p.m.
"	4/30, 5 to 7 a.m.	
"	5/28, 5 to 7 a.m.	5/29, 5 to 7 a.m.
"	7/ 4, a.m.	7/15, a.m.
"	8/ 9, 5 to 6 a.m.	8/10, 12ʰ30ᵐ p.m.
"	10/31, 10 a.m.	10/31, 2 p.m.
"	1/ 6, 12 to 3ʰ30ᵐ p.m.	1/ 6, 2 p.m.
"	3/ 7, 5 to 6 a.m.	

52 occurred before 9 a. m., 5 between 9 and 12 a. m., 4 between 12 and 1 p. m., 19 between 1 and 4 p. m., and 3 at noon. The proportion of morning hatchings is greater for the second egg than for the first. Of the 34 cases in which the data are given for both eggs of the clutch, 11 pairs were hatched on the same day, 20 on successive days, and 3 on alternate days. These data illustrate once more the fact that the incubation period of the second egg tends on the whole to be the shorter; but this phenomenon can not be due *wholly* to the irregularity of early incubation, because in 4 cases the second egg was hatched first, unless we suppose that the irregularity of incubation not only prevents but positively *checks* the development of the first egg.

METHOD OF HATCHING.

In hatching, the shell is broken pretty evenly around its large end, so that this is often completely severed, but it sometimes adheres to the body of the shell at one point, and then when the young gets free this cap-like part is often turned into the larger part of the emptied shell. The break in the shell in one case, was 23 to 25 mm. from the small end, or 7 to 9 mm. from the large end. This is the usual way in all pigeons' eggs. Only in a few cases have I seen the break nearer the small end than the large end. The egg is usually first pricked about 24 hours or more before the young liberates itself. (R 33.)

INCREASED INTEREST AT HATCHING.

Both birds exhibit an increase of interest in the nest at hatching-time. This is not necessarily due to the presence of the young, as it may manifest itself before the eggs are hatched. The phenomenon is mentioned but briefly in several of the records.

The first egg of a pair was hatched between 5^h 30^m and 6^h 30^m a. m. At 9^h 50^m it was noted that the female has not once left the nest, evidently having an increased interest in the contents of the nest. At 11^h 15^m the male, after calling for 2 or 3 minutes on the floor, went to the nest, but the female was loath to leave and he again retired. The female was not off the nest to evacuate during the whole morning, thus showing how much the young has increased her interest in the nest.[1] At 1^h 05^m p. m. the male went to the nest and the female resigned for the first time.

At 10^h 45^m a. m. it was noted that the male of a pair of bronze-wings had been trying to get over the eggs for an hour, but the female kept solidly to the nest. Both were evidently ready for the young to hatch. At 2^h 30^m p. m., I helped the young bird out of the shell; it was evidently ready to emerge and was impeded by a little unnatural drying and sticking to the shell as a result of an injury on the previous day. On another occasion it was noted that, at the time the young was due to hatch, this male was very attentive and anxious to have the nest and its care. Indeed, he appeared to be remarkably solicitous, and he not only tried to get the nest, but called quite a number of times while sitting beside the female, as if he wanted to feed the young before it was quite out of the shell.

A male mourning-dove sat beside the female most of the time for 3 days before the hatching of the young. The female seemed loath to leave her nest for more than a short time. The male continued to sit close beside the female for 2 days after the first egg was hatched. (R 33, Em 7.)

---

[1] Normally the female leaves the nest early in the morning, before the first relief by the male, evacuates the cloaca, and then resumes her duty.—EDITOR.

CHAPTER V.

INCUBATION BEHAVIOR.

The time of beginning incubation is not always synchronous with the appearance of the first egg; it differs for the two birds, it varies with the species, and it seems to be highly variable within a species. The early incubation is often irregular, but in the later stages the eggs are covered almost continuously. Copulation ceases with the advent of the eggs, but nest-building is continued for the first half of the period. Both birds participate in the incubation of the eggs. At night the female covers the eggs, while the male normally roosts on the perch as far from the nest as possible. During the day the male and female alternate in the task, though the male occupies the nest the major portion of this time. These activities are described in detail under the topics which follow.

EARLY INCUBATION.

The wild passenger-pigeon (*Ectopistes*) begins to incubate a day or two in advance of laying, and the male takes his turn on the nest just as if the eggs were already there. In the common pigeon the sitting usually begins with the first egg, but the birds do not sit steadily or closely until the second egg is laid. The birds do not, in fact, really sit on the first egg, but merely stand over it, stooping just enough to touch the egg with the feathers. This peculiarity has an advantage in that the development of the first egg is delayed so that both eggs may hatch more nearly together.[1]

A female passenger-pigeon began to make a nest on a Monday. She sat much on that day and almost constantly all day on Tuesday. She was sitting again on Wednesday; on this latter date the male seemed to be off duty and did not come near the female on the nest, although he sat for a long time on the nest during the middle of Monday and Tuesday. The egg was laid after 4 p. m. on Wednesday. In another instance, a female passenger-pigeon was on the nest in the early morning. The male sat during the middle of the day, as if he were in charge of an egg, though the nest was empty. I found the female on the nest at 3 p. m., and she remained on from this time, laying her egg at $4^h 52^m$ p. m. of this same day. In still another case a pair of passengers accepted a nest on one day. On the next, I saw the male on the nest at $11^h 30^m$ a. m., and he remained there until 3 or 4 o'clock, or perhaps until later. The egg was laid that day between 4 and 5 p. m. (SS 4.)

Fulton (*op. cit.*, p. 41) comments upon this subject as follows:

"As a rule, it is found that the sooner pigeons' eggs are allowed to commence the process of incubation after being laid the better, certainly not later than 5 or 6 days. Further, as to the time during which they may be allowed to remain uncovered after incubation has once commenced, this is regulated by the stage which has been reached. In the early days eggs may have become cold and remained so for 24 hours, and even more, and yet not be injured; but as the date of hatching approaches even 1 or 2 hours of desertion by the covering bird may cause the egg-tenant to perish; though even within 24 hours of the time of hatching we have known marvelous instances of the vital power of squabs being preserved, even though the egg may have been stone-cold for a few hours."

On the third day of incubation, *i. e.*, on the day of the laying of the second egg, a pair of bronze-wings were in full swing proceeding in regular order with incubation, not leaving the nest except by exchange of relief, and sitting (not standing). The day following the laying of the first egg was one of fairly regular incubation, but the sitting was not

---

[1] Woods Hole Biological Lecture, p. 327.

54 BEHAVIOR OF PIGEONS.

quite so close; the egg was left uncovered once or twice when both birds went to feed together. (R 33.)

In various records it is noted that the female bronze-wing *stood* over the first egg until the second was laid, and that she did not really sit. The female of a crested × blond ring pair also "stood" over the egg the first night. A female geopelia left the nest at $4^h 15^m$ p. m. and roosted on the perch beside the male the night before the second egg was laid. No record was given for the first night. In another cycle this same female roosted on the perch during the first night. The female of a second crested × blond ring pair "stood" over the first egg until the second egg was laid. A bronze-wing male began incubation on the second day of one cycle and on the third day of another. A male white ring sat on the egg the first night it was laid. A male crested pigeon began incubation on the second day, a male geopelia on the third day, and another male crested on the third day after the second egg was laid.

Since the second egg may be laid as late as 10 a. m. on the third day of the incubation period, it is possible that the male's participation in incubation may interfere with this function. Sometimes the male does not begin to participate until after this event. This means no relief for the female during the second day and a postponement of the first relief on the third day several hours later than the normal time. This was true for two of the pairs (bronze-wing and crested) mentioned above. In the first and third cycles of a pair of bronze-wings the male participated in the incubation regularly on the second day. On the third day he relieved the female for some time during the early morning, but the female had the nest at the usual time for the dropping of the second egg. Two cases are also recorded in which the male's tendency to relieve interfered with the female's duties. In the bronze-wing's fourth cycle the male relieved early in the morning. At the time for laying, the male attempted to sit and made some trouble, but the female refused to resign until after the egg was laid. In the second cycle of a crested × blond ring pair the first egg was laid at the usual time and the male participated regularly in the incubation on the second day. On the third day, the date of laying of the second egg, the male relieved at $6^h 40^m$, $8^h 10^m$, and $8^h 59^m$. At $9^h 10^m$ the female crowded into the nest and forced the male off. The male relieved again, and the female returned at $9^h 17^m$, but the male refused to leave. The female returned at $9^h 19^m$, crowding herself on while the male yielded reluctantly. At $9^h 25^m$ the male was sitting beside the female and trying to take the nest, but the female refused to resign and laid at $9^h 48^m$ a. m. The male was back at the nest at $9^h 55^m$, but the female did not resign for several minutes. The author notes that "this male's instinct is not attuned to the needs of the female in laying the second egg. I had to keep the male away from the nest, as he insisted on taking possession several times just as the female was about to lay."

TYPICAL INCUBATION RECORDS.

The various excerpts and the data on incubation have been taken from the detailed daily records. As illustrative of the nature and detail of these observations, the two following daily records are given as typical.

INCUBATION BEHAVIOR. 55

At 6^h 19^m a. m., Dec. 22, 1906, the female bronze-wing came off the nest to the perch to discharge her load; this being done, she went back to the nest. At 6^h 30^m the male came down to the floor for seed, but soon went back to the perch. At 6^h 32^m the male gave two calls, but I can see no reason for it. The female made no response. At 6^h 34^m the male was again on the floor trying to get into the next pen, running back and forth along the wire-netting partition. He sees a green-wing (*Lophophaps*) eating in the next pen, and this incites him to try to get through. At 6^h 39^m the male again gave two calls, nodding his head strongly with each call as usual, and then flew to the perch with his landing call. At 6^h 41^m he again went to the floor and to the seed-dish. I put fresh seed in dish at 6^h 48^m and the male came at once for his breakfast. On returning from my own breakfast at 8 a. m. I found the male on the nest and the female on the floor. At 8^h 20^m the male called three times and the female went to the nest and the male came down to feed. Probably feeding him early (at 6^h 48^m) led to his taking the nest. At 8^h 26^m the male returned to the nest and the female was again on the floor. The male resumed nest duty and in a moment or two gave two calls which were not answered. At 9^h 26^m the male gave one loud call. The female was still on the floor and gave no answer. At 9^h 28^m the male gave one loud call, no answer; the female was tramping about. Perhaps the female's noise incited the male to call. At 12^h 13^m the female relieved and the male went to the floor. During this morning the male relieved twice: 8 to 8^h 20^m and 8^h 26^m to 12^h 13^m. Since the female once held the nest only 6 minutes, the male's two times count really for once. The sun rose on this date at 7^h 17^m, and set at 4^h 23^m. (R 33.)

On Feb. 12, the male went on the nest at 7 a. m.; he left the nest at 7^h 12^m and carried straw to the female. He took the nest at 8^h 50^m and came off at 9^h 06^m, the female going on at 9^h 07^m. The female came off at 9^h 20^m, and the male went immediately to the nest. At 9^h 37^m the male was off, but soon returned with a straw; he was off again at 9^h 42^m and brought a straw to the female, which had at once taken the nest. The male resumed the nest at 11^h 25^m and the female came off at 11^h 26^m; the male followed at 11^h 28^m, went back at 12^h 03^m and came off at 12^h 18^m. At 1^h 20^m the male took the nest and stayed until 2^h 05^m; the female went on at 2^h 06^m. She was relieved at 2^h 50^m by the male, which kept the nest until 3^h 07^m; the female went on 2 minutes later. The male relieved from 3^h 15^m to 3^h 33^m, and the female went on for the night at 3^h 35^m. (R 18.)

ROOSTING HABITS.

Before the eggs are laid, both birds sit together at night; after the first egg is laid the male sits at night as far away from the female as is possible.

A male crested pigeon mated with a ring-dove took up his place every night on the perch at the corner farthest from the nest-box where the female was sitting. Up to the time of laying both were accustomed to sit together on the edge of the nest-box. The male changed his sleeping place the first night after an egg was laid.

This instinct seems to be general among all species. It is the more remarkable in those social pigeons, like the crested pigeons and geopelias, which are so fond of roosting together. To-night the female of a pair of *G. humeralis* has laid an egg and is sitting on it. Her mate sits at the opposite side of the pen all alone. It would seem as if this was great self-denial, for the two have been roosting together constantly and they appear to take great pleasure in each other's company. The male sees his mate, makes loving little calls, and adds those movements of the head and beak which seem to say "come here and I will fondle your head." The female remains faithful to the egg and makes no response. The male does not yield to his desire for his mate—to go and sit beside her—but remains at the greatest distance possible. Does he have any idea of why he must deny this pleasure? In the native state his action would mean that the nest is safer if he remains away from it. But, of course, in a small pen of a few feet the distance is nothing and the sitting apart has no sense. Something moves the bird to do thus, but what? Has his love cooled?

56 BEHAVIOR OF PIGEONS.

No; for he calls for his mate and he is as loving as ever. I can think of no reason or feeling that should move him to sleep apart from his mate. But certain it is that from the moment he sees his mate on the nest, he keeps away from her at night and also in the day, except when he wants to sit. It is curious and mysterious. How could such an instinct arise? Suppose birds have been accustomed to sleep in a certain place; that is enough to establish a strong preference for the place. If the female has laid her egg in a nest in some other place, the male will have two desires—one to roost in the old place and one to go to the female. If the two motives were equally strong, the male might do either. But natural selection would favor those that remained away from the nest. (B 2c, R 17, R 33.)

Deviation from normal conduct is characteristic of the male's attempt to break up the incubation cycle. Such behavior was frequently noted in the daily record of several incomplete incubations. The male sits on the perch close to the nest-box, sits on the edge of the nest-box, or may attempt to crowd the female off the nest. This tendency was associated with many other deviations from normal masculine behavior—such as refusal to participate in incubation during the day, attempts at copulation, etc. For further details the reader is referred to the excerpts from the incubation records given in Chapter VII.

The first egg of the season was laid by a passenger $\times$ blond-ring pair at 4 p. m. The female remained over the egg that night. The next night, at 8 o'clock, I found the male on the nest and the female on the perch. I can not say how it happened. Possibly the light in the room led the male bird to think it was morning and so he went on to relieve the female. It may be that he is again beginning his irregular sitting of last year. When I drove the male passenger off and put the female on the nest he did not try to return. This male passenger-pigeon sat on the eggs regularly of nights, the female meanwhile sitting on the edge of the nest-box. (R 17.)

ALTERNATION.

Fulton, on page 36 of his work previously cited, made the following statements, which apply to fancy or domestic pigeons:

"And now the merits of her mate grow apparent. He does not leave his lady to bear a solitary burden of matrimonial care, while he has indulged in the pleasures only of their union. He takes a share, though a minor one, of the task of incubating; and he more than performs his half share of the labour of rearing the young. At about noon, sometimes earlier, the hens leave their nests for air and exercise as well as food, and the cocks take their place upon the eggs. If you enter a pigeon loft at about 2 o'clock in the afternoon you will find all of the cock-birds sitting—a family arrangement that affords an easy method of discovering which birds are paired with which. The ladies are to be seen taking their respective turns in the same locations early in the morning, in the evening, and all the night. The older a cock-pigeon grows, the more fatherly does he become. So great is his fondness for having a rising family that an experienced unmated cock-bird, if he can but induce some flighty young hen to lay him a couple of eggs as a great favor, will almost entirely take the charge of hatching and rearing them by himself."

A female passenger-pigeon left her egg at 9 a. m. to feed for a few moments. The male saw her, but did not offer to sit. She soon returned and sat until about 10 o'clock, when he came and relieved her. She remained off until 4 p. m., then flew to the nest, but soon walked off to a perch near by when the male did not resign. At $4^h 18^m$ the male, after bowing a few times in recognition of his mate or to invite her to take the nest, walked off and flew to the farther end of the cot; she at once took her place on the nest. It was interesting to see the males of several varieties—two fantails, an owl-pigeon, and a common dove—all resigning their nest at about the same time, i.e., about 4 p. m.

INCUBATION BEHAVIOR. **57**

A crested male relieved his blond-ring female between $6^h 50^m$ and $8^h 40^m$ in the morning and relinquished the nest for the night between $2^h 40^m$ and $4^h 15^m$ in the afternoon. The average time of relief in the morning was $7^h 30^m$, and the average time in the afternoon was $3^h 30^m$. The total time during the day devoted to incubation by the male varies from $2\frac{1}{2}$ hours to $8\frac{3}{4}$ hours; the average period being 6 hours daily. During the period of alternation (daytime) the male occupied the nest three times as long as the female. The number of reliefs by the male during the day varies from 1 to 9, with an average number of $3\frac{1}{2}$. The length of time spent on the nest in these reliefs varies from 1 minute to $6\frac{1}{2}$ hours. There were 8 intervals of 4 to 7 hours, 23 intervals of 1 to 3 hours, and 25 intervals of less than 1 hour in length. As a general rule the early reliefs were short and the later reliefs rather long.

A bronze-wing male began relief between 7 and $8^h 45^m$ in the morning, the average time being at 8 a. m. He retired for the night from $12^h 15^m$ to $3^h 20^m$ in the afternoon, the average time being at 2 p. m. The average number of reliefs during the day were two. The total time spent on the nest during the day varied from $3\frac{1}{2}$ to $6\frac{3}{4}$ hours; the average being $5\frac{1}{2}$ hours. The shorter intervals of relief occurred in the morning, while the later periods were generally the longer ones. (SS 4, R 18, R 33.)

The time of early-morning relief, as well as the time when the male retires for the night, is probably influenced by light conditions, such as the length of the day, clear or cloudy weather, etc. The bronze-wing male put in a shorter day than did one of the passenger males of the first pair; his early-morning relief averaged a half-hour later, while he retired for the night much earlier. He also spent less actual time on the nest during the day. The bronze-wing record covered the period from Dec. 16, 1905, to Jan. 3, 1906; the passenger record concerns incubation during February, when the days were appreciably longer. The daily records sometime state the character of the weather, but the cases are too few to allow of any conclusions as to the effect of the clearness or cloudiness of the day. In the bronze-wing record it is noted that the male once relieved at $6^h 30^m$ a. m., shortly after lighting the gas during an early-morning inspection. It is stated that this very early relief was probably due to the light.

INITIATIVE IN INTERCHANGE.

In the majority of cases the records do not state which bird was responsible for the interchange at incubation. From the available records it may be stated that either bird may take the initiative in leaving the nest or in resuming nest duty. In the bronze-wing, both birds took the initiative in resuming incubation more frequently than in leaving the nest, while the reverse was true for a crested-blond-ring pair. In the latter pair the male showed more initiative, both in leaving and in taking the nest, while in the bronze-wing pair both birds initiated the changes a nearly equal number of times. The female often leaves the nest early in the morning, before the first relief, in order to defecate, but she returns to nest duty at once.

When a bird takes the initiative in resuming nest duty, the mate often exhibits some stubbornness in giving up the nest upon demand. The female exhibits the most stubbornness and reluctance in leaving. Often the male is forced to give up the attempt to take the nest, and he is sometimes forced to crowd in and push her off the nest. In one case the female resisted for 15 minutes before leaving.

58 BEHAVIOR OF PIGEONS.

When one bird leaves, this departure is the signal for the other bird to take the nest, and as a rule this is done immediately. Sometimes one bird refuses to go to the nest when the mate leaves it, and the latter is then forced to return; otherwise the eggs are left uncovered until the first bird awakens to its responsibility. These periods in which the eggs are left uncovered vary from 1 to 6 minutes and they usually occur in the early part of the incubation period. The female was responsible for this lack of care in the majority of cases. While on the nest either bird may give the nest-call as a call for relief, and this call is sometimes heeded and sometimes not.

When one bird takes the initiative, either in leaving or taking the nest, this act serves as a stimulus to its mate. Under the caption "Incubation left to young," an instance is given in which a young bird goes to the nest, and this serves as the stimulus for the old bird to resign. During the early stages of an incubation period a pair of doves may be still feeding the young of the former cycle. The title of this note might indicate that the young bird's action in going to the nest is to be interpreted as an attempt to participate in the incubation. Such an interpretation is hardly necessary.[1] The note contains a seeming discrepancy of statement.

A pair of wood-pigeons have young able to fly and feed, but they are still fed by the parents. One young is in the nest-box and both old birds are on the perch [? a mis-statement.—EDITOR]. The young goes into the nest to sit beside the old bird, and the old bird resigns as she would for her mate. I drove the young off the nest and the old bird went back to duty. I have seen this behavior in the case of ring-doves and in some other species. (R 18.)

DEFECTIVE ALTERNATION.

A Japanese turtle female, mated to a homer, deserted her eggs 5 days after the first egg was laid. I had already transferred them to another pair and put other eggs in their place. The male homer has continued up to the present (for 5 days) faithful to his own duty, incubating during the day, and has tried to fulfil the duty of his mate besides. He has sat *every night* so far, while she has done nothing since her desertion. It is really remarkable that a male dove should undertake double duty. This is not the normal course of incubation, and one would not expect pure instinct to provide in one sex against the abnormal in the other. When instinct once ceases to acknowledge eggs, nothing can induce the bird to pay them any attention. Why is it that a faithful bird, accustomed to only regular hours of day, feels impelled to take the nest even at night when its mate deserts it? Is the sitting instinct continuous, and is the usual exchange regulated only by a regular round of needs? That is, does the female leave her eggs in the morning because her mate comes to relieve her, and would his leaving the nest call her back to it? This is certainly true in many cases. The male continues to sit at nights as well as during the day for 4 more days, at which time the female laid again in another nest. (BB 5.)

A male will often sit on the eggs at night in case the female deserts or dies; he will also sit overnight on the young as well as on eggs. An example of the latter behavior has just occurred where a male ring-dove is sitting at night on young only a few days old. (R 7.)

In the bronze-wing record the editor finds several cases of defective behavior on the part of the male. He fails to cover or feed the young during the day. He

---

[1] A case, however, is elsewhere (Chapter IX) reported by Dr. Riddle, in which a young bird—38 days old—nested eggs, and engaged in sexual billing with its two male foster-parents.—EDITOR.

INCUBATION BEHAVIOR. 59

roosts near the female on the nest at night, fondles her head when she is on the nest, follows her to the floor, and attempts copulation, etc. The female is thus forced to do double duty. In this connection an instance is noted in which "the female is absolutely faithful and sticks to the nest, doing double duty, while the male loafs about, occasionally visiting his mate and fondling her head without showing a particle of interest in the little one."

In a fourth case the incubation was normal from February 28 to March 15, shortly before the eggs were due to hatch. The male then began to sit irregularly and attempted to entice the female to begin a new cycle. To prevent this the male was removed from the cage early on the morning of March 16. After being on the nest all night, the female remained on the nest all of the following day and during the next night, a period of about 40 hours. On the morning of the 17th, the day the first egg was due to hatch, she left the nest and refused to sit another moment.

The female does not always do double duty when her mate fails to do his duty. There would seem to be a limit to endurance. In the first cycle of a crested-ring-dove pair whose record is given in Chapter VII, no eggs were laid. The female persisted in incubating an empty nest for 20 days, while the male did not participate. In this record it is noted that "she takes the nest at about the same time that she would if she were alternating with the male." The same conditions probably obtained in the second cycle of the same pair, and in two cycles of a similar crested-blond-ring pair; while no definite statements are made, the fact is emphasized that the female persisted in sitting at night. Sitting at night and indifference to the male are regarded as the proofs of the contention that the female was really going through the incubation stage of the cycle.

In the hybrid-*Zenaidura* pair whose record is given in Chapters I and VII, the male courted unsuccessfully for a month and then began incubation alone, without eggs, and on the floor of the cage. The records state that "this male sat steadily night and day" for a period of nearly 2 weeks.[1]

COPULATION.

Copulation persists practically up until the first egg is dropped and it then, or very soon after, ceases. Normally there is no courting or copulation during the incubation period. When such activities are manifested by one bird, it is a sign that it is attempting to renew the cycle. If both birds participate, a new cycle begins at once and the eggs are deserted (see Chapter VII). However, one copulation was recorded on the seventh day of the incubation period of one pair and no disturbance of their incubation activities resulted.

NEST-BUILDING.

The nest-building which occurs during the mating period ceases during the egg-laying period, but is resumed as soon as alternation of sitting begins. The "free" bird spends much time in carrying straws to its sitting mate. At first the

---

[1] Some males are so hyperdeveloped in the tendency to sit that they hardly give the females a chance. (Conv. W. C.)

BEHAVIOR OF PIGEONS.

activity occurs very persistently throughout the day, but it soon becomes mainly confined to the early-morning period between 8 and 10 o'clock. This activity persisted for 8 days in the bronze-wing and then stopped. Both birds participated for the first 5 days, but the male alone was active thereafter.

NEATNESS IN NEST.

When the young hatch, the old ones—I saw the male do this once—take the shells in their beaks and carry them off to the farther corner of the yard and drop them. This is done to save the young from being cut or incommoded.

When roosting, doves defecate quite frequently, but when incubating the female allows nothing to pass the cloaca during the night, waiting until the male comes to take his turn in the morning; then flying to a remote part of the yard, she relieves herself of a monstrous load—often enough to fill a good sized spoon. The weight in one case taken at random was 11.75 g. A ring-dove laid her first egg at the usual time and came off the nest at 10 o'clock in the evening to defecate and then returned. In the morning, before it was fairly light, she came off again to relieve herself; it was evident that she felt the strain. She soon returned to the nest.

I have noticed that the male is also equally careful to attend to this matter only after leaving the nest. He does not, however, have to carry so large a mass, as he is not so long on the nest at one time.

The young, when defecating, reach back just as far towards the edge of the nest as they possibly can, thus keeping the center of the nest perfectly clean. The young, after they get to be a week or more old, push back as far out of the nest as possible. Before this age, the young reach back less, but the anus is protruded like a tube and thrust down into the bed of the nest so far that none is seen on the surface. I have often wondered how the nest was kept so clean during the first week until I noticed this habit. This habit is perhaps correlated with the habit, in the old birds, of adding new straw to their nest after the young are a few days old.

I learned that the female of a pair of archangels, unlike any other dove I have had, piles up her dung around the nest. As it is now cold weather, this does not matter so much, but I presume she would do the same in warm weather, when it might make a most filthy place of the nest. This seems to be a case where an instinct of a very fixed character has weakened and become obsolete.

One day, at $7^h 45^m$ a. m., I saw the male bronze-wing take the emptied shell of the just-hatched egg to the floor. On the next day it was noted that one of the young was dead and that the female had just taken it out of the nest and dropped it on the floor, where she had deposited the second egg shell. The young of a pair of mourning-doves was dragged out of the nest with the egg-shell and got cold before being discovered; the bird revived, but died on the same day. (R 33, Em 7.)

The following similar incidents are reported by Dr. Riddle:

"Two *alba-orientalis* hybrids had been given eggs to hatch. In hatching, a small piece of the shell became attached to an umbilicus. Two hours later both bird and attached shell were found on the floor of the cage. While the act was not observed, there is reason to believe that the old birds, in attempting to remove the shell from the nest, had carried away the young as well. In another case, when one young had been hatched, the other egg was just nicely 'pipped.' In removing the shells of the first egg, the parents also removed, and deposited on the floor, the egg which was partly hatched. This egg was discovered shortly afterwards and the young was saved."

INCUBATION BEHAVIOR. 61

INFLUENCE OF TEMPERATURE.

A pair of blond and white ring-doves hatched a pair of eggs on January 19 and 20 in the aviary behind the house. The egg-shells were not removed from the nest on January 23, when I found the birds and removed the shells myself. I have never known doves to neglect this point during summer, nor in winter if they are kept in a warm room. Evidently the bitter cold weather of the week of hatching must have been the condition that prevented action. In the previous set the sitting was very irregular, owing to the cold, and the male neglected his duty altogether on the colder days. That a low temperature suspends breeding in *Ectopistes* and retards the process of breeding in all species is well known. The secretion of pigeon's "milk" is also checked by cold. (R 17.)

HIDING ON THE NEST.

A male mourning-dove from California is now sitting in the first pen on the west side of the house. The eggs were laid by a white ring-dove, 1 and 3 days ago. This is the "tamest" of all my mourning-doves. He always flies straight to me and alights on my hand or head or shoulders quite fearlessly. If I clasp him in my hand to carry him from one place to another, he makes no struggle beyond trying to keep his equilibrium. To-day I was astonished as I walked past his pen to see him exhibit the "instinct of hiding." He sat on the eggs (this is the first time that he has taken part in sitting) facing the front side of the pen. As I approached he drew down his head, closed his feathers, raised the wing next to me, and as I passed by to the other side the other wing was raised. I passed back and forth several times in order to see him perform. He kept up the hiding, and raised first one wing then the other as I went from side to side. The wing is raised without being opened at all. The shoulder is thrown up a little above the level of the head, so as to alter the figure and thus lessen the chances of discovery. The habit of lowering the head as far as possible is common in the crested pigeon and the common dove.

I brought in a young white-faced pigeon of 18 days to put a ring on its leg, and while I prepared the ring I left the bird in a cage near by. It soon took the characteristic "hiding attitude," resting on its breast with tail up, and held its head low and still. There it sat without moving, except for a slight breathing movement, for nearly 10 minutes, and would probably have sat there for an hour had I remained and left it to act its way. (R 17, Sh 8/13.)

VOICE.

NEST-CALL.

The nest-call is given frequently by both birds throughout the incubation period. It is almost invariably given upon taking the nest; it is sometimes given as a signal for relief, and frequently no purpose is apparent. These statements are evident from the following excerpts taken from the record of the bronze-wing pigeons:

The male gave the usual nest-call as he took his place over the egg. The female gave two to three calls as she placed herself over the egg. She gave the call three times while she was taking her place on the nest. The female is thinking of returning to the nest, and the male has called once for her. The male gave two calls a moment or two after resuming nest duty. The female went to the perch beside the nest and called twice, at which the male came off. The male had just settled on the eggs when he gave several calls. The male took his place and gave one nest-call. The male gave a call before leaving the nest, and I think this call was for the female to relieve him; he seems hungry. The female gives the nest-cell, or a call very similar to it, just before she takes her position to drop the second egg. Hence this is not a call for hay, but perhaps a call that means, "I am in the nest, don't disturb me." Other species also do this; at least some others do.

62 BEHAVIOR OF PIGEONS.

The nest-call is also used in connection with egg-laying and the feeding of young. The crested pigeon gave the call-note almost continuously just before laying. A mourning-dove likewise gave a low call several times just before she took a position to lay. The call here was the *usual call to nest-making*. The feeding-call, which is given by adults during the act of feeding the young, is essentially the same as the nest-call for straw. (R 19, R 28.)

During a period of 165 minutes that a male bronze-wing was on the nest there were recorded 55 nest-calls on the part of the male to 7 for the female. During 39 minutes in the afternoon, while the male was on the nest, 17 calls were noted for the male and 1 for the female. During 55 minutes while the female was on the nest, the male called 12 times and the female 8 times. During incubation the male thus seems to call more frequently than the female. Probably calls are more frequent while the bird is on the nest. Either bird may take the initiative in calling and usually the calls are not answered by the mate.

ALIGHTING, OR SHORT-NOTE CALL.

The short-note call is a regular thing on landing, whether on the perch or on the floor, for both sexes of bronze-wings. The above generalization is amply supported by many notes in the record of the bronze-wings, a few examples of which are given:

The male went to perch near the nest and emitted three or four short notes; these were rolled off quickly without other demonstration. Then he returned to the floor and repeated these peculiar quick, sheep-like notes and began looking for straws. The female flew to the floor and immediately on alighting gave the short quick notes—four to six—uttered about as rapidly as possible without blending. The male returned to the nest and gave the short notes upon arrival at the perch. The male flew to the perch in front of the nest and gave the short-note call—two short grunts. The alighting-note of these birds is a short note repeated rapidly. This is homologous with the threatening note of the white-wing (*M. leucoptera*) and other species. (R 33, R 1.)

CHAPTER VI.

FEEDING AND CARE OF THE YOUNG.

During the first week after the hatching of the eggs the old birds continue their alternation of nest duty. At the end of this time the young can be left uncovered for some time without harm, and the period of "close sitting" characteristic of the incubation period ceases. At the end of the second week the young begin to venture from the nest and become more and more independent of parental care. The young are fed by regurgitation. The food at first consists of "pigeon's milk," a secretion whose appearance is well timed with the end of the incubation period. Later the young are given the partially digested food of the parents. While in the nest (2 weeks) the young rely entirely upon this food. After leaving the nest they begin to pick up food of their own accord, and they can be "weaned" at the end of 4 to 5 weeks. Both parents participate in this feeding for the first two weeks, and in case they do not begin a new cycle, both may continue the feeding for some time later.

With a renewal of the reproductive cycle, the order of events is changed. The cycle may be started at the end of the first week, when close sitting ceases. The female is then ready to lay at the end of the second week, just as the young are venturing from the nest. The female then stops feeding and devotes her entire energy to the task of incubation. The male continues the feeding and also participates in the incubation of the second set of eggs. When the eggs are hatched, the male devotes his attention to the new set of young, and the first set are forced to rely upon themselves for their sustenance. "Driving" is sometimes necessary to accomplish this weaning of the first young. If a series of cycles follow each other in immediate succession, the male bird will thus be continuously engaged in the task of feeding his various broods of offspring.

GENERAL NATURE OF THE ACTIVITIES.

At the end of the period of incubation (2 weeks) and a further week or more in care of the young, the pair renew the cycle of events. The young are fed by both parents until the female is about ready to lay again, then the male continues the work alone and the young begin to help themselves. As soon as the time of hatching arrives, the previous young begin to learn that they are no longer wanted and, if they do not leave, the male takes them in hand and drives them without mercy. All this is to the end that the newcomers may be safe in their nest from attacks by their elder brother and sister when the parents are away. The bird has no idea of what its actions mean, for its actions are according to "feelings" which follow each other in regular serial order, making the same round each time. The close sitting normally lasts for about 21 days—two weeks to hatch and one week on the young.

A pair of bronze-wings were brought into my library, about the middle of November, in order to save the young, then about 4 weeks old. The young and old had done well, although the young have not developed flying power as they would if they had lived

64 BEHAVIOR OF PIGEONS.

outside in viable conditions. The old birds kept on feeding the young until about Dec. 7, or between 7 and 8 weeks.[1]

I notice that a pair of young mourning-doves, 1 and 2 days old, are sleeping quite uncovered in front of the male. The young birds are in the nest, and the parent bird seems to have drawn back a little to one side of the nest so that the young can sit uncovered. The heat is oppressive for the first time this season, and the birds are left uncovered because they are more comfortable so. In cold weather this would not happen.

When a nest-box with young is placed on the floor of the pen, the young will usually begin to get up on the edge of the box a few days before they are 2 weeks old. At 2 weeks they will often venture to jump from the box to the floor of the pen, a height of 3 to 4 inches. A pair of blond ring-doves got out of the box 2 days before they were 2 weeks old. The young are unable to fly at 2 weeks and these young were plainly prematurely out of the nest. Similarly a young hybrid from a white fantail and a ring-dove, at just 2 weeks old—a full week before it would venture to fly from its nest—stepped out of the nest-box, which was kept on the floor, on to the floor of the pen, and walked around with the foster-parents, which were eating their breakfast. The young bird then, without experience, appreciates the conditions which make it safe or unsafe to leave the nest. If the nest were several feet above the floor it would not have ventured out for at least a week.

At two weeks of age, and the first or second day after they get out of the nest, the young quite generally learn to pick up seed and bread crumbs, if these are placed near them; but they are almost invariably, if not always, led to do this by seeing the parents eat. The parental example is the guiding stimulus.

A female passenger-pigeon left her young early in the morning at the age of about 8 days, and neither parent covered the young during the day, although the mother continued to cover the bird for two nights more. Two days later the parent birds began a new cycle. The young of this second cycle were left uncovered when 9 days old. When their young were only a week old, a pair of fantails ceased to sit continuously and started a new cycle. Sitting continued intermittently until 3 days later, when the female took the perch at night, leaving the young uncovered. Both birds of a pair of mourning-doves came off the nest during the daytime, leaving the young alone at the ages of 6 and 8 days. Five days later the female left the young at night also and sat on the perch with the male. They were thus left uncovered before they were quite 2 weeks old.

A pair of white-face pigeons (*Leucosarcia picata*) gave, in contrast with the above cases, remarkable and unceasing care to a young bird hatched by them. One or the other of the parents remained every minute with the young until it was 19 days old; this youngster, moreover, was kept "covered" during the whole time, except for a short time towards the last, when it sometimes sat beside the parent rather than under it. I have never known any other pigeons to keep close to the nest after the young got to be 10 or 12 days old; frequently the old birds begin to leave the nest a little at the end of 6 or 7 days. A new egg was laid 2 days later, but it did not develop. Evidently the close care of the young did not give the male a fair chance to fertilize this egg. One such young of this species, when 6 days old, was put in a cage with the parents and taken on a railway journey of nearly 1,000 miles. The old birds took care of it on the way, covering it as usual. On arrival, I left the young and old in the cage over-night. On the next day I moved them to a new pen, placing the nest-box with the young in it on a shelf. In this new position the old birds did not seem to feed it and refused to cover it.

---

[1] This pair did not renew the cycle immediately, and this may partly account for the long period of feeding. A new cycle was started on Dec. 10.—EDITOR.

FEEDING AND CARE OF THE YOUNG.

65

The following incident was observed in November, in a pair of young common pigeons that were hatched on Oct. 26 and 27. These birds were about $3\frac{1}{2}$ weeks old, not ready to fly. The old birds wanted the nest for a new set of eggs and began to drive the young. These, wonderful to say, bore it for a while and then began to resist, and fought with such desperation that the old ones left them in peace. I saw this fight repeated several times.

After feeding, the young usually turn so as to sit with the head pointing backward under the parent. This position is the one almost invariably taken by the passenger, ring-dove, crested pigeon, and the domestic dove.[1] (R 17, R 33, R 6, R 7, R 19, C 7/33, Em 7, Sh 8/13.)

FEEDING OF YOUNG.

Most people know something of the way the pigeon feeds its young. There are, however, some rather extraordinary things that happen in connection with feeding that deserve mention. Suppose we place the young of a small species under the care of a larger species—a young ring-dove, for example, under a common pigeon or homer. The old birds will take care of this young ring-dove just as faithfully as they would take care of their own young. But when this young bird gets out of the nest, at a week or 10 days, he is not able to take all the food that the old birds want to get rid of; the homer can not feed this young and small bird as much as he desires to feed it, and we can imagine that this gives the homer a quite unpleasant feeling, for he behaves in a way to indicate this. When the young bird does not accept all the food that is offered to him, then the foster-parent begins to tease the young to accept it. The parent will pull the feathers of the young very gently and bite its beak, or give it a gentle pinch, just to stimulate it to feed. The little bird will respond to these things until it has so much that it can hold no more; but the old bird urges it to accept still more. Finally the parent begins to pinch the young bird's beak a little more severely, and to pull its feathers a little more strongly, and—being a larger species—behaves in a way rather rough for the smaller species, and in the end alarms the young bird, which now tries to get out of the way. The old bird follows it up—he can not give up, but is fully determined to get rid of all his food. Naturally it troubles and startles the young bird to be pursued in this rough way and the old bird sooner or later gets angry and begins to peck the squealing, retreating young very severely, sometimes pulls out its feathers, sometimes pulls off the skin of its head, neck, and back, and if the young bird is not taken away it is very often killed.

Now, I am perfectly certain that the old bird behaves in this way, not from any malicious motives, but just for its normal relief. There are a great many ways of becoming sure of this fact. This behavior, of course, is found in birds of different species. I have tried some of them in many different ways and found this view of the behavior confirmed by other behavior which is analogous. In further illustrations of this, we may consider a situation which is sometimes met with in the case of a common pigeon and her own young. When one of the two young of a brood is hatched a little too long after the first one, the first hatched is apt to get quite an extra start in growth and be much stronger than the second one; when the second one is hatched, it is fed a "little" and the other one is fed "more," and so from day to day the first one continues to outgrow the second one to such an extent that the second one has not the strength or ability to stand up and get as much of the food as the first one; so the difference increases from day to day. The second bird is more and more hungry, because the old bird is satisfied with the vigorous bearing and

---

[1] When the bird is sitting the eggs are usually placed end to end in the median line. They are usually too far back under the abdomen to come into uncomfortable contact with the keel of the breast bone. The young commonly face toward the tail of the sitting parent. It seems as if they can be better covered by the feathers in this position. The parent easily turns round to feed the young. (Conv. 8/6/08, W. C.)

BEHAVIOR OF PIGEONS.

desire and energy on the part of the stronger bird. The second one does not satisfy the old bird and is more and more neglected and in the end it becomes a dwarf bird, or it may die.

On the question as to the part played by intelligence in these cases, I may say that it does not seem to me that the birds exercise intelligence; they simply act in accord with their feelings. They appear to be very fond of the young birds, but their fondness for the young is all determined by their feelings, or desire for relief. The moment they get over their desire to feed they also get over their fondness for the young. If the eggs do not hatch they have a desire to feed, but it is not so strong as to lead to bad results and they soon outgrow it; it does not then make them sick. In those cases, however, where parents really get started in feeding the young, the need to feed is most pressing; and if the young die in two or three days after hatching, then the old birds are not only frequently made sick as a result of not being able to feed, but frequently sick to death.

The special secretions in the pigeon's crop seems to be stimulated in part by the sight of the young and the amount of stimulation, or rather the amount of food which the parents want to relieve themselves of, and it rapidly increases in amount during the days which follow the beginning of feeding. If they do not begin actual feeding they get over it, but if they once get started it is necessary to go on; otherwise they suffer.

I have noticed in pigeons that the "weak are neglected" and the strong favored. This is seen in the feeding as noted above. To get the full benefit of the parent's ability to feed the young must *push, squeal, and flap its wings—and all this with vigor*. The moment these acts are not well performed, the parent's exertion dwindles for lack of stimulus.

The feeding process is performed—at least in many cases—purely *to get relief*. The old bird gives "milk," and at intervals this secretion must be thrown out. I have seen a parent try to induce young to feed when the latter had no desire, having been well filled by the other parent. The old bird gets into the nest and calls; if there is no response it takes hold of the beak of the young and begins to pump vigorously. If the young die, or if they are taken away, one may see after 6 to 10 hours how eager the parents are to relieve themselves of the food reserved for the young. They are ready to feed anything that will put its beak into their mouths; they will often return to weaned young (crested pigeons) and feed them for a second time. They will try to feed an adult bird if that bird's beak is only held in their mouth, and held low enough to simulate young in the nest.

On the other hand, the old birds will often try to feed when they have nothing to give, *e. g.*, when young are given to them before the regular time for hatching has come. Thus the act is performed sometimes for relief, sometimes in answer to the teasing of a hungry young.

The theory that the act was primarily one for relief from too much or from indigestible food, and secondarily turned to use in feeding, has one great difficulty, namely, to account for the "milk." I do not think that could have been at first a product of a useless nature, like ejected food. It is something that has probably been developed in conjunction with the feeding. The dove's method of feeding occurs also in some other birds.[1]

As the young get larger, their feeding becomes for the parent more and more of a dread, as they are ravenous and push with all their strength to get the food. The old bird becomes wary and makes haste to finish quickly and retire, going out of the cot often before it has full relief. It then continues to call, but hesitates to go in. The young stand at the hole and squeal. The appearance is as if the old bird wanted to entice the young outside. Later the old one grows still more cautious and the young venture out and are fed. The next time they go out quicker and the old bird retreats. It then looks as if the old bird wanted to teach the young to fly. It is evident, however, that this is no thought-out art,

---

[1] Lucas states (Mental Traits of the Pribilof Fur Seal, V, 1899), that the young of the fur seal was fed by the mother for her own relief.

FEEDING AND CARE OF THE YOUNG. 67

but an art that grows out of the situation—young clamoring for food, old ones anxious to relieve themselves, and fear of the push of the young.

The old bird normally feeds two birds at the same time, and it seems to need the two-sided contact to get full relief.[1] If there is only one young, the old bird after feeding from one side may walk off to the other side of the nest and thus give a chance for a change in position. (SS 10, R 24, B 2b, R 7.)

This "feeding from both sides" has been mentioned in a previous topic (Billing and feeding in uniting, Chapter II), under which are described a few cases in which the male was observed to "feed" the female. This sort of "feeding" is, however, connected with the sexual billing which precedes a copulation. But the close similarity of the activities in the two kinds of "feeding" is certainly remarkable; for it is stated that "the male feeds the female with the same up-and-down shake of head and crop as is used with the young, and then she shifts to the other side," and also that the male opens his beak and the female inserts hers first on one side and then on the other.[2]

Fulton, on page 42 of the work already cited, states:

"The pigeon's 'milk,' which has pointed so many a joke, is no myth, but a veritable existence; the fact being that as the time for hatching approaches the crops of both old birds secrete a soft substance closely resembling curd, which forms the solid food of the young pigeons for some days, after which its quantity slowly diminishes, and it becomes gradually mixed with the grain more or less softened, till by degrees the young pigeon is thus introduced to hard food and can feed itself. This 'soft food,' as it is called, is pumped up by the old ones with a sort of vomiting action, and the little pigeons have just sufficient sense to feel about for the bills of the old birds, into which they insert their own, and are thus fed; they will feel in the same way for the finger if held to them. It is singular, but true, that the beak of a young pigeon, being thus almost entirely intended for a kind of suction, is much *thicker and larger* in proportion to the body than in after life, besides being of a soft and fleshy character. It looks immense at first in proportion to the bird, but gradually shrinks and hardens."

ANOMALOUS FEEDING BEHAVIOR.

Two young hybrids, one white (*H*) and the other blond (*J*), were with their foster-parents in a cage. The old birds were at the time out of the nest. The white young (*H*) appealed to *J* for food, whereupon the latter several times opened his beak to receive that of his nest-mate, and shook his crop and wings as if it would give up food. Soon the white young actually inserted its beak into that of *J* and the latter fed it in a vigorous manner, pumping up food liberally until I interrupted, thinking it could not be well for *J* to part with its food. *J* is only 12 days old, and it is at least 3 days behind its companion in the development of its feathers. It was a strange sight to see this unfledged bird, with only pin-feathers on its head, and much of its body bare, feeding another bird more advanced in its feathers, although of about the same age and weight. I have never before seen or heard of such a performance.

I have seen both young and old throw up food that was indigestible, especially when sick. I have seen them in good health overeat and cram themselves with more than could be readily swallowed, and then seek relief in throwing up. In so doing the movements may all be the same as in feeding the young—the head is held down, the beak open, the

---

[1] The parent takes care to feed both young. I am not sure that this is intentional, but it looks almost so. The parent feeds for a time, then stops, disengages, and moves around a short distance before commencing to feed again, so that it usually happens the other young gets the second feeding. (Conv. W. C.)

[2] This statement is made for the bronze-wing, which is a species that copulates on the ground. For those species which "bill" and copulate on a perch, or branch of a tree, the shifting of the billing from one side to the other would seem to be a rather difficult or awkward matter. Possibly, however, it occurs in these latter species also. It certainly sometimes occurs in the case of ring-doves when these birds copulate on the ground.—O. R.

68 BEHAVIOR OF PIGEONS.

crop is shaken, and with it the whole body, especially the wings. The power to regurgitate is, then, common to doves, old and young, and *it has come secondarily into service in the care of the young.*

What prompted *J* to feed its white companion? I think the crop was a little overloaded, and that, together with the stimulus of a teasing beak, led it to give up food. It was not, however, an act of vomiting merely; for *J* offered its open beak several times to the companion, and in a way that was unmistakable, so that I wondered at it before the feeding began. When the beak was inserted in the open beak the whole machinery of correlated movements was set in motion and the young bird behaved in all respects like an adult bird. The beak inserted in the throat may have much to do with stimulating the process.

A hybrid between a ring-dove and the European turtle was 11 days old; it had as a nest companion a ring-dove 1 week old. The ring was small and covered with pin-feathers; the hybrid had many wing-coverts and scapulars unfolding. These birds were under the care of a pair of ring-doves; both were perfectly healthful and strong. I noticed the young ring teasing the hybrid with its beak, as young birds scantily fed often do with a nest-mate. The vigorous billing about the hybrid's beak and neck led it to feel like feeding, and it opened its beak several times for the ring, and once after offering the open beak, it put its head down and shook its wings and crop as an old bird does in feeding. The young ring did not get its beak into that of hybrid, but came near doing so. (R 24.)

TRANSFERENCE OF YOUNG TO FOSTER PARENTS.

The young of any species may be transferred to foster-parents, provided they are put under the foster-parents at the time the eggs of the latter are due to hatch. It does not seem to make any difference whether the young birds are transferred when they are just hatched, or at a week or 2 weeks old, provided only that they are not old enough to stand up straight and raise the head too high. The old birds do object to taking care of any young birds that stand up and look too much like old birds. If the young simply sits down, holds its head down in the proper position for care, that is all that is required; the old birds will feed it just as well as if it were hatched out under them. If eggs are transferred one must always be sure that they are properly timed; that is, timed to hatch with the eggs which are removed; if they hatch too early, or are due to hatch too long after the time of the eggs removed, the transfer is not successful. The foster-parents are as well satisfied with the eggs of other species as with their own; they do not know the difference.

The necessity of exactly matching the time of hatching of the transferred eggs with that of the eggs removed is one of the complications that is met with in attempts, such as my own, to obtain and hatch unusually large numbers of eggs from particular pairs of birds. I have had some trouble of this sort. The common pigeons, however, are a little less particular in the matter of the exact time the eggs are due to hatch than are the wild species. Also, in crossing common pigeons with the wild species one finds that the former will usually continue the incubation a few days after their mate's usual time. The wild passenger-pigeon never waits more than 10 or 12 hours. If the egg does not hatch within that time he leaves it; even if the shell is broken and the bird is nearly ready to hatch it is deserted. If young are put into their nests before they are due to hatch they are not able to feed them; much care in this matter is necessary. "Pigeon milk," as it is called, seems to be ready at the proper moment. Everything is well-timed, and if there are young birds in the nest before this time arrives they will get no food. (SS 10.)

Fulton, in pages 42-43 of the work previously cited, contributes the following on the subject under discussion:

FEEDING AND CARE OF THE YOUNG.

"Hence the practice of employing 'feeders' or nurses, which are necessary to all fanciers of the 'high-class' varieties, and to which the young are transferred when a few days old to be reared, only being left long enough with their own parents to 'feed off the soft food,' which would otherwise make them sick and cause the hen to be much longer in laying again than if allowed to feed young for a few days. The young require to be left with the old birds, in general from 6 to 8 days, in order to relieve them of their soft food, when they should be shifted to the feeders. But in shifting, one caution is very necessary, viz, not to shift to old birds which have hatched *before* the young ones it is desired to rear. Should this be done, the young will in all probability perish, through the food now supplied being too 'hard' or too far advanced for them, in conformity with what we have already explained as to the gradual change in its character, by increasing mixture with grain, which the young can not digest till the proper age. On the contrary, should the feeders have hatched three or four days *after* the breeding-birds it will be all the better, and do the young a great deal of good, since nothing brings on a young pigeon so well as this extra allowance of soft food."

"Another caution may be necessary. We have seen how easily, in the case of most pigeons, the young may be 'shifted' at almost any time desired within a fortnight; and pigeons will also take to and sit upon other eggs than their own; but it will *not* answer to give to any pair eggs partly hatched, unless laid at the same time as their own, and therefore due to hatch at the same date. The reason is obvious; the eggs hatching before the ordinary time of incubation is expired, there is *no soft food* ready for the young, and they must therefore perish. One day or perhaps two does not matter; but success when the shifted eggs have been sat upon more than this is very doubtful."

VOICE.

Food-Call of Young.

The call for food in the bronze-wing is a cry resembling that of young pigeons in general—a sort of mild whistle given in a beseeching manner, from a fraction of a second to a second and a half long, and varying in loudness and shrillness according to the eagerness for food. In general, the manner is very deliberate and free from the excitement and hurry shown by common pigeons. If the young does not get the attention of the old bird, it may stop in front of the parent and give a few of the polite bows so characteristic of the old bird. The young bows with the same motion as the adult, and quite or nearly to the floor. It is a comical thing to see this bow from a bird only 2 weeks old, and before it has had any opportunity to learn from the parents. The call is repeated at varying intervals and is often continued for some minutes.

As just noted above, the call of the young for food is very calmly delivered, but with earnestness, and no flurry or scramble as in common pigeons. If the old bird, after giving the young a taste, walks off, the latter looks earnestly for more, but does not rush and flap its wings against the old bird; it moves towards the old bird with a slow, hesitating step, lifting its wings only a little and wagging them slowly up and down as if pleading, and it again gives the beseeching whistle as it approaches.

When the old bird first approaches the young to feed them, these welcome him with their affectionate and pleasing little twitter—the "whistle" broken into a ripple of few or many sounds; these are generally low, but the same sound may be quite loud. A good demonstration of this loud whistle was obtained in the following instance. A young bronze-wing escaped, but came back and alighted on the top of its old pen. Here it sat looking down at its mate and the old bird, whistling loud to get back. The whistle was delivered with the beak quite wide open, and sometimes it was broken into a twitter, the whole frame seeming to shake at the sound. The voice of the young reminds one of the voice of the sandpiper. The wing-movements of the young, when appealing to the old birds for more food, are the same as those given in conjunction with the nest-call by the adult male.

Food-Call of Adult Bronze-Wing.

A female bronze-wing came several times to the near (feeding) side of her cage, at about 3 p. m., and gave a peculiar little grunt of impatience for lack of food. This was about the time for her to return to the nest for the night, and there was no seed in her dish; she

70 BEHAVIOR OF PIGEONS.

was anxious to eat before returning, and hence expressed her want in the short guttural oo sound. This sound was made with the mouth closed, and was repeated rather quickly several times as she stood looking expectantly for me to give her food. As soon as I did so she fed and I heard no more from her. I heard the same sound, only stronger, from a bronze-wing kept in the basement of my home, and on looking I found the bird had neither water nor seed.

The female referred to above called again for food 6 days later, and came to the side of the cage nearest me and tried to get through. I then learned that she repeats the call at a rate of two to three notes a second, and sometimes she brings her effort to an end with several notes cut short and run off close together as rapidly as the tip of the tongue vibrates in giving the sound of *r*. Thirteen days still later I saw this female go to her nest and use this same call to her mate to leave the nest; she then "wanted to feed the young."

Feeding-Call of Bronze-Wing.

A female bronze-wing was heard calling, and at the same time it was noted that her young also were calling for food. Glancing at them, I found that the old bird's note was given as the young reached up towards her beak to be fed. She repeated the call several times before taking the beak of the young. The note was essentially the same as the nest-call for straw. A week later at 9 a. m., I saw the female feeding her young. With every shake she gave the usual call, but it was *very low*, as if half-suppressed and it was given without dropping the beak of the young; *i.e*, the calling was continued *while* feeding, only very *quietly*. In ring-doves and other species I have heard feeding-calls given while in the act of feeding, and have observed that this is often an expression of the "satisfaction of the old bird in the process."

Resistance to Intruders.[1]

A detailed record, made on two different days, of the behavior of the bronze-wing in resisting a hand directed toward the incubating bird, is given herewith: (1) I move my hand slowly towards the bird, on a level with the top of the nest-box—never above the bird, as that alarms her too much. As the hand comes within a few inches of the nest-box, she places herself sidewise or at right angles to the line of approach, gives a growl, and raises her wings straight up, prepared to strike if approached more closely. By moving the hand very slowly, and taking care to move steadily, without jerks, she may permit me to get my hand within 3 or 4 inches of the eggs, but she is afraid and retreats enough to allow a sight of one or both eggs. Usually, however, she strikes several times sharply if the hand comes within an inch of the eggs. In all this she is in a threatening attitude, with wing ready to deliver a quick blow, and she growls more often and viciously the nearer you get to her. Between growls she "puffs" like a young dove that is old enough to be frightened when approached. She may permit you to touch the eggs without being frightened off, but she protests with vigorous growls and blows from the wing. (2) As I approach the female with my hand, she is careful when she strikes with her wing not to stir her feet and thus endanger the young resting between her legs. Her growl is a rough rumbling, guttural sound, in making which the bird opens its beak but slightly and raises both wings over its back; the feathers of the back, including the upper tail-coverts, are raised, reminding one of the way a dog "bristles." The tail also is more or less spread and held horizontally, or raised very slightly and rigidly.

A "growl of warning" is given by the bronze-wings when the bird is nesting eggs, and the same note is still more strongly given after the eggs are hatched. The note of threat is a growl, or better, a grunt, expressing fear and a disposition to resist intrusion to the nest. It is made when one puts his hand near the nest.

---

[1] See topic on "Periodicity of Disposition to Fight," Chapter I.—Editor.

FEEDING AND CARE OF THE YOUNG.

NOTE OF ALARM[1] OF BRONZE-WING.

A male bronze-wing that was sitting on the nest, over the 1-day-old young, saw a cat run along the sidewalk; the bird stretched his neck at full length, nearly vertically, and held his head a little aslant, with one eye fixed steadfastly on the cat. The female was on the floor and unable to see the cat. The male gave a very low short muffled note of "anxiety" or "alarm." The female was at once alert, with feathers held tightly, as if danger was expected. The note is not only low and short, but quite smooth, no vibration being noticeable. *Geopelia humeralis* gives a similar note on like occasions, but it is not quite smooth, is just a little hoarse, though not loud. The note is uttered by a short, quick expulsion of air with the "beak closed." All species seem to understand this alarm-note, no matter which species gives it.

FLOCK WHISTLE OF YOUNG BRONZE-WING.

The young bronze-wing has another note—a soft, pleasant twitter—that is hard to describe. It almost continuously gives this note when it is on the ground, and I incline to think that it facilitates the movements of the family and enables them to keep together. These birds spend all their time running about on the ground, and some such note would enable the old birds to keep track of the young. This mellow whistle of the young reminds one of the notes emitted by the Bartramian sandpiper (*Bartramia longicauda*). Chapman describes, in his Birds of Eastern North America (p. 168), this sandpiper's note, when flushed, as "a soft bubbling whistle." (R 28, R 33.)

---

[1] Descriptive material may be found in Chapter X.

CHAPTER VII.

DEFECTIVE CYCLES.

The reproductive cycle consists of numerous activities which, when normally related to each other in a definite temporal order, are nicely adapted to achieve that essential result—the production and rearing of young. While harmony and adaptation are the rule, yet certain faults, defects, and abnormalities, serious and trivial, frequently occur. In the normal series of events it is evident that these activities must stand in some sort of a mutual relation of cause and effect. To the analysis of this causal interdependence the normal series of events can furnish but little help. The key to this analysis lies here as everywhere in experimental control and alteration of the order of events. The defects and abnormalities which are described in this chapter possess not only an interest *per se*, but they may be regarded as isolated bits of nature's own experimentation which may furnish some help towards the proper analysis of that complex organization of activities constituting the reproductive cycle. For the most part, these accounts consist of excerpts and digests from the various records which present the essential facts pertinent to our purpose.

BRONZE-WING.

FIRST CYCLE.

The eggs were laid on December 16 and 18, 1905. The incubation record was normal up to December 17. The eggs were hatched on January 3 and 4. During the last week of the incubation period the male participated fairly well in his incubation duties, but deviated from normal behavior by attempting to entice his mate to desert the eggs and start a new cycle. After hatching, the male refused to cover or feed the young properly and consequently both died within a few days. A new cycle was started immediately afterwards.

The male thus discontinued his cycle of activities, without any apparent external cause, 15 days before its natural end. The female continued her cycle for 11 days, or until the death of the second young on January 7, in spite of a number of disturbing factors. These were, (a) the necessity of doing extra duty in the care of the young, (b) the continual solicitations of the male, and (c) the death of one young. With the death of the second young, the normal sequence of activities was interrupted 4 days before its normal completion and a new cycle was started.

The above facts are verified, and the necessary details supplied, by the following excerpts from the daily incubation records:

Dec. 27.—At $3^h 45^m$ p. m. the male calls again five times and the female answers once. The male this time does not attend to the call of his mate, but walks back and forth on the side of the cage. His many calls evidently indicate that he has a sexual inclination. At $4^h 44^m$ p. m. the male walks nearer to the female, getting onto the edge of the nest, but she sticks to the nest and gives a low call as much as to say: "I must be left alone." At $5^h 46^m$ p. m.[1] the male is again on the edge of the nest and the female protests by two more

---
[1] This is the normal time for the male to be on the perch for the night.—EDITOR.

74 BEHAVIOR OF PIGEONS.

calls, and he again retires to the opposite end of the perch. It is now after sunset, getting dark; but I have the room lighted, and this perhaps incites the irregular behavior in the male, for he is already back to the nest again at $5^h 48^m$. Two or three times more, between $5^h 30^m$ and $5^h 55^m$, the male returned to the nest after I had lowered the light; the female protested every time and he called as if uneasy at something. At $6^h 30^m$ I find, on going to the room, which has been dark since I left and locked so that no outside disturbance could occur, that the male is sitting on the perch close in front of the nest instead of at the most distant end of the perch, as I should expect.

Dec. 29.—At $7^h 34^m$ a. m. the male is on the side of the nest, calls twice, waits a moment or two, walks off the perch, and is now walking uneasily back and forth, as if he would like to get out of the window. The same behavior was noticed for the last two or three days.

Dec. 30.—The male is standing in the nest beside the female, fondling her head. I presume he wants to relieve her again.

Dec. 31.—After keeping the room locked from $1^h 46^m$ p. m., I returned at 6 p. m. and found the male sitting on the perch directly in front of the female, instead of sitting at the distant end of the perch.

Jan. 2.—At $7^h 35^m$ a. m., the male went to the nest and fondled the head of his mate while standing on the side of the nest. He then pushed the female off the nest, but refused to sit. At 10 a. m. the first egg is hatching. The female has been off the nest for 30 minutes, and meanwhile the male has not offered to sit. In fact, he has stood for 20 minutes on the nest without sitting, and he walked to the perch just before the female stepped to the nest. The male is ready to renew the nesting cycle. I noticed this as early as yesterday, but more plainly to-day. His way of going to the nest and fondling the head of the female as if she were not doing serious duty, sometimes carelessly walking over her, and also sitting near her at night, all indicate this fact. Besides, he sits very perfunctorily. To-day he left the egg and came down to his mate on the floor and began courtesying to her as if he desired to copulate.

Jan. 3.—The first young hatched this morning. The male went to the nest and fondled the head of the female, but did not relieve her till $1^h 05^m$ p. m. He gives no attention to the young bird and does not sit down to cover it. His behavior confirms the conclusion of yesterday that he prematurely arrived at the end of his incubating period and has now become totally indifferent at the very time when he should be most attentive. The female is absolutely faithful and sticks to the nest, doing double duty; the male meanwhile loafs about, visits the female, and fondles her head, but shows not a particle of interest in the little one.

Jan. 4.—The second egg has hatched. One young, probably the first one, is dead.

Jan. 5.—The male relieved the female several times during the day, but he does not really sit; he "stands" over the young or on the edge of the nest. He makes no attempt to feed the young. He bows to the female and solicits her frequently. He feeds the female once, tries to copulate with the seed-dish several times, and attempts to mount the female.

Jan. 7.—The male has refused to cover or feed the young. The second young bird is dead this morning, the female not being able to cover it continuously. The male has been trying to entice the female to a new nesting cycle. This new cycle started shortly after the death of the young bird. (R 33.)

SECOND CYCLE.

The first egg was laid on January 16, but it was thin-shelled and broken. The second egg was laid on January 18. The incubation record was normal for 5 days. The egg was then gradually deserted during a period of 3 days, and a new cycle began on the day following. The cycle was thus terminated 10 to 13 days before

DEFECTIVE CYCLES. 75

its normal end. The only known external defect was the loss of one egg, but this factor had no appreciable effect upon the incubating impulse for at least 5 days. While the male led in the desertion, the female must have been similarly predisposed or she would not have responded so quickly to his sexual advances. The following excerpts from the records are apropos:

Jan. 23.—In the morning the male bowed in front of the female, very strongly striking the floor at each bow with his beak.

Jan. 24.—At 4 p. m., both birds were on the floor, hugging, mounting, and strutting, but without contact.

Jan. 25.—Before 11 a. m. both birds have been off the nest several times, and I have not seen the male sitting at all. They are interested in courting and copulating.

Jan. 26.—Hugging, bowing, and "feeding" of the female by the male without coitus occurred in the morning. The egg was finally deserted in the afternoon. Little attention was paid to the egg during the day, and when night came the female did not sit on the egg. Desertion has been gradual with the female. The male has led in the desertion; he enticed the female from her work. This behavior is similar to that observed earlier in the crested pigeons. These cresteds usually sat only a few days and then began over again. In one case the female laid four eggs with but little interruption between the sets. (R 33.)

THIRD CYCLE.

The incubation record was normal until after the death of the first young on Feb. 20. The egg was injured in handling on the 19th, and the bird died shortly after hatching on the 20th. The male's cycle terminated shortly after this event and he began soliciting the female to renew the cycle. The female resisted his advances until after the death of the second bird, which occurred during the night of the 21st. The birds began copulating on the morning of the following day. The termination of this cycle is evidently connected with the death of their young.

Feb. 21.—Yesterday, at the time the young was due to hatch, the male was very attentive and anxious to have the nest and care. Indeed, he appeared to be remarkably solicitous, and not only tried to get the nest, but called quite a number of times while sitting beside the female, as if he wanted her to get off, and as if he wanted to feed the young before it was quite out of the shell. This morning his behavior is already decidedly changed. He runs over the female and the nest carelessly, and when the female left the second egg for a few moments he at first charged at her, uttering his scolding notes, and then he mounted her twice and went through the routine, but without coitus. I believe that the male was so closely timed with the hatching period that the slip of yesterday (death of first bird) ended his course and that he is now ready to renew another course.

Feb. 22.—The fourth cycle began this morning immediately after the death of the second young. The birds were copulating right away, although no actual union took place at first.

FOURTH CYCLE.

The eggs were laid on February 28 and March 2. The male's behavior was slightly irregular from the first, though he participated in his incubation duties. With no apparent external cause, the male gradually terminated the cycle shortly before the eggs were due to hatch. His sexual advances finally broke up the cycle for the female.

76 BEHAVIOR OF PIGEONS.

Mar. 15.—Contrary to usual behavior, the male sat every night beside the female in the nest-box. To-day he tried to copulate with the female while she was sitting on the egg. He tried this also yesterday morning. The first egg is due to hatch 2 to 3 days hence. Probably the male will be unable to feed the young in case they hatch. The female is faithful.

Mar. 16.—The male was taken away because he had succeeded in getting the female weaned from the nest so that she would stay with him on the floor and copulate. After removing him the female sat one day and night; but on the next day, when the first egg was due to hatch, she refused to sit another moment. I shall keep this pair apart for a while to see if they will fall into regular work next time. (R 33.)

GEOPELIA HUMERALIS.

The eggs of the first two cycles (of 1906) were thin-shelled and were broken within 2 days after the second eggs were dropped. The cycles were terminated immediately. In the first case, a renewal started immediately; but it was delayed several days in the second case, probably owing to sickness of the female.

The male is already in the nest calling the female to a new nesting cycle. How quickly the renewal of these things takes place. At once the male invites a renewal of the nesting cycle. The female, however, does not seem to feel quite well—perhaps somewhat exhausted, and possibly her digestion is not normal. I saw her throwing up her food the evening after she laid the first egg. (R 29.)

In the third cycle of the above pair both eggs failed to hatch, and they were deserted on the seventeenth day, shortly after they were due to hatch. Since the period of sitting continues (with feeding of young) for a week after the eggs hatch, evidently the termination of the activity is connected with the failure of the eggs to hatch.

PASSENGER-PIGEON MALE AND RING-DOVE FEMALE.
FIRST CYCLE.

The account starts on January 9, when the female was expected to lay. The pair had evidently been mated previously, and had entered the first part of the mating period. This record is unusual in the length of this mating period; it covers 17 days, exclusive of that portion preceding the record. The female persisted here in continuing the incubation activities for 11 days in spite of a number of defective conditions. Only one egg was laid, which was broken after 3 days; she was subject to the sexual attentions of the male; probably the male failed to alternate in the task of incubation; she was driven from the nest for 5 nights and forced to take the perch. This driving finally broke up the incubating impulse, and the female took the perch of her own accord and began to receive the male. The male participated in the incubation regularly until the egg was broken (3 days). Although no definite statements are made, it is probable that this event very soon terminated the incubating impulse of the male. He certainly made sexual advances to his mate, and it is highly improbable that he continued to alternate with the female without the fact being noted.

On Jan. 9 this female was expected to lay for the first time in life. I found her on the nest at $3^h 50^m$ and kept watch in order to get the exact time. She behaved as if she was

DEFECTIVE CYCLES.

just ready to lay. She remained on the nest until $5^h 30^m$, came off for a minute, returned, and came off again in about a minute. She went back almost immediately, but stopped on the edge of the nest-box. Here she sat quietly until $7^h 25^m$, when frightened by something—probably an owl appearing at the window—she flew to the floor and her mate flew to another corner of the pen. After a few moments the female went back to the edge of the nest-box, where she remained all night, returning to the nest early in the morning. She evidently went through the preliminaries to laying, but was a little premature in her actions. By experience she will learn to waste less time in fruitless formalities over such a small matter as laying an egg.

Jan. 10.—To my surprise the female pays little attention to the nest as 4 o'clock draws near. She was on the nest early in the morning and nested for considerable periods during the day, but when the time for laying came, she was off and is now on the perch, apparently for the night.

Jan. 12.—This female has not laid yet. She works at the nest a good deal in the forenoon, but less in the afternoon. She goes to the nest towards 4 o'clock but does not stay more than a few minutes, certainly not more than half an hour. She is on the perch to-night.

Jan. 19.—After 10 days there are still no eggs. The female has recently spent less time on the nest, and sometimes she seems to have given up nesting for the present.

Jan. 23.—The female spent some time in the forenoon in making a nest, her mate bringing the straw. She has not been on the nest of afternoons to stop long, and has taken the perch every night.

Jan. 26.—To my surprise the female (*L 2*) has laid her first egg this afternoon, between 3 and $5^h 30^m$—17 days after I expected it. The time has dragged on at such length, and she has given so little sign of laying, that I did not keep close watch of her to-day.

Elsewhere the editor finds a detailed daily record of this pair covering 3 days, a brief synopsis of which is here given: The first egg was laid on Jan. 26 between 3 and $5^h 30^m$. She sat over night on the egg, but not closely, and kept the nest until $10^h 20^m$ a. m. of the next day, when she was relieved by the male. On the 27th the pair alternated on the nest and in carrying straws. Similar behavior obtained for the 28th. The egg was broken on the 29th, and the detailed record was terminated. There was no second egg laid.

Feb. 1.—The female began yesterday to sit at night, and I made her sit on the perch. She did the same to-night. Whether she sat on the nights of the 29th and 30th I am not certain. The egg was broken and removed on the 29th. *Her sitting is therefore certainly a part of the regular routine on which she was started when the egg was laid. She now keeps it up although the egg is removed.*

Feb. 4.—That *L 2* is still in her course of incubation is shown also by her indifference to the male. She has taken her nest every night thus far and I have removed her every night. Yesterday a union took place, probably the first since the incubation period began.

Feb. 6.—To-night is the first time that *L 2* has taken her place on the perch without being driven from her nest. She has been trying to sit at night ever since her first egg was laid on January 26, i. e., for 10 days. Driving her off every night has at last broken up the incubation course, and to-day I noticed several sexual unions. (R 18, R 19.)

SECOND CYCLE.

In this cycle the female continued the incubation for a period of 10 days (probable) after a normal mating period, in spite of the following defective conditions: Absence of both eggs, without even the stimulus of the act of laying, the absence of interchange with the male (probable), the probable sexual advances of her mate, and

78   BEHAVIOR OF PIGEONS.

being forced from the nest and driven to the perch. Apparently the only possible stimulus of the incubating impulse in this case must be found in the previous activities of courting and mating. The author makes no specific reference to the male. In all probability the incubating impulse was not awakened in the male.

The previous cycle was broken up by driving the female from the nest at night. The new cycle began on the 6th; on this date she first took the perch at night of her own accord and sexual unions first began to occur freely. The later records are given in the following excerpts:

Feb. 7.—The female takes her place on the perch to-night for the second time without help.

Feb. 8.—*L 2* went on the perch to-night, of her own accord, for the *third* time.

Feb. 9.—*L 2* is again on the perch. The male tried to induce her to build a nest to-day, but she did not stop long.

Feb. 24.—After sitting on the perch at night for a week or so (since Feb. 6), the female again returned, now some days since, to sitting at night without laying. I have driven her off every night, and have sometimes had to cover the nest to keep her off. Still she has kept on trying to sit up to the present. On Feb. 25 she abandoned sitting at night and of her own accord took the perch. The same occurred on the nights of the 26th and 27th. On Feb. 27 she spent some time making a new nest, and on the 28th she spent nearly the whole forenoon receiving straws, the male working almost continuously. (R 19.)

THIRD CYCLE.

In this cycle the male's incubation record was normal for 3 days. He then began to deviate from normal conduct by making sexual advances to his mate. This sexual impulse arose gradually and increased in strength. Its origin can not be due to any external objective conditions, and the author attributes it to much rich food. The sexual impulse does not at first entirely destroy or terminate his impulse toward incubation; it merely interferes with the normal expression of the latter. Incubation was probably not terminated entirely until the female began to respond and unions resulted. The female continued the incubation activities for 9 days in spite of the advances of her mate, his defective participation in incubation, the substitution of a set of old eggs, and the breaking of one egg. The removal of the second egg was apparently the final stimulus necessary to break up the cycle. This cycle is described with much detail in a diary record. It began on February 25, and after a short mating period the first egg was laid on March 1, between 4 and 6 p. m. The second egg was delivered at $9^h 48^m$ a. m. on March 3. The record was entirely normal for both birds until 5 p. m. March 4. The deviations of the male and the termination of the cycle are described in the following excerpts:

Mar. 4.—At $5^h 02^m$ p. m. the male tried to crowd into the nest. He fondled the head of the female and appeared to take great delight in his paternal caresses. He pressed so hard to get possession of the nest that I felt anxious for the eggs. He continued to sit beside the female until long after dark, until $8^h 45^m$ p. m., and then took a place on the edge of the nest-box, close by the female and with his head turned towards her.

Mar. 5.—At $6^h 27^m$ a. m. the female came off the nest, and the male flew up to the nest and back to the floor of the pen four times. He seemed undetermined what to do.

DEFECTIVE CYCLES. 79

Once he picked a straw out of the nest and carried it away. The record was normal for the remainder of the day.

Mar. 6.—The male did not offer to go on the nest during the entire day. The female was off and on many times. She was frequently led to resign by the male coming to the box, but she was mistaken as to his purpose. He paid no attention to the nest when she left it, except to tear it to pieces and walk roughly over the eggs. I removed the eggs early in the forenoon to another pair, and gave him a pair of old discarded eggs. The female kept on the nest all day, except for short intervals when she left expecting the male to do his part. Several times the male visited the nest and tried to satisfy his passion on his mate, thus forcing her off the nest.

This strange and sudden desertion of the nest by the male was accompanied by attempts to get out of the pen, by flying again and again against the window and then against the wire screen. He appeared extremely restless, and his whole behavior was very different from what it had been hitherto.

Is it possible that too rich food brought his course of incubation to a premature close and stimulated him to renew the cycle of his paternal functions? Is it the same cause in the case of the crested pigeons which leads them to desert their nest after 6 or 7 days? I notice that the desertion of the nest in the latter case begins with a sexual union. When this has happened the birds may keep on for a day or two in care of the nest, but gradually they leave it for a longer and longer time, and in the course of two or three days they cease to return to it. The union may be stimulated by too much hemp seed and (once started) it brings the incubation course to an end and introduces a new cycle.

On Mar. 8 I found that the female had broken one of the old eggs given to them and I removed the other. As soon as she left the nest and began to receive the male he quieted down and eagerly called her to the nest-box. This shows that he is fully prepared for a new course. (R 18.)

CRESTED-PIGEON MALE AND RING-DOVE FEMALE.

FIRST CYCLE.

This pair had an unusually long courting period. It covered 11 days in addition to a period of unknown length which preceded the record. The incubation period began on January 20, and ended on February 8, a period of 20 days. As in the preceding pair (passenger × ring), the incubation activities continued over a long period, in spite of a number of abnormal conditions—the absence of the act of laying, the absence of eggs, lack of interchange with her mate, and the solicitations of the male. The incubation, furthermore, extended over into the period devoted to the care of the young, so that the latter part of the activity continued also in spite of the absence of the young, and during a period of need for feeding them. Evidently the incubating impulse did not even arise in the case of the male.

On Jan. 9 I expected the female (GF 1) of this pair to lay for the first time. I found her on her nest at $3^h 50^m$ p. m. and kept watch in order to get the exact time. She behaved as if she was just ready to lay. She came off the nest at $4^h 30^m$, flew to the floor, and then took her place on the perch beside her mate until $5^h 45^m$. At $5^h 45^m$, after dark, she went to the nest-box and sat quietly until $7^h 50^m$, when she got up on the edge of the nest-box and soon stepped upon the perch close by. She remained on the perch all night, returning to the nest early next morning. She evidently went through the preliminaries to laying, but was a little premature in her actions.

Jan. 10.—To my surprise the female pays little attention to her nest, at the time she should take the nest and lay. She was on the nest early in the morning and during

80   BEHAVIOR OF PIGEONS.

much of the day; but when the time for laying came, she was off, and is now on the perch apparently for the night.

Jan. 12.—*GF 1* has not laid yet. She works at the nest a good deal in the forenoon, but less in the afternoon. She went to the nest a little before 4 p. m. but remained only a few minutes, or half an hour at the most. She is on the perch to-night.[1]

Jan. 19.—After 10 days there are no eggs. *GF 1* has been busy of mornings more or less every day, and to-day her wings droop, showing that she is about ready to lay.

Jan. 20.—At $4^h 30^m$ p. m., *GF 1* went upon the nest, but came off at about 7. At $7^h 58^m$ she went on the nest again and remained on all night.

Jan. 21.—During the morning the female was on the nest as usual; she was found on the nest also at $4^h 30^m$ p. m., but there were no eggs. She came off within 5 minutes and took her usual place on the perch.

Jan. 22.—The female has spent much of the forenoon on the nest; the male meantime has carried straws. About $3^h 30^m$ p. m. *GF 1* went on the nest, but came off soon and then went back again. At $7^h 15^m$ I found her on the nest, apparently for the night, but at $10^h 30^m$ she left the nest and took her usual place beside her mate. At midnight I found her again on the nest.

Jan. 23.—*GF 1* worked on the nest considerably during the morning. She went on the nest about $2^h 30^m$ in the afternoon, but did not remain steadily, coming off now and then for a few minutes. To-night she is on to remain, but as yet there is no egg.

Jan. 24.—To-day *GF 1* acted, during all the morning, as if she had deserted the nest she had made. She acted like a dove that, after rearing young, is looking for a place at a distance for a new nest. She flew back and forth in a very uneasy manner, trying to get out of the pen. Instead of going to her nest, she went into a box at the opposite side of the pen, where there was no straw, and spent some time there with the male, but no straws were brought to her. At 5 p. m., however, I find her on the nest, and apparently she will remain on overnight, as she did last night.

Jan. 25.—During the morning *GF 1* and her mate were building a nest in the box opposite the one hitherto occupied. This evening she is back again on the old nest for the night. On Jan. 26 she behaved again in the same way. On Jan. 27 she was on and off her nest. She went on at $3^h 30^m$ p. m., came off at $4^h 25^m$, returned at $4^h 26^m$, came off at $4^h 45^m$, returned at $4^h 53^m$, and remained on overnight.

Jan. 30.—The record for the 28th, 29th, and to-day has been about the same as for the 27th, the female sitting every night on the nest. She takes the nest at about the same time that she would if she were alternating with the male.

Feb. 1.—In the morning the female is driven about by the male and the latter is uneasy and evidently is looking for a place for a new nest. He tries very hard to get out of the pen and to interest the female, but she seems comparatively indifferent. In the afternoon the female went on the nest early—at about 3 p. m. She was on at $3^h 30^m$ when I left and at $5^h 30^m$ when I returned; she is now on for the night. *The case of (the previously described pair) L 2, first cycle, seems to clear up that of GF 1. GF 1 made a slip in not bringing forth an egg, and has since continued sitting every night just as if she had laid.*

Feb. 4.—*GF 1* has gone on sitting every night. I have allowed her to remain on just to see how long she will continue. Of Feb. 6 I note that she still takes the nest every afternoon about $3^h 30^m$ to 4 and remains on overnight. This incubation without having laid an egg has now continued since Jan. 20, *i.e.*, for 18 days. She will probably sit a few nights more. The close sitting normally lasts for about 21 days—2 weeks to hatch the eggs and 1 week on the young. On Jan. 7, *GF 1* went on to her nest at $4^h 30^m$ p. m., which is later than usual.

---

[1] The records of this female (*GF 1*) are practically identical with those for *L 2*, described in the previous section. *Both* of these females *failed* to lay their expected eggs on the *same* date, Jan. 9, 1897.—EDITOR.

DEFECTIVE CYCLES. 81

Feb. 8.—To-night *GF 1*, for the first time since Jan. 20, takes her place on the perch beside her mate. She went on the nest at first, but came off of her own accord. Thus ends her incubation of an empty nest for a period of 20 days. The time is so nearly the same as is usually given to eggs and young that there can be no doubt that she has taken a regular course, just as if she had laid. On the following night *GF 1* took the perch for the second time. The male tried during the day to induce her also to build a nest, but she does little as yet.

SECOND CYCLE.

After a normal mating period this pair repeated a part of their previous performance. The female incubated for a week under the same defective conditions. This activity was finally terminated by persistently driving her from the nest.

Feb. 25.—On Feb. 8, *GF 1* ended her 20 days' incubation of an empty nest. On Feb. 10 she paid more attention to the male and spent a short time on the nest receiving straws. After taking the perch for 3 or 4 nights she began sitting again and, although driven off every night, she followed it up for about a week; but on Feb. 19 she took the perch again of her own accord. After taking the perch regularly every night from Feb. 19 to Feb. 24, she laid an egg this afternoon at the normal hour, between $4^h 30^m$ and 6 o'clock. This is her first egg in life, and it comes after two premature rounds of sitting. She laid a second egg after the usual interval. (R 19.)

BLOND RING MALE AND WHITE RING FEMALE.

This record presents some rather unusual and ambiguous features. The two females *W 1* and *W 2* (*St. alba*) had been together previous to the record, and both were nearly ready to lay. Since the two laid at practically the same time, there being a difference of only one day, it is probable that we here have another case of the pairing of two females resulting in the production of eggs on the part of both. A male called *X* was introduced into the cage with *W 1* two days before her first egg, or five days after she had started on the reproductive cycle of activities. The male attempted sexual advances and persisted in the sexual activity in spite of the lack of an adequate response on the part of the female. The male's incubation activity did not start with the advent of the eggs, but only upon the "cessation of his sexual activity," *i.e.*, after a normal period of 6 days. The female's incubating activity persisted, although there was a lack of interchange with the male, and in spite of the sexual advances of the latter.

This male was later transferred to another female, *W 2*, who, like the male at this time, was in the incubating stage of activities. But the two birds that had separately attained and begun the incubating activity refused to continue it together; the new mating broke the cycle for both, and a new cycle was initiated almost immediately. It is thus probable that the continuance of incubation on the part of the male depends to some extent upon a definite set of external conditions, a particular female, nest, or nest-location, etc.; for a change from one set of conditions to a very *similar* set of conditions was sufficient to break up the activity. The female *W 2* responded very quickly. Probably her discontinuance of incubation was not due entirely to the solicitations of the male, since in the pairs previously discussed it was frequently noted that the female effectively resisted the solicitations of the male for long periods. A predisposing cause may

82   BEHAVIOR OF PIGEONS.

have been the lack, in the previous cycles of this female, of a masculine companion and participant in the task of incubation; her impulse to sit may have thus been weak at the time. Probably the introduction of a "novel stimulus," namely, of a male to which she was not accustomed, had much to do with the disturbance. This latter fact would account for the disruption of the incubation, but it alone would not account for her ready acceptance of the male. The detailed records which justify the above analysis follow:

Mar. 28.—The male blond ring-dove (*X*) was purchased to-day. I have placed him with a female white ring-dove called *W 1*. The latter is one of two white rings bought in the previous November and then thought to be male and female; the second white bird, which also proved to be a female, I designated as *W 2*. *W 1* is nearly ready to lay and is inclined to mate. The male is fierce and will not tolerate her presence, so I have to keep her in a small cage within his cage. On the following day the male was still intolerant, but began to yield a little. He went to the box and called; she at once responded and went to him, tried to take the nest, and began cooing in her turn. He endured it a while and then drove her off. He next went to the opposite box and repeated the same behavior with her. She is patient and takes all his abuse. By night he finally gets reconciled to her and condescends to sit beside her.

Mar. 30.—The female laid an egg at about 5 p. m. The male has behaved towards her to-day about the same as yesterday, driving her about a good deal and not permitting her to remain long in the nest. He seemed to accept her when she answered his call to the nest; he often resigned it to her, but would soon return and drive her off and then call her back. Yesterday, and once to-day, I saw him on the perch with her and soliciting her, but without result. I do not think the egg had any chance of being fertilized.

Mar. 31.—This morning the male has been to the nest and the female resigned. He examined the egg, but did not take any interest in it. He did not cover it, but began to call for the female. After a few moments he went over to the opposite box and called, and the female soon returned to her egg. The male is getting more tolerant, leaving the female more quiet on her nest. But he is evidently not in the spirit of sitting, and the presence of the egg does not stimulate him to the act. The decisive stimulus for such an act is thus not external but internal—probably a feeling which comes over a male "periodically," and which he will manifest perhaps only if the external stimulus is also present. This seems to me to be a not unimportant point. At $9^h 45^m$ a. m., the male went to the nest again, and this time he did not disturb the female, but fondled her head affectionately and then went off as if fully reconciled to her as a mate. All this is the more interesting, as he still has no impulse to sit. He is ready for making a nest and to accept a mate, *but he requires time to generate the impulse to sit.* This impulse naturally follows the period of sexual activity, and he is now in the latter period.

Apr. 1.—The second egg was laid at $8^h 15^m$ a. m. The male behaves as on yesterday, allowing the female peace on the nest. If she goes to the floor of the cage when he is there he may behave as if he had accepted her or he may drive her unmercifully. At $1^h 30^m$ p. m. I find the male on the nest and the female on the floor. He sits on the eggs now, but he does not hesitate to come off three times within half an hour in order to pay his attention to a female in the adjoining cage. Each time, however, he goes back to the eggs, and thus seems to have a rising impulse to the function of sitting. Nevertheless, at $2^h 20^m$ p. m. he came off the nest and, finding the female on the floor of the cage, attacked her fiercely. She flew to the nest, leaving him to his pleasure. The impulse to sit, if there is one, must still be very weak.

Apr. 2.—The male relieved the female very early, at about 7 a. m., and remained about 10 to 15 minutes on the eggs. He went on the nest again during the middle of the day.

DEFECTIVE CYCLES.

Apr. 3.—The male takes his part in sitting and has, so far as I can see, fully accepted the eggs. This impulse to sit has arisen gradually in the course of 6 days.

As an experiment in mating, I to-day took away female *W 1* and put female *W 2* in her place. *W 2* is the one I first took to be a male, and she is a little lighter in weight than is *W 1*. *W 2* laid one egg on Mar. 31 and the second on Apr. 2. She is thus one day behind *W 1* in egg-laying. Both of the birds of the new pair, male and female, are now in the beginning of the sitting period.

When the new female (*W 2*) was introduced to the cage of the male at $9^h 30^m$ a. m. the male chased her around for a time on the floor of the cage. I covered up the box in which the eggs of *W 1* had been laid so that the male would not try to sit.[1] After a short time the male went to the opposite box and called. *W 2* responded after a few moments, but seemed indifferent and soon left. The male allowed her to walk about on the perch and the box without attacking her. At $9^h 45^m$, while sitting on the perch, the male actually induced *W 2* to come to him, and she put her beak in his. This looks like dispatch as compared with the behavior of this male toward *W 1*. Shortly, however, his disposition to attack returned and he drove her about, though not so violently as he did *W 1*. In the course of the day the male modified his behavior, becoming quite affectionate and attentive. The match is evidently made for good. On Apr. 9, 6 days after mating, female *W 2* laid an egg. (C 7/15.)

HYBRID MALE AND MOURNING-DOVE MALE.

These birds were paired on April 8. The male hybrid unsuccessfully attempted courting during a month. His lack of success was better understood later, when it was learned that his consort was also a male. On May 9 the hybrid began incubation on the floor of the cage and sat steadily night and day. He was given eggs on the 15th and accepted them. He persisted in the incubation for a week longer, or until he and his consort were transferred to a cage out of doors. This hybrid had never been mated. The incubating impulse thus developed and persisted without eggs, nest, interchange with a mate, nest-building, or any sexual intercourse with a mate. The cage of this pair was so placed that none of their own species was visible. (Summarized from C 7/48.)

LEUCOSARCIA PICATA.

A pair of white-faced pigeons kept up their care of the young until it left the nest at the age of 18 days. Two days later the egg of the succeeding cycle was dropped, but it failed to develop. It is noted that "evidently the close care of the young did not give the male a fair chance to fertilize the egg." (Sh 8/13.) Usually the old birds begin to leave the nest near or at the end of 7 days, and cease covering the young entirely by the twelfth day. In this case the unusual persistence of the incubating impulse of one cycle disrupted the normal activities of the succeeding cycle.

MOURNING-DOVE MALE AND WHITE-RING FEMALE.

A male mourning-dove refused to mate properly when paired. He finally courted and united with a female, but took no part in nest-building and incubation. This behavior was repeated in several cycles. The female attempted incubation,

---

[1] The subsequent record shows, however, that the male made no repeated or prolonged attempt, possibly no attempt at all, to continue sitting in or near the old nest.—EDITOR.

84 BEHAVIOR OF PIGEONS.

but the eggs failed to develop because of probable lack of fertilization. Thus the initial act does not necessarily stimulate and arouse the succeeding activities of nesting and incubation in the male. The female, however, completed the cycle without the coöperation of a mate in nesting and incubation. "I do not understand this male. Finding that he used the female white ring (*W 1*) for his pleasure, but never mated with her properly, so as to take any part in sitting, I gave him another female." (C 7/7.)

HOMER MALE AND HYBRID FEMALE.

This pair, consisting of a male homer and a hybrid, was mated on May 29. "They paired, courted, united, built a nest, but *never* laid or sat." (BB 5.) This phenomenon, according to Dr. Riddle, occurs perhaps more frequently among hybrid females than among non-hybrids. Dr. Whitman cites at least one such case in domestic pigeons, and notes that this failure on the part of the female was a mark of "degeneracy."

ECTOPISTES.

In crossing common pigeons with the wild species one finds that the former usually keep up incubation for a few days after their usual time. The wild passenger-pigeon never waits more than 10 or 12 hours. If the egg does not hatch within that time he leaves it; no matter if the shell is broken and the bird nearly ready to hatch, it is deserted. The common pigeons, however, are a little less particular in this respect than are the wild species.

The egg of a ring-dove mated to a passenger-pigeon developed up to a few days of hatching, but died for some unknown cause. The male passenger was then flying back and forth, calling as he flew. He was evidently at the end of his period, and as he got nothing to feed, his impulse turned in the direction of seeking a place for a new nest. His incubation period is thus seen to be cut short if the egg fails to hatch. The same is true of the crested pigeons. The ring-dove will keep on sitting for 20 days in many cases, or even longer. (SS 10, SS 4.)

MISCELLANEOUS.

(1) The pairing of two males, as described in Chapter III, constitutes a defective cycle. Two males may pair, court, unite, and incubate an empty nest. If given eggs, they may hatch them and feed and care for the young. The cycle is thus completed without the presence or production of eggs, and with an unusual and abnormal sexual response. Upon the desertion or death of the female, the male may continue incubation, doing double duty, in spite of the absence of a partner and of her lack of participation in incubation.

A male will often sit on eggs or young at night, in case the female deserts or dies. An example of the latter has just occurred where a male ring-dove is sitting at night on young only a few days old.

(2) In a pair of female ring-doves (pair *D;* see Chapter III), the first egg was laid on January 26. The supposed male attempted to take the nest at this time, but was driven away. He then went to an empty nest and persisted in sitting in spite of being driven off until the act was broken up by covering the nest. He

DEFECTIVE CYCLES. 85

then began incubation of the eggs on January 29, and normal conduct was exhibited thereafter. In the second cycle the one female laid on February 27 and 29 and the supposed male did not begin incubation until March 3, when she too laid an egg. Another pair (*E*) mated and went through all the preliminaries, even to the symptoms of laying. Neither bird laid, however, but incubation began at the usual time. For the most part both birds sat on the nest at night and exchanged with each other during the day. This incubation persisted for the usual time, when a new cycle was started and one of the pair laid eggs. In another case both females laid in one nest and exchanged with each other as if male and female. The preliminary activities of courting, uniting, and nesting are abnormal in one bird, and they find no normal reciprocal response in the other. Following these, the production of eggs may be lacking in one or both of the pair, although some of the correlated behavior may be present. The production of eggs may be stimulated in both birds, and when this occurs the previous masculine behavior is associated with delayed laying. The impulse to incubate develops in both birds, although eggs are lacking. This impulse was not awakened in one bird until after the delayed laying. Incubation persisted in spite of defective alternation, and also, in the case of one of the females of "pair *D*," in spite of an empty nest and being driven away and having the box covered.

(3) Several times this season and in different pairs, such as ring-dove × Japanese turtle, *tur-orient.* × *tur-orient.* hybrids, *orientalis* × *turtur*, *guinea* × *guinea* hybrids, etc. (and formerly crested pigeons, which laid several times before sitting steadily), I have seen eggs laid and incubation begun, and in the course of a few days or a week the eggs were deserted.

In the case of the *turtur-orientalis* hybrids, the offenders were young birds. They began by laying and sitting well for a few days or a week, then beginning a new nest and laying again, and again incubating for a short time. I believe this is due to having "an abundance of rich food," and to eating more than is really needed, thus bringing forward a set of eggs that would, under normal nourishment, not develop until the previous set hatched and the young were reared. After the birds have repeated this several times, and as the season is more advanced, they become exhausted to an extent that allows of a normal course of incubation. As an example of this, two pairs of Japanese turtle × European turtle, and also one of the reciprocal cross, have repeated the short abnormal course four or five times, but they are now at work in normal time.

(4) The time of incubation, or rather the time that the old bird will continue her sitting, can be varied somewhat as the result of excessive feeding. The bird becomes unsteady in sitting and then begins a new cycle, and in several cases I have found pairs of birds producing a second and even a third set of eggs in the same nest. One pair of crested pigeons, for example, after they had sat a week on one set of eggs, laid two more in the same nest; and then after a week or ten days more laid a third pair of eggs in the same nest. These birds were kept indoors and had plenty of stimulating food, hemp and canary seed; and I saw no other reason than the easy conditions under which they were kept which should lead them to break the cycle in this way—to stop the sitting on one set of eggs and renew the sitting on another set of eggs in the same nest.

(5) A pair consisting of a ring-dove and a Japanese turtle have twice raised young, and each time they have laid again before the young were out of the nest. As a result, the later eggs were deserted and the young were thus given more time to get out of the way, and then other eggs were laid which were properly incubated.

7

86 BEHAVIOR OF PIGEONS.

(6) Any serious fright or disturbance is likely to cause desertion. In a pair of mourning-doves it was noted that the eggs were deserted on the second day of incubation as a result of disturbance by dogs. A pair of homers deserted their young when 10 days old in order to return to a former nest. Other pairs, however, failed to desert their eggs in similar circumstances (Chapter X). A change in the position or character of the nest may also cause desertion of eggs or young (Chapter XII). (R 7, R 18, SS 10, Em 7.)

(7) Two male mourning-doves, after the normal end of their breeding season, indulged in all the preliminaries of courting, uniting, and nesting, but failed entirely to incubate, or else did so quite spasmodically. It is noted that this phenomenon occurred only with males which were unusually prolific and unusually successful in fertilizing eggs (see under "Prolongation of the Breeding Season in Wild Pigeons," Chapter I). At the period of the subsidence of the reproductive impulses, it was found that the sexual proclivities were still vigorous and found expression, while the incubating impulse was extremely weak and sometimes failed altogether. It is thus possible that, in the disintegration of the reproductive series of acts at the end of the season, the incubating impulse tends normally to disappear first, or that we are here dealing with males in which the sexual impulse is relatively much stronger than usual. From the short account of the phenomenon the latter interpretation is to be preferred, though one is not justified in making a decision.

(8) In his breeding experiments the author frequently removed the eggs shortly after being laid and had them hatched under a pair of "brooders." This removal of the eggs generally disrupts the cycle immediately. To assure the disruption, however, the nest-box is usually temporarily displaced or removed. In the treatment of the topic, "Length of the Mating Period," in Chapter I, 27 such cases are listed. Many hundreds of cases could have been obtained from the "breeding records." In one case it is stated that the female persisted in sitting for some time (probably 10 days) afterwards. The breaking of the eggs usually produces the same effect; 4 such cases are listed in the same place cited above, while in one case the new cycle was postponed for about 10 days.

CHAPTER VIII.

THE GENETIC STANDPOINT IN THE STUDY OF INSTINCT.

This chapter is composed entirely of a selection from Professor Whitman's lectures on Animal Behavior delivered at the Marine Biological Laboratory at Woods Hole in 1897 and 1898. Although these lectures have been published,[1] it has been deemed advisable to insert this selection at this point, as it presents in a very succinct form the author's view of instinct in general as well as an admirable treatment of the instinct of incubation.

GENEALOGICAL HISTORY NEGLECTED.

The problem of psychogenesis requires a more definite genetic standpoint than that of general evolution. It is not enough to recognize that instincts have had a natural origin, for the fact of their connected genealogical history is of paramount importance. From the standpoint of evolution as held by Romanes and others, instincts are too often viewed as disconnected phenomena of independent origin. The special and more superficial characteristics have been emphasized to the exclusion of the more fundamental characters.

Biologists and psychologists alike have very generally clung tenaciously to the idea that instincts, in part at least, have been derived from habits and intelligence; and the main effort has been to discover how an instinct could become gradually stamped into organization by long-continued uniform reactions to environmental influences. The central question has been: How can intelligence and natural selection, or natural selection alone, initiate action and convert it successively into habit, automatism, and congenital instinct? In other words, the genealogical history of the structural basis being completely ignored, how can the instinct be mechanically rubbed into the ready-made organism? Involution instead of evolution; mechanization instead of organization; improvisation rather than organic growth; specific *versus* phyletic origin.

This inversion, or rather perversion, of the genealogical order leads to a very short-focussed vision. The pouting instinct is supposed to have arisen *de novo*, as an anomalous behavior, and with it a new race of pigeons. The tumbling instinct was a sort of *lusus naturæ*, with which came the fancier's opportunity for another race. The pointing instinct was another accident that had no meaning except as an individual idiosyncrasy. The incubation instinct was supposed to have arisen after the birds had arrived and laid their eggs, which would have been left to rot had not some birds just blundered into "cuddling" over them and thus rescued the line from sudden extinction. How long this blunder-miracle had to be repeated before it happened all the time does not matter. Purely imaginary things can happen on demand.

THE INCUBATION INSTINCT.

1. *Meaning to be sought in phyletic roots.*—It seems quite natural to think of incubation merely as a means of providing the heat needed for the development of the egg, and to assume that the need was felt before the means was found to meet it. Birds and eggs are thus presupposed, and as the birds could not have foreseen the need, they could not have hit upon the means except by accident. Then, what an infinite amount of chancing must have followed before the first "cuddling" became a habit, and the habit a perfect instinct!

---

[1] Biological Lectures, Woods Hole, 1898, pp. 285-338, Boston.

BEHAVIOR OF PIGEONS.

We are driven to such preposterous extremities as the result of taking a purely casual feature to start with. Incubation supplies the needed heat, but that is an incidental utility that has nothing to do with the nature and origin of the instinct. It enables us to see how natural selection has added some minor adjustments, but explains nothing more. For the real meaning of the instinct we must look to its phyletic roots.

If we go back to animals standing near the remote ancestors of birds, to the amphibia and fishes, we find the same instinct stripped of its later disguises. Here one or both parents simply remain over or near the eggs and keep watchful guard against enemies. Sometimes the movements of the parent serve to keep the eggs supplied with fresh water, but aeration is not the purpose for which the instinct exists.

2. *Means rest and incidental protection to offspring.*—The instinct is a part of the reproductive cycle of activities, and always holds the same relation in all forms that exhibit it, whether high or low. It follows the production of eggs or young and means primarily, as I believe, *rest* [1] with incidental *protection to offspring.* That meaning is always manifest, no less in worms, mollusks, crustacea, spiders, and insects than in fishes, amphibia, reptiles, and birds. The instinct makes no distinction between eggs and young, and that is true all along the line up to birds, which extend the same blind interest to one as to the other.

3. *Essential elements of the instinct.*—Every essential element in the instinct of incubation was present long before the bird and eggs arrived. These elements are: (1) the disposition to remain with or over the eggs; (2) the disposition to resist and to drive away enemies; and (3) periodicity. The birds brought all these elements along in their congenital equipment and added a few minor adaptations, such as cutting the period of incubation to the need of normal development and thus avoiding indefinite waste of time in case of sterile or abortive eggs.

(1) *Disposition to remain over the eggs.*—The disposition to remain over the eggs is certainly very old and is probably bound up with the physiological necessity for rest after a series of activities tending to exhaust the whole system. If this suggestion seems far-fetched, when thinking of birds, it will seem less as we go back to simpler conditions, as we find them among some of the lower invertebrate forms, which are relatively very inactive and predisposed to remain quiet until impelled by hunger to move. Here we find animals remaining over their eggs, and thus shielding them from harm, from sheer inability or indisposition to move. That is the case with certain mollusks (*Crepidula*), the habits and development of which have been recently studied by Professor Conklin.[2] Here full protection to offspring is afforded without any exertion on the part of the parent in a strictly passive way that excludes even any instinctive care. In *Clepsine* there is a manifest unwillingness to leave the eggs, showing that the disposition to remain over them is instinctive. If we start with forms of similar sedentary mode of life, it is easy to see that remaining over the eggs would be the most likely thing to happen, even if no instinctive regard for them existed. The protection afforded would, however, be quite sufficient to insure the development of the instinct, natural selection favoring those individuals which kept their position unchanged long enough for the eggs to hatch.

(2) *Disposition to resist enemies.*—The disposition to keep intruders from the vicinity of the nest I have spoken of as an element of the instinct of incubation. At first sight it seems to be inseparably connected with the act of covering the egg, but there are good reasons for regarding it as a distinct element of behavior. In birds this element manifests itself before the eggs are laid, and even before the nest is built; and in the lower animals the disposition to cover the egg is not always accompanied by an aggressive attitude. This attitude is one of many forms and degrees. A mild self-defensive state, in which the

---

[1] This is an important point in connection with the phenomenon of "weakened germs," resulting from rapid egg-laying without intervening incubations—a subject dealt with in Volume II.—EDITOR.

[2] Journ. of Morph., Vol. XIII, No. 1, 1897.

GENETIC STANDPOINT IN THE STUDY OF INSTINCT. 89

animal merely strives to hold its position without trying to rout intruders, would perhaps be the first stage of development. In some of the lower vertebrates the attitude remains defensive and is aggressive only in a very low degree, while in others pugnacity is more or less strongly manifested. Among fishes the little stickleback is especially noted for its fiery pugnacity, which seems to develop suddenly and simultaneously with the appearance of the dark color of the male at the spawning season.

In pigeons, as in many other birds, this disposition shows itself as soon as a place for a nest is found. While showing a passionate fondness for each other, both male and female become very quarrelsome towards their neighbors. The white-winged pigeon (*Melopelia leucoptera*) of the West Indies and the southern border of the United States is one of the most interesting pigeons I have observed in this respect. At the approach of an intruder the birds show their displeasure in both tone and behavior. The tail is jerked up and down spitefully, the feathers of the back are raised as a threatening dog "bristles up," the neck is shortened, drawing the head somewhat below the level of the raised feathers, and the whole figure and action are as fierce as the bird can make them. To the fierce look, the erect feathers, the ill-tempered jerks of the tail, is added a decidedly spiteful note of warning. If these manifestations are not sufficient, the birds jump toward the offender, and if that fails to cause retreat, wings are raised and the matter settled by vigorous blows.

The pugnacious mood is periodical, recurring with each reproductive cycle and subsiding like a fever when its course is run. The birds behave as if from intelligent motive, but every need is anticipated blindly; for the young pair, without experience, example, or tradition, behave like the parents.

It seems to me that this mood or disposition, although in some ways appearing to be independent of the disposition to cover the eggs, can best be understood as having developed in connection with the latter. It has primarily the same meaning—protection to the eggs— but the safety of the eggs and young depends upon the safety of the nest, and this accounts for the extension of its period to cover all three stages—building, sitting, and rearing.

(3) *Periodicity.*—The periodicity of the disposition to sit coincides in the main with that of the recuperative stage. Its length, however, at least in birds, is nicely correlated with, though not exactly coinciding with, the time required for hatching. It may exceed or fall short of the time between laying and hatching. The wild passenger-pigeon (*Ectopistes*) begins to incubate a day or two in advance of laying, and the male takes his turn on the nest just as if the eggs were already there. In the common pigeon the sitting usually begins with the first egg, but the birds do not sit steadily or closely until the second egg is laid. The birds do not, in fact, really sit on the first egg, but merely stand over it, stooping just enough to touch the egg with the feathers. This peculiarity has an advantage in that the development of the first egg is delayed so that both eggs may hatch more nearly together. The bird acts just as blindly to this advantage as *Ectopistes* does to the mistake of sitting before an egg is laid. *Ectopistes* is very accurate in closing the period, for if the egg fails to hatch within 12 to 20 hours of its normal time, it is deserted, and that too if, as may sometimes happen, the egg contains a perfect young, about ready to hatch.

Pigeons, like fowls, will often sit on empty nests, filling up the period prescribed in instinct, leaving the nest only as the impulse to sit runs down. It happens not infrequently that pigeons will go right on with the regular sequence of activities, even though nature fails in the most important stage. Mating is followed by nest-making, and at the appointed time the bird goes to the nest to lay, and after going through the usual preliminaries brings forth no egg. But the impulse to sit comes on as if everything in the normal course had been fulfilled, and the bird incubates the empty nest and exchanges with her mate as punctiliously as if she actually expected to hatch something out of nothing. This may happen in any species under the most favorable conditions. It is possible by giving an abundance of rich food to wind up the instinctive machinery more rapidly than would

90   BEHAVIOR OF PIGEONS.

normally happen, so that recuperation may end in about a week's time, when incubation will stop and a new cycle begin, leading to the production of a second set of eggs in the same nest. This has happened several times with the crested pigeon of Australia (*Ocyphaps lophotes*).

Schneider says: [1] "The impulse to sit arises, as a rule, when a bird sees a certain number of eggs in her nest." Although recognizing a *bodily disposition* as present in some cases, sitting is regarded as a *pure perception impulse*. I hold, on the contrary, that the bodily disposition is the universal and essential element, and that sight of the eggs has nothing to do primarily with sitting. It comes on only secondarily and as an adaptation in correlation with the inability in some species to rear more than one or two broods in a season. In such species the advantage would lie with birds beginning to incubate with a full nest.

The suggestions here offered on the origin of the incubation instinct, incomplete and doubtful as they may appear, may suffice to indicate roughly the general direction in which we are to look for light on the genesis of instincts. The incubation instinct, as we now find it perfected in birds, is a nicely timed and adjusted part of a periodical sequence of acts. If we try to explain it without reference to its physiological connections in the individual, and independently of its developmental phases in animals below birds, we miss the more interesting relations and build on a purely conjectural chance act that calls for a further and incredible concatenation of the right acts at the right time and place, and is not even then completed until its perpetuation is secured by a miracle of transmission.

A FEW GENERAL STATEMENTS.

(1) Instinct and structure are to be studied from the common standpoint of phyletic descent, and that not the less because we may seldom, if ever, be able to trace the whole development of an instinct. Instincts are evolved rather than involved (stereotyped by repetition and transmission), and the key to their genetic history is to be sought in their more general rather than in their later and incidental uses.

(2) The primary roots of instincts reach back to the constitutional properties of protoplasm, and their evolution runs, in general, parallel with organogeny. As the genesis of organs takes its departure from the elementary structure of protoplasm, so does the genesis of instincts proceed from the fundamental functions of protoplasm. Primordial organs and instincts are alike few in number and generally persistent. As an instinct may sometimes run through a whole group of organisms with little or no modification, so may an organ sometimes be carried on through one or more phyla without undergoing much change. The dermal sensillæ of annelids and aquatic vertebrates are an example.

(3) Remembering that structural bases are relatively few and permanent as compared with external morphological characters, we can readily understand why, for example, 500 different species of wild pigeons should all have a few common undifferentiated instincts, such as drinking without raising the head, the cock's time of incubating from about 10 a. m. to about 4 p. m., etc.

(4) Although instincts, like corporeal structures, may be said to have a phylogeny, their manifestation depends upon differentiated organs. We could not, therefore, expect to see phyletic stages repeated in direct ontogenetic development, as are the more fundamental morphological features, according to the biogenetic law. The main reliance in getting at the phyletic history must be comparative study.

(5) Instinct precedes intelligence both in ontogeny and phylogeny, and it has furnished all the structural foundations employed by intelligence. In social development also instinct predominates in the earlier, intelligence in the later stages.

(6) Since instinct supplied at least the earlier rudiments of brain and nerve, since instinct and mind work with the same mechanisms and in the same channels, and since

---

[1] Der Thierische Wille, pp. 282, 283, as cited in Professor James's Psychology, p. 388.

GENETIC STANDPOINT IN THE STUDY OF INSTINCT. 91

instinctive action is *gradually* superseded by intelligent action, we are compelled to regard instinct as the actual germ of mind.

(7) The automatism, into which habit and intelligence may lapse, seems explicable, in a general way, as due more to the preorganization of instinct than to mechanical repetition. The habit that becomes automatic, from this point of view, is not an action on the way to becoming an instinct, but action preceded and rendered possible by instinct. Habits appear as the uses of instinct organization which have been learned by experience.

(8) The suggestion that intelligence emerges from blind instinct, although nothing new, will appear to some as a complete *reductio ad absurdum*. But evolution points unmistakably to instinct as nascent mind, and we discover no other source of psychogenetic continuity. As far back as we can go in the history of organisms, in the simplest forms of living protoplasm, we find the sensory element along with the other fundamental properties, and this element is the central factor in the evolution of instinct, and it remains the central factor in all higher psychic development. It would be strange if, with this factor remaining one and the same throughout, organizing itself in sense-organs of the keenest powers and in the most complex nerve mechanisms known in the animal world—it would be strange if, with such continuity on the side of structure, there should be discontinuity in the psychic activities. Such discontinuity would be nothing less than the negation of evolution.

(9) We are apt to contrast the extremes of instinct and intelligence—to emphasize the blindness and inflexibility of the one and the consciousness and freedom of the other. It is like contrasting the extremes of light and dark and forgetting all the transitional degrees of twilight. In so doing we make the hiatus so wide that derivation of one extreme from the other seems about as hopeless as the evolution of something from nothing. That is the last pit of self-confounding philosophy.

Instinct is blind; so is the highest human wisdom blind. The distinction is one of degree. There is no absolute blindness on the one side and no absolute wisdom on the other. Instinct is a dim sphere of light, but its dimness and outer boundary are certainly variable; intelligence is only the same dimness improved in various degrees.

When we say instinct is blind we really mean nothing more than *it is blind to certain utilities* which we can see. But we ourselves are born blind to these utilities, and only discover them after a period of experience and education. The discovery may seem to be instantaneous, but really it is a matter of growth and development, the earlier stages of which consciousness does not reveal.

Blindness to the utilities of action no more implies unconsciousness in animals than in man. It is the worst form of anthropomorphism to claim that animal automatism is devoid of consciousness, for the claim rests on nothing but the assumption that there are no degrees of consciousness below the human. If human organization is of animal origin, then the presumption would be in favor of the same origin for consciousness and intelligence. Automatism could not exclude every degree of consciousness without excluding every form of organic adaptation.

(10) The clock-like regularity and inflexibility of instinct, like the once-popular notion of the "fixity" of species, have been greatly exaggerated. They imply nothing more than a low degree of variability under normal conditions. Discrimination and choice can not be wholly excluded in every degree, even in the most rigid uniformity of instinctive action. Close study and experiment with the most machine-like instincts always reveal some degree of adaptability to new conditions. This was made clear by Darwin's studies on instincts, and it has been demonstrated over and over again by later investigators, and by none more thoroughly than by the Peckhams in the case of spiders and wasps.[1] Intelligence implies varying degrees of freedom of choice, but never complete emancipation from automatism. The fundamental identity of instincts and intelligence is shown in *their dependence upon the same structural mechanisms and in their responsive adaptability*.

---

[1] Wisconsin Geological and Natural History Survey Bulletin No. 2, 1898.

CHAPTER IX.
REPRODUCTIVE CYCLE—SUMMARY AND ANALYSIS.

The present chapter attempts, for the convenience of the reader, an editorial summary of the various facts, principles, and interpretations of the previous material, with occasional additional comment and suggestion. The reproductive cycle may be conveniently divided into four groups of activities whose temporal relations are represented in figure 1. The sexual activities are represented by M; N and F refer to the nesting and feeding activities respectively; while I stands for the incubation of the eggs and young. The variation in thickness expresses the gradual rise of the impulse to its maximal strength and its gradual decline and final disappearance. The length of the lines expresses the relative duration of the activities, each unit of length representing a day. Since these periods are highly variable in length, we have arbitrarily chosen values which approximate an average.

DESCRIPTIVE SUMMARY.

(1) *The sexual activities* extend over a period of 7 days. They are difficult to describe in any fixed temporal order, since the composition and order of events seem to vary with the state of excitement, the reciprocal response of the mate, and the general progression of events in the cycle. The same bit of behavior may occur in several connections and have a variable meaning and purpose. Only a logical analysis and summary of the simpler elements of behavior is possible. The preliminary acts mentioned are billing or pecking at their own feathers on the wings and certain parts of the tail; preening and shaking the feathers; elaborate bowing and cooing; going to the nest and giving the nest-call; approaching the mate; giving amorous glances; wagging the wings; lowering the head; swelling the neck; raising

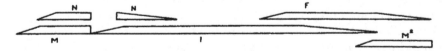

Fig. 1.—M, mating period; N, nesting activities; I, incubation of eggs and young; F, feeding of young; M², mating period of second cycle.

the wings; raising and spreading the tail and feathers on the back and rump; alternately stamping and striking the feet and wagging the body from side to side, and strutting with drooping wings. Charging and driving may be resorted to in the courtship. The male walks or rushes at the female, holds the head high, lowers the wings, exhibits excitement, elevates the back, erects the feathers, pecks perfunctorily or petulantly, clucks, and gives the driving coo consisting of three notes,[1] with raised wings, raised and spread tail, while the beak is on the floor.

---

[1] This and some other features of behavior apply particularly to bronze-wing pigeons.—EDITOR.

94 BEHAVIOR OF PIGEONS.

As the period of consummation approaches, the composition of the activities changes with the addition of new elements. Along with bowing, there is billing and fondling of each other's head, hugging or necking, jumping over the female without any attempt at mounting, opening the beak by the male, inserting of female's beak in his, and often the shaking and rattling of the crop as if the male fed the female. The female stoops with lowered head, the male mounts with a jump, the female raises her wings as a support and lifts the tail, while the male reaches back, moving the tail from side to side until contact is effected. The subsequent actions vary with the species; some slip off at once, while others recover the position and remain still a moment; and, in addition to this, the bronze-wings lower the head and wings, give a series of seven rising notes, and jump off with a wing-slap at the final note. After dismounting, some species lower the tail and wings, raise and arch the neck, and strut around the female; others bristle up and drive the female, and some raise the head with the beak pointing upwards.

(2) *The nesting activities* are initiated two days after the beginning of the cycle and thereafter the nesting and sexual impulses alternate in their dominance of the bird's behavior. The onset of the impulse is manifested by uneasiness, restlessness, indecision, and restrained flying movements which finally eventuate into an overt search for a nesting site. In a second cycle some birds invariably seek a new location, and this instinctive tendency is so strong that it persists in a cage with no opportunity for adequate expression. So far as the records go, the male appears to take the initiative in the search. Either bird may become satisfied with a site, while the other remains undecided for some time. The selection is rendered evident by the bird's remaining near the chosen spot and giving the nesting-call to the mate. The selection becomes certain with the initiation of nest-building. The nest-building activities under the artificial conditions of close confinement are exhibited in a rather rudimentary and spasmodic manner with varying degrees of strength and completeness.[1]

Usually the female stays on the nest and works at its construction, while the male carries the straw. One straw only is carried at a time, and in delivery the male of some species mounts the back of the female and places it in front of her. The female fashions the nest with certain movements of the legs, feet, and body. The nest-building ceases for several days at the time of egg-laying, but is resumed again with the initiation of incubation and extends throughout about half of that period. During incubation either bird may carry straws to the one on the nest. The nest-call is given frequently during these nesting activities and this probably influences the activities of the other bird to some extent. The male's call, in bronze-wings, consists of a single note, one second long, clear and hollow and like the moan or groan of a cat. It is given at a varying rate and with a varying loudness and

---

[1] It is a general rule that the female remains in the nest and receives straws which are brought by the male. If, however, the female while on the ground happens to notice a straw, she may seize it and carry it up. After laying, the female not uncommonly brings straws to the male in the nest. If two males become mated, usually the stronger, more masculine bird plays the part of male, while the other becomes docile and in all respects like a female. In such cases the docile male will sit in the nest and receive straws brought by the other bird. (Conv. 9/?/07, W. C.)

REPRODUCTIVE CYCLE.

95

earnestness. It is sometimes accompanied with nods of the head, the beak being held vertically downward. These nods are the more pronounced as the calls increase in loudness and earnestness. The call is also accompanied by wing-movements similar to those of the young in appealing for food. These vary in amplitude with the earnestness of the call. The female's call is, in these forms, a single husky, jarring, vibratory note with a duration of three-fourths of a second. Its strength is less than that of the male, and it is given at a variable rate. It is accompanied by slight head nods and the beak is slightly opened.

(3) *In egg-laying* the bird exhibits diagnostic symptoms for several days previous to ovulation, and apparently the length of this period can be curtailed as a result of experience. The symptoms mentioned are, sitting in the nest, drooping wings, sickly appearance, and heavy movements. In laying, the bird moves well forward in the nest, assumes an erect position with the head and fore-parts raised and the rump lowered at an angle of 45°, raises the tail, exhibits an attitude of strain and sometimes of pain and agony, exhibits intermittent moments of labor, gives in some cases the nest-call occasionally throughout the operation, raises the wings to the horizontal with the head thrown back and half around and with beak raised as the egg drops, and then stands motionless for a variable time with closed eyes, cuddles the egg with the bill, and then usually settles down on the nest. The egg invariably comes small end first. The number of eggs depends upon the species. The first egg is invariably dropped in the afternoon, the exact time varying with the species and the time of the year. The time of the second egg and the interval between the two eggs is a function of the species and the time of the year.

(4) *The onset of incubation* is not necessarily synchronous with the appearance of the first egg; the time varies with the species. With *Ectopistes* both birds start incubation previous to egg-laying. Others begin after this event, the time being somewhat variable. The impulse gradually rises in strength; at first, the birds may merely stand over the eggs and sitting is somewhat intermittent, but shortly after the second egg is dropped incubation becomes continuous. Both birds participate in the nesting duties. The onset of the impulse seems to develop rather independently in the two birds. Generally the male begins incubation later than the female. The female takes the nest during the night, while the male roosts on the perch as far away from the nest as is possible. During the daytime the two alternate on the nest, with the male performing the major portion of the work during this time. The length of this period in which alternation occurs is somewhat variable, probably being somewhat dependent upon conditions of light.

With any defection on the part of either bird, the mate usually attempts continuous incubation until endurance is no longer possible. The exchange is frequently stimulated by the mate's act of taking or leaving the nest. The incubation impulse seems to reach its maximum at the time of hatching and persists for about a week, when incubation becomes intermittent and finally ceases. Apparently the male desists from his duties sooner than does the female. The length of the incubation period is highly variable. Its duration, as represented in figure 1, is

96   BEHAVIOR OF PIGEONS.

27 days, 16 of which are devoted to the eggs and 11 to the young. The old birds defecate out of the nest and remove the vacated shells and any dead young from the nest. The young also manifest instinctive behavior conducive to the cleanliness of the nest.

(5) *Both birds feed the young by regurgitation.* These activities begin with hatching and the duration of the period is highly variable. Feeding invariably continues after incubation has ceased. Normally the feeding is terminated by the events of the succeeding cycle. The female usually stops feeding with the beginning of the second incubation period, while the male may continue well up to the point of hatching. The food consists at first of "milk," a secretion of the crop. Later this secretion becomes mixed with partially digested food. The young birds stimulate the feeding response by certain attitudes of the body, their cries, flapping of the wings, and the teasing stimulus of their beaks around those of their parents. The old birds open and present their beaks, while those of the young are inserted with vigorous thrusts. The machinery of regurgitation consists of a shaking of the crop, involving movements of the entire body and especially of the wings.

SPECIES DIFFERENCES.

For purposes of reference the various comparative statements of the manuscripts may be summarized. There are probably specific differences in the time and duration of the breeding-season. The essential similarity of *Leucosarcia, Geopelia,* bronze-wing, mourning-dove, and the crested pigeon in their display and preliminary courting activities is frequently commented upon. Band-tails deviate from the usual procedure of mouth-billing as a preliminary to mounting. Mounting behavior, up to the point of contact, is uniform, only differences in speed and vigor being noted. The acts subsequent to union are highly variable with the species. The recovery of position by the male is peculiar to the bronze-wing. In some species the male drives the female away, while the opposite attitude is exhibited by others. Uniformity is asserted as to the symptoms of nesting, the tendency to seek a new nesting-site for subsequent cycles, the number of straws carried at a time, and the male's manner of delivery. Apparently each species exhibits distinctive voice characteristics, as is evident in their nesting-calls. Uniformities are mentioned as to the method of egg-laying, the feeding activities, the roosting habits of the male during incubation, feminine incubation at night, and the time of interchange. Differences are noted in the length of the incubation period, the number of eggs laid, the time of laying, and the time of beginning incubation.

One can hardly regard this account as an exhaustive comparative study. The manuscripts indicate that Professor Whitman was apparently more interested in the general uniformities of behavior than in the matter of specific differences. Close confinement under highly artificial conditions would tend to obscure or distort many specific modes of response, such, for example, as the nesting activities of wild species. A note in one of the later manuscripts indicates, however, that the author at that time contemplated a very extensive study of species relationships by means of comparative behavior.

SEX DIFFERENCES.

In the normal reproductive cycle many acts are performed by both birds. Either bird may make advances, bill its own feathers, bow, coo, bill the other's head, stamp and strike the feet, hug and neck, and, in one species, strive to obtain the upper hold for mounting. Under certain conditions, bronze-wings of either sex may stoop and receive the mate, and either may mount and exhibit all of the characteristics of uniting behavior. Both participate in the search for and selection of the nesting-site, and during the incubation period each bird takes its turn in carrying straws and arranging them in the nest. Both incubate the eggs and the young and both participate in the feeding of the young.

Within this *common group* of activities, the sexes normally differentiate themselves in the characteristics of initiative, vigor, energy, and aggressiveness, and in the frequency and completeness of many of the acts. The male, even in the bronze-wings, is the more initiative and aggressive; his acts are performed with more energy and vigor; the male bows, coos, stamps his feet, and mounts more frequently. The female spends more time on the nest; she begins incubation somewhat earlier than the male, continues it longer, and puts in more time per day. The mounting activities of the female bronze-wing are infrequent, rather incomplete, and much reduced in energy and life.

Certain activities in the normal cycle are also *peculiar* to each sex. The activities normally manifested by the male alone are: Jealousy, display, charging and driving, jumping over, presenting the open beak in billing, carrying straw for the nest in the period prior to incubation, incubating by day only, and roosting away from the nest at night. The acts peculiar to the female are retreating from the driving male, insertion of the beak in billing, nest construction in the period before incubation, egg-laying with its preliminary symptoms, and incubation by night.

In the unnatural pairings of like sexes, however, it has been found that most of those acts which are normally characteristic of the one sex may be exhibited by the opposite sex. Under these conditions, a female may also charge and drive, exhibit jealousy, jump over, present the open beak and receive that of the mate, carry straw, incubate by day, and roost away from the nest at night. The only masculine act not noted for the female was *display*. Under these unnatural conditions the male may also retreat, insert the beak in billing, construct the nest, and incubate at night. The egg-laying activities, from the nature of the case, can not be (fully) manifested by males playing the feminine rôle, and possibly this fact is due merely to the absence of the necessary stimulating intraorganic conditions (ovulation). When either bird thus plays the part of the opposite sex it does so rather unwillingly and under protest, as it were, and the resultant acts often lack something of their normal vigor, finish, and completeness. Especially is this true of many of the males forced to play the feminine rôle in copulation.

So far as *potentialities* of *kind* of behavior are concerned, the two sexes are almost on a par, and possibly we may correlate this with the fact that these birds usually exhibit but little *sex dimorphism*. As a useful device for the comprehension of this complex situation, the following conception may be suggested: There are types of conduct distinctive of each sex; these may be termed masculine and feminine traits. Each bird possesses its own distinctive sex-traits deeply and thoroughly ingrained in its organization. These tendencies function with a high degree of readiness, ease, finish, and perfection. The organization of each bird also contains in a more or less embryonic fashion the traits of the opposite sex. These tendencies function only under unusual situations and the resultant behavior lacks the normal degree of ease, vigor, and completeness of expression. The relative strength of the two systems of tendencies varies with the individual, and we may say that male birds differ in their degree of masculinity, while the females likewise vary as to the dominance of feminine traits.

These two systems are reciprocally related to each other at many points of contact and hence are mutually exclusive in large part. They also differ as to the stimuli to which they are susceptible. Aggressiveness, vigor, and determination in demeanor and act tend to arouse the feminine traits, while submissiveness and coyness make their natural appeal to the masculine tendencies. The type of conduct manifested by any bird will thus be a function of the strength and nature of its sexual impulse and the reciprocal behavior of its mate. In a natural mating each bird will usually manifest the behavior distinctive of its sex. When the male is temporarily exhausted from his endeavors the female may take the initiative and perform the mounting. Often the sexual impulses do not develop synchronously in a pair, and thus we may have a female dominated by passion mated with a male who is in a state of relative unreadiness. In such a situation the female may make the advances and possibly assume the masculine rôle in courting and copulation. If incubation is defective in either bird, the mate will attempt to remedy the deficiency by doing double duty. Unnatural matings are thus possible with this conception. Each will attempt to act in a manner characteristic of its sex, but when the acts are mutually exclusive a contest will result and the bird with the weaker sex-traits—or with sex-traits nearest to those of the opposite sex— will be forced to play the rôle of the opposite sex. Since the degree of sexuality is an individual variant, the same bird may play a different rôle in two unnatural pairings.

MATING PREFERENCES.

The sexual activities are aroused by and are directed towards certain stimulating objects. What is the nature of these stimuli, and what are the reasons for their effectiveness? While no complete and final analysis of mating preference is possible on the basis of these notes, Dr. Whitman's work establishes a few general principles which determine sexual choice.

Previous social environment is undoubtedly one factor. As a matter of fact, pigeons normally pair with members of their own species, and this preference has generally been regarded as instinctive in character. But the data of this volume show rather conclusively that the species preferences exhibited by birds at maturity are to a large extent acquired and are functions of the social environment in which the birds were reared. We are told that young birds raised under foster-parents

REPRODUCTIVE CYCLE. 99

of a different species are very apt to prefer a mating not with their own kind, but with a member of the species among which they have been reared. The author's phrase, "very apt to prefer," indicates that such means of social education are not always efficacious, and this fact shows that *some degree* of innate preference probably exists. Adult preferences must thus be regarded as the result of two factors, *instinct* and *experience*.

This fact that the range of stimuli to which an instinctive act is susceptible may be modified by experiences previous to the first expression of the act develops a novel and important principle of instinctive modification for the more prevalent doctrine assumes that instincts become modified only through the influence of simultaneous activities.

It is possible that previous experience is efficacious in part by removing fear and distrust or indifference and substituting therefor a more positive attitude of familiarity. There are some facts which indicate a fear and distrust of unfamiliar species. A pertinent example is described in Chapter XII. A young geopelia reared under ring-doves was placed with a young dove of its own species at the age of 7 weeks. It immediately manifested fear and terror. The second dove was reared with geopelias and found no cause for alarm in its new companion. Fear and distrust tend to prevent matings, as is evident from the account of a pair consisting of a mourning-dove and a white ring-dove (found in manuscript C 7/7). On the other hand, there is evidence that the normal attitude of some species towards members of some other different species is one of indifference. Under the topic "The Disposition to Fight," in Chapter I, it is stated that the wood-pigeons and white-faced pigeons, during the period of nesting, manifested hostility *only* towards members of their own species.

Behavior is the means of the selection or recognition of the sexes in mating. A male desirous of mating makes advances to various birds, and the outcome is determined by the response elicited. Continued hostility and indifference will in time discourage the wooer, and the search is prosecuted elsewhere. A certain type of response is essential to the mating. This preference for certain types and modes of behavior in the mate is probably based in large part upon innate conditions. The incident reported by Fulton (quoted in Chapter III) indicates that "vigor" makes its natural appeal to the female.

Behavior differentiates not only between the sexes but also between sexually responsive and sexually indifferent individuals. Although the sexual impulse probably may be stimulated to some extent by the advances of a potential mate, yet in the main it tends to develop automatically. The rise of this impulse is essential to the act of pairing. The choice of any male will thus be limited to those females whose sexual periodicity is synchronous, or comes in the course of wooing to be synchronous, with his own.

Contiguity is also a factor. The continued confinement and isolation of two birds will secure a mating when otherwise it would not occur. Confinement alone is sometimes efficacious, while at other times isolation from the sight and sound of other birds is necessary. Even inter-species matings can be secured in this manner. Under natural conditions of freedom the selection of a mate is probably determined in large part by chance proximity at the time of sexual readiness. The contiguity secured through confinement operates in several ways. It keeps the birds together until their sexual impulses become synchronized. It tends to eliminate any possible fear and distrust. Which matings a bird will accept depends partly upon the strength of the sexual impulse. Confinement with a certain bird will thus in time overpower the usual canons of preference and secure matings which would not occur in conditions of freedom.

Selection of a mate is influenced by the *strength* or *potency* of the sexual impulse. When the impulse is weak, at the onset of its development, it responds only to the normal or adequate stimuli; when the disposition waxes strong, due to lack of expression or other causes, and the usual stimulus is absent, it overflows the normal bounds of preference and the bird may of necessity accept almost any sort of an object with which to gratify its impelling passion. As noted above, confinement will thus force matings which would not otherwise occur. Pairings between like sexes are secured in this manner. One can thus explain some of the unusual cases of sexual behavior described in Chapter III. The male becomes dominated by the rise of the sexual impulse, but his mate repels his endeavors. Stimulated by her presence and acts—working himself up into a state of frenzy by his endeavors—he finally attempts satisfaction on the young, on the seed-dish, or on another convenient object. Given an unrequited and dominant passion, what is more natural than to make advances to his own shadow on the floor or his image in a bottle?

The case of the male mourning-dove that regarded the author as his mate (Chapter III) presents some difficulty of explanation. The bird was purchased from a dealer when a few months old. It may have been reared in isolation or with pigeons of a different species. No data are given in the records. It was kept in the author's study, after its purchase while young, until sexual maturity was reached. Other mourning-doves were in the room, though no statement is made as to whether they were kept in separate cages or were reared in common. Evidently this bird received a good deal of personal attention, for it became quite tame and well acquainted. It is thus possible that this male had been reared with birds of a different species and its preferences had become fixed by this experience, so that birds of its own kind failed to attract it. Solitary and alone, but accustomed to the presence and attentions of its benefactor, its interest and attention centered upon him for companionship. The bird may have been reared, while with the dealer, in entire isolation from pigeons, and the human environment was perhaps the only one in which it lived with any degree of intimacy; and this early training may have so fixed its habits of interest and attention that they persisted for some time after being given companions of its own kind. These habits were finally broken up, and after some effort this male was induced to pair with a female of a different species.

FIDELITY OF PAIRING.

A pair of birds normally remain faithful to each other during the reproductive cycle and then maintain their relations in the succeeding cycles of the season. It has been noted, however, that the female may desert a mate defeated in fight for the stronger male. We are not definitely told whether the matings are spontaneously continued in subsequent years, but often probably they are not. This fidelity of pigeons is at once explicable on the basis of the principles developed in the previous section. One does not need to postulate an "instinct of fidelity" to account for the circumstance that pigeons act as if actuated by well-developed ethical ideals. During a reproductive cycle there is little opportunity for illicit intercourse, for the reason that the sexual impulse is suppressed during incubation, i.e., it is limited to the first week of each cycle. Their reciprocal activity in courting and nest-building keeps them in proximity to each other and relatively isolated from others. At the time there is little likelihood that any other birds would be simultaneously disposed, except when such pairs are members of large flocks. At the end of the first cycle the rise of the sexual impulse will be closely synchronous in the two members of the pair, and this impulse generally develops while the pair is still kept together by the necessity of caring for the young. Fidelity is thus a necessary result of the synchroneity of impulses and the proximity to each other and the isolation from others which result from the cycle. As a matter of fact, illicit copulations with paired birds do occur; and we know further that a pairing may be broken up and a new mating be almost immediately obtained. These facts are readily explicable on the basis of the conception already developed.

FUNCTIONAL INTRA-RELATIONSHIP OF ACTIVITIES.

The various activities of the cycle are presumably woven together in some sort of a causal nexus. In the analysis of these relations we need to distinguish between the impulse or disposition, the objective sensory stimuli which excite it, and the resulting behavior. By an impulse we mean any intraorganic condition predisposing the organism to a certain line of behavior. Both the stimulus and the impulse necessary to any act may thus be a result of previous activity. The utility and validity of this distinction will be obvious from the subsequent discussion.

FEEDING.

The initial act in feeding on the part of the old birds consists of presenting the open beak to the young. The conditioning factors of this act are both internal and external. The external stimuli are an attitude of helplessness, certain cries, flapping of the wings, and the teasing contact of the beak of the young. The favorable internal condition is a full crop. The relative amount of coöperation of the two is highly variable. On the one hand, the parents may respond to vigorous and insistent appeals of the young when they have nothing to give. Again, the internal stimuli may become so strong, the desire for relief so compelling that the parents will attempt to force food upon their unwilling progeny, may return to

102   BEHAVIOR OF PIGEONS.

young which have been weaned, may make advances to adults, or they may react to bill-contact stimuli (finger-tips) which are normally totally inadequate. The range of potential stimuli is wide, and inside of this range the stimuli vary in potency. When the internal situation is weak only the most potent of the stimuli can release the response. When the impulse is sufficiently strong almost any objective stimulus will suffice. This organization is innate, and may appear in the young long before maturity, since one young bird may open the beak to the contact stimulus of another. The behavior of the young birds is likewise the expression of the internal conditions of hunger and certain objective stimuli. The range of potential stimuli is again a function of the strength of the internal situation. The regurgitating reflex is similarly the result of two independently variable factors, namely, the fullness of the crop and the contact in the rear of the buccal cavity which results from the thrust of the beak. Apparently this mechanism is somewhat similar to the vomiting reflex in the human.

The feeding activity develops from the previous activities of the cycle *in two ways*. Its adequate stimulus—the helpless birds in the nest—is an obvious product of the earlier activities. But an impulse to feed is also necessary to the act, and this impulse is *in part* an outgrowth of the previous conditions, for birds will not feed young unless they have participated in the cycle, and even then they will feed only at a certain stage in the cycle. The very last few days of incubation are quite essential to the impulse, for it will fail to develop if the birds do not persist in their incubation duties to the end. The onset of the impulse is due to the "milk-secretions" of the crop, and this is probably bound up physiologically with the previous activities in a way analogous to the mammary-gland secretions of mammals, though one must recognize that incubation and intra-uterine development are radically different situations. Although the impulse originates in prior conditions, its further development into functional potency is a result of its own activity.

INCUBATION.

Incubation is likewise dependent upon *two sets* of conditions. The sensory situation to which the bird responds is quite complex; it comprises the eggs, the young, the nest in a given environment, and the various activities of the mate. The "potency" of these factors is proved by the fact that their removal or alteration will disrupt the act at times. For examples the reader is referred to Chapter VII. The removal or breaking of one or both eggs, the death of one or both young, the failure of the young to hatch, may each produce a disruption of the cycle. The necessity of doing double duty, the sexual advances of the mate, the introduction of a new mate, sexual union, a new nest, a new position for the nest, the introduction of novel stimuli inducing fright, may each and all prevent a continuance of incubation. The *modus operandi* of many of the stimuli is ambiguous. We do not know the relative efficiency of sight and contact in the reaction to the young and the eggs. It may be that neither the sight nor contact of the young is the effective stimulus, but rather that the cessation of incubation is here due

REPRODUCTIVE CYCLE. 103

to the stimulus of an unrelieved crop resulting from their absence. Neither can any assertions be made as to the "relative" potency of the various objective factors.

The existence of an "impulse" as an essential condition of incubation is likewise obvious. Mating birds will not incubate at all times, even though all the objective conditions are present. If the objective stimuli were the only decisive factors, incubation should persist until the young desert the nest. A pair may enter the incubation stage and then desist without any objective defect. Also, incubation may persist for the normal period when most of the objective conditions are absent. Rich food may terminate the act before its normal end, and the author has interpreted this fact to mean that the disposition to incubate finds its primary root in the "exhaustion" resulting from the previous sexual behavior and that the disposition will tend to persist until recuperation occurs. On this basis rich food will hasten recuperation and shorten the duration of the period.

The great variety of results (Chapter VII) may be explained by supposing that the various conditioning factors vary independently of each other in potency. If the disposition be "weak," the removal of any one of the objective factors will disrupt the act; when the disposition is "strong," the same objective defect will be impotent and disruption will result only from a number of deficiencies. Given an impulse at its maximum strength, incubation will persist in the absence of practically all of the objective factors.

Incubation is a result of the previous mating and nesting activities. The causal nexus is mediated in *two ways*. The previous activities furnish the objective stimuli essential to the act, viz, the mate, the eggs, and the nest in a particular environment. Likewise the disposition to sit is a physiological outgrowth of these former acts. Numerous lines of evidence may be adduced in support of this latter proposition. There is no case of a bird manifesting a disposition to sit without some indication of previous sexual activity. The male of the blond × white ring pair (*X-W 1*) was slow in his sexual response and, as a consequence, began incubation 4 days late. All of the objective conditions essential to incubation were present, but no disposition was aroused until the usual period of sexual activity was completed. Normally the birds do not always begin incubation coincident with laying. As to the relative efficiency of the various constituents of the sexual and nesting activities in contributing to the development of the incubation impulse, no very confident assertions can be made. Probably "every phase" of these prior activities contributes somewhat to the result. Undoubtedly both the prior dispositions, as well as their behavior manifestations, are effective. On the one hand, the impulse to sit sometimes develops when the sexual and nesting impulses are denied any adequate expression, and, on the other hand, deficient expression often results in a very "tardy" development of incubation. Several pertinent facts may be mentioned. The nesting activities, in these conditions of close confinement, are, for the wild species at least, far from normal. Females may incubate without having laid eggs. Both males and females may incubate when they were forced to assume the rôle of the opposite sex in mating and nesting.

104   BEHAVIOR OF PIGEONS.

The male of the pair $X-W\ 1$ did not participate in nesting and his sexual advances were repelled, yet incubation developed in due time. A hybrid male paired with another male by mistake, courted for a month without inducing a response, and then began incubation with objective deficiencies. Inadequate sexual expression may result in delay or lack of incubation. The male hybrid cited above illustrates delay. A bronze-wing pair were separated and each remained in a state of sexual readiness for 45 days without inducing the impulse to sit. When the rise of the sexual passion is not synchronous in the two birds, the rise of incubation is timed in reference to the beginning of "sexual activity" and not with the rise of the sexual impulse.

Though incubation is a result of preceding activities, it is not an invariable result. A male mourning-dove courted and united with his mate in several cycles, but refused to participate in either nesting or incubation. A pair may mate, court, unite, and construct a nest, but proceed no further with the cycle. Other cases are mentioned in which the only defect consisted of a lack of incubation on the part of the male. We are thus forced to assume that incubation and sexual activity may vary in relative strength, even though they stand in a causal relation. Incubation results from the sexual activities, but the two impulses are not necessarily proportionate in strength. Incubation may be normal when the preceding conditions were somewhat deficient, while incubation may be weak or absent when the previous acts were normal.

Incubation and sexual activity are also *mutually exclusive* and antagonistic phenomena. The two never occur together. Coition ceases immediately as incubation begins. The rise of sexual activity during incubation disrupts the cycle, and the sex activities generally appear shortly after incubation terminates. The resultant advantage of this relation is obvious; but one can not explain the mechanism of the antagonism in terms of its consequents or advantages. Neither can the relation be explained in terms of the mutual exclusiveness of the activities *per se;* for, in the early periods of incubation, the eggs are often left uncovered for sufficient time to allow coition. The antagonism must be conceived as obtaining between the two "dispositions."

Whitman has suggested a conception (Chapter VIII) which is not wholly unsatisfactory in explaining these relations. Incubation is due to "exhaustion" resulting from the previous sexual or reproductive activity. Incubation is thus a result, and the two must necessarily be mutually exclusive impulses. Neither does it follow that the strength of the two tendencies are always proportionate, for exhaustion and recuperation could well depend in part upon factors other than the degree of sexual activity. In fact, the author regards exhaustion merely as the *primary* or *germinal* condition from which incubation arose. Other supplementary factors were added in the process of evolution before the primary condition could be utilized in the manner in which it is manifested in pigeons. Whitman would not only admit, but also assert, that the incubating behavior of pigeons is to be explained only "in part" in terms of exhaustion and recuperation.

REPRODUCTIVE CYCLE.

In Chapter VIII the author gave but two proofs of his hypothesis. These were the phylogenetic history of incubation and the fact that the incubation period can be shortened by over-feeding. The conception is further supported by the phenomenon of "pumping"; the cycle is disrupted after the eggs are laid, and the birds are thus kept in a continued state of sexual activity throughout the season. Whitman (Vol. II) and later Riddle have found that this procedure develops germinal weakness, a condition which results in an increase of infertility, a greater percentage of partial embryonic developments, and an excessive proportion of females. The following quotation from Fulton (p. 35) is also apropos:

"The result is likely to be the ruin of the constitution of the hen; for if she is what is called a free breeder, or lays her eggs fast, before the season is over she becomes so weak as in many cases to become ruptured, and in other cases barren, when she is of course valueless. The cause of this is not only excessive laying—indeed a young and rank hen will often lay, like a fowl, whether she be mated or not—but the cock-bird continually driving her to nest and teasing her while in her weak state, which causes her weakness of course to increase, until the ovary gives way, and she becomes what is termed "down behind." . . . . We have known some persons, by what is called 'pumping' a hen, or breeding from her as long as possible, to obtain 8 or 9 pairs of eggs from her in one season; but we have seldom known more than half reared, and often some of these would have crooked breast bones, which is a great fault as well as a sign of weakness. And as to the hen herself, she is, as already stated, if not entirely, seriously debilitated for life, so that none of her after progeny will be as vigorous as they ought to be."

There are certain features as to the division of labor in incubation that deserve comment. The impulse seems to develop rather independently in the two birds, though later there is certainly some degree of interaction. It is suggested that the impulse to sit is continuous in both birds, that each bird is desirous of sitting at all times, and in fact would do so if it were not for the need of food, the necessities of bathing and defecation, the desire for some form of alleviating activity, and the insistence of the mate in participating in these duties. This conception accounts for the fact and mechanism of interchange, and the tendency for each bird to do double duty in case of defection on the part of the mate. The female, because of her more *exhausting* sexual activities, which involve the forming and laying of eggs, is dominated by the stronger impulse, with the greater need for rest and recuperation, and as a consequence she begins earlier, stops later, and puts in much more time during the day. The early irregularity of incubation, we are told, delays the hatching of the first egg relative to the second, so that both hatch more nearly at the same time than they otherwise would. This result possesses the advantage of securing a greater equality in the feeding of the two young. The delay on the part of the male tends to secure a further advantage in that the male's activity does not interfere with his mate's duties in the matter of the laying of the second egg. In this connection we may note the fact that in *Ectopistes*, which lays but *one* egg, both birds start incubation previous to egg-laying.

NESTING.

In the nesting activities the existence of an impulse and its development from the previous sexual activities is evident. Nesting occurs only as a part of the sequence of activities, and when the impulse is satisfied the activities cease. The

106 BEHAVIOR OF PIGEONS.

acts persist when no necessity is present, for the birds are forced to choose their old and ready-made nests. The impulse to seek a new site is manifested even when there is no opportunity for gratification. This tendency to seek the site in a new locality can be correlated with the advantage accruing from the resultant weaning of the previous set of young. Both parents may be feeding at this time and the previous young may not yet be entirely weaned from the nest. If the old nest be utilized, the second cycle may be disrupted in this manner. Such an incident is reported in Chapter VII. Results, however, can not explain the existence and mechanism of the tendency. One would need to conceive this behavior somewhat in the light of a negative reaction to the old environment.

In the matter of the selection of a site, we can do little but ask a number of questions indicating the problems involved. What are the objective conditions necessary to the satisfaction of the birds? Must the seeking impulse run a certain temporal course before it can be satisfied, and is it then easily satisfied by almost any condition present at the time? Which bird takes the initiative in the selection? Must the impulse run a certain time in each bird independently of the other? The records make it probable that one bird may become satisfied with a site while the other remains undecided for some time. If they do not influence each other as to the time of choice, do they influence each other as to what the site shall be? And which of the pair exhibits the greater initiative in this regard?

Evidently the two tendencies do as a matter of fact become harmonized and adjusted to each other; little can be said, however, as to the means by which this is accomplished. Is the choice purely instinctive, or is it highly adaptive to variable conditions? To what extent may experience play a part? The impulse can adapt itself to changed conditions, as is evident from the final selection of the old site and the adoption of a ready-made nest which, in many of the species studied, is far removed from the sort of nest used under natural conditions. The nest-constructive acts are highly instinctive, being observed in a young bird when resting on the floor. It is suggested that the stimulus to these movements is the uncomfortable contact situation which the resultant acts relieve.

SEXUAL ACTIVITIES.

The nature of the objective stimuli in the sexual activities has been discussed under the topic of mating preference. A disposition is also present here, since the acts are not always manifest when the objective conditions are present. The impulse arises in part spontaneously and automatically, but it is also stimulated to some degree by the persistent advances of the mate. The stimulating influence of the mate is made evident by several instances, cited in Chapter VII, in which the male was able to disrupt the cycle and entice his mate into sexual relations within a few days. The sexual passion further develops from its own expression and from the reciprocal stimulus of the mate. Without *expression* the cycle *may* not develop further, or the sexual period *may* be greatly prolonged before incubation is aroused.

REPRODUCTIVE CYCLE. 107

The impulses arise in the two birds somewhat independently of each other. Synchronization of the two cycles is effected in two ways. The two birds stimulate each other to some extent, and each bird will *remain* in a state of sexual readiness for some time when interaction is absent. The initiation of the subsequent stages of the cycle is timed primarily in reference to the beginning of sexual interaction rather than with the onset of the sexual impulse. This conception involves the assumption that many of the preliminary courting activities serve in part to attract, interest, and sexually excite the mate. The author is definitely of the opinion that the display activities serve this function. Necessarily the exact function of each act and the mechanism whereby the result is achieved must remain somewhat speculative. There are four possible functions of the activities: (*a*) to excite the sexual impulse in the mate; (*b*) self-excitation; (*c*) to arouse in the mate the attitudes and behavior necessary to coition; or, (*d*) to serve as motor outlets of energy incidental to the sexual act. A few speculative suggestions may be offered.

(*A*) The act of "billing" probably serves the first purpose. This act of taking the beak of another bird into the mouth occurs in both courting and feeding. The act *per se* is nearly, if not quite, identical in the two cases. The differences lie in the situation in which the impulse develops, the nature of the stimulus, and the functional result. In many organisms there seems to be an intimate functional relation between the sexual activities and those processes involved in the care and feeding of the young. The sexual activities and their physiological consequents stimulate and arouse the food secretions. Nursing may suppress the sexual impulse. The stimulation of the sensory regions involved in the feeding and care of the young tends to excite the sexual passion. The vigorous thrust of the beak stimulates *regurgitation* with one internal situation, but arouses *passion* when the bird is sexually disposed. Though the primary result of the act in courting is sexual excitement, yet *feeding* does occasionally occur as an incidental by-product when the internal conditions are such as to favor it. In the later stages of the cycle the primary purpose of the act is to feed the young, and likewise we might expect at this time a secondary result of sex-excitement if the conditions are at all favorable. Such conditions are not present during the first week or so, while close incubation is the rule; for, as we have seen, incubation and sexual activity are mutually exclusive functions. As incubation gradually terminates, however, this possibility exists, and as a matter of fact sexual activity frequently appears at this point. This conception of an incidental sex stimulation resulting from the feeding activities will thus explain the very general tendency toward an immediate renewal of the cycle and the *synchronous* appearance of the sexual impulses in the two birds.

The conception presented above is further supported by an observation furnished by Dr. Riddle:

"Two male blond rings had been paired and given eggs to incubate. The young were hatched and fed, and the pair were again given eggs in due time. The previous young had

108   BEHAVIOR OF PIGEONS.

left the nest, but were still being fed during the second incubation period. One of these young birds, No. 560, was observed to participate in this incubation when only 38 days old, and the activity was continued for more than a week. This act was a genuine case of incubation, as was shown in several ways. It occurred after the nest had been deserted by both of the young; the young bird took up such a position as to cover the eggs completely; and it exhibited the usual incubation behavior of ruffled feathers and an attitude of holding its ground, when the hand was placed in the nest. Further observation showed that the two old males were driving the other young bird (a nest-mate) in the attempt to wean it, but that they were, at the same time, most anxious and eager to feed No 560, and that this feeding was almost invariably followed by attempts to mount and copulate with the young bird. This situation continued for some time, and finally the young bird was itself observed to attempt the complete sexual response; only its muscular inability to bear the weight of the male prevented any copulatory success. The first successful coition was observed when the young bird was about 3 months old. The motive to this unusual prolongation of the feeding on the part of the old males was primarily *sexual*. The young bird was at first primarily interested in the *food*, but the continuance of the activity finally aroused a sexual response before maturity. This abnormal sexual attitude of the old birds toward the young is probably a result of their unnatural sexual relation; the pair consisted of two males. Possibly the awakened sexual impulses would have found a normal outlet in a pair consisting of male and female."

(*B*) Some of the activities are designed to arouse the appropriate attitudes in the mate. As noted previously, each bird possesses the behavior potentialities of both sexes, and the system awakened depends upon the behavior of the mate. Driving and charging stimulates coyness and submissiveness. Hugging and "jumping over" tend to arouse the necessary stooping attitude in the female; and the movements adapted to secure sexual union are the outcome of the contact stimuli incident to the mount.

(*C*) The billing, preening, and pecking at certain feathers on the wings and tail seem more of the nature of a self-excitatory process. These parts are the sensory regions involved in certain reflexes incidental to mounting, and it is thus possible that the act of preening is designed to stimulate these areas and arouse the sexual inclination.

(*D*) The activities preceding coition are highly uniform for various species, and this fact will suggest the conception that they are adapted to secure certain results in the progression of events in the cycle. The activities immediately "subsequent" to contact, however, exhibit many specific variations, and one may therefore suspect that they serve no particular function in the cycle, but are the specific modes of expression of the neural energy released in the orgasm. When no definite result is to be achieved, variability in response may be permitted.

EGG-LAYING.

Some of the acts in egg-laying are adapted to the purpose at hand, while others are probably incidental but necessary results of the labor involved. The preliminary symptoms of ovulation are stimulated mainly by the presence of the egg, but probably in part by antecedent conditions, because these symptoms were more than once observed when no eggs were produced.[1] The stimulus to ovulation

---

[1] The possibility that ova were set free in the body-cavity is not excluded by the author's data.

REPRODUCTIVE CYCLE. 109

is to be found in the *preceding* sexual activities. Fertilization is not necessary, as a pair of females may stimulate each other. When a female is stimulated by another female acting as a male there is a more frequent lack of eggs than in normal conditions. This deficiency may be due either to the lack of sperm or sperm effects or to the inadequate masculine behavior of the mate. Feminine modes of behavior constitute a favorable though not an essential condition, for the female which assumes the masculine rôle does not lay as frequently as her mate; moreover, in those cases in which she does lay, her eggs are often several days late. Contact is efficacious, but not essential. As Fulton says, "neither contact nor any of the activities of a mate are essential; a young and rank bird will occasionally lay without a mate." Undoubtedly ovulation may occur in a female that occupies a cage alone. These cases were almost certainly preceded by a rise of the sexual impulse. Probably ovulation is normally a result of all the preceding conditions, the sexual impulse, its various modes of expression, and the stimulus resulting from the behavior of the mate. The relative efficiency of these factors may be variable, and at times a deficiency in any one may prevent ovulation, while in other cases ovulation may occur when but one condition is present.

MISCELLANEOUS.

The motive to any act is an ingrained impulse or disposition toward some sensory stimulus. The bird acts as it does because it "feels" disposed to do so; it acts in harmony with its feelings and impulses of the moment. The act brings certain sensory results which are satisfying, and these results may enter into the motive subsequently. The acts also achieve other results with a biological utility; but these advantages may constitute no part of the actuating motive and bring no satisfaction to the bird. To the bird these results are mere incidental by-products, without meaning or significance. Many proofs of this conception are offered. Such activities as seeking a nesting-site in a new locality, construction of a nest, and roosting away from the nest at night are manifested under environmental conditions in which they are entirely gratuitous and unnecessary. Birds will incubate without eggs or young; or they may desert either eggs or young. In satisfying their impulse to remove the shells, the parents have been known to deposit the fledglings on the floor of the cage and leave them to perish and the young may be injured or killed in the act of feeding.

While the organization of the cycle of activities has been perfected, probably by natural selection, to achieve certain results, the adaptation need not be absolute and letter-perfect. The theory of natural selection demands only a practical perfection sufficient to secure the survival of the species in their conditions of life. Not every egg need be hatched nor every young be reared. Moreover, the utility refers only to those conditions in which the organization was developed. On this basis certain acts, which appear unutterably stupid and non-intelligent from the human point of view, are rendered more comprehensible. Although the young birds may be cast from the nest along with the shells, or seriously injured in the process of feeding, or eggs and young be heartlessly deserted, or the

110   BEHAVIOR OF PIGEONS.

nesting activities be manifested when they are useless, these consequences are insignificant from the standpoint of the birds, and they do not occur with sufficient frequency to militate against the practical utility of the bird's organization in the long run.

The instinctive organization, however, does possess a high degree of plasticity and adaptiveness at many points. Acts are adapted to meet novel conditions and the bird may persist in its duties in spite of many defects. The mating preferences are quite plastic. Natural preferences may be overcome and a bird will pair with a member of another species or with one of its own sex. Each bird may assume the duties of the opposite sex throughout the cycle whenever necessary. The old nest and site may be adopted in spite of a strong inclination to the contrary. Continuous incubation may be attempted when the mate deserts. Incubation will be continued in spite of serious defects and obstacles. Acts may be modified to some degree by experience. The effect of experience has been noted chiefly in connection with the mating preference, the preliminary symptoms of egg-laying, the preference for a nesting-site, and the removal of fear and distrust of strange birds. The effect of experience in mating has been discussed. It is remarked (Chapter VII) that the female of the passenger-ring-dove pair "will learn by experience to waste less time in fruitless formalities, and make less ado over such a small matter as laying an egg." The supposed male of "pair D" was driven from his nest and then sat for a time in an empty box. In a few hours he developed a preference for this site which was difficult to break, although the box contained no eggs and was filled with dry dung.

The author has developed what one may term an orthogenetic conception of instinctive development. Instincts are not novel and unique constructions which spring, without ancestry, into being; rather each new instinct[1] is but a slight modification or organization of tendencies already in existence. This conception is well depicted in his treatment of the phylogeny of incubation (Chapter VIII). Each of the prior elements or stages in the process of development has its own meaning and survival value. Any complicated instinct is built up by small increments; but natural selection is operative throughout, for each stage as well as the final product has a selective utility of its own. The mutation conception is thus unnecessary, and we are relieved of the difficulty of assuming a gradual or integrative development over long periods in which natural selection is powerless to operate. On this conception the same act with slight modifications may function in widely different situations, and any act may have several utilitarian results. The consequences—bringing satisfaction to the bird—may be far different from those upon which natural selection has operated. Many illustrations are given in the manuscripts. A pertinent example is the case of "billing," which occurs in both courtship and feeding. There is a marked similarity and intimacy of connection between charging and driving, display, jealousy, pugnacity, and the behavior subsequent to dismounting. For the details of these relations the reader is referred to the appropriate topics.

---

[1] In Chapter XIII this same principle is applied also to "intelligence."

CHAPTER X.

VOICE AND INSTINCT IN PIGEON HYBRIDIZATION AND PHYLOGENY.[1]

If Professor Whitman had completed his work, he would have produced an extensive treatise on the phylogeny of the pigeon group. All of his studies would have been brought to bear upon the problems of phylogeny. The voices and the behavior of the various species would have been used, like their color-patterns, to throw light on the relationships, derivation and method of origin of pigeon species. To this end, Professor Whitman was interested in discovering similarities and differences of voice, and in learning which elements are homologous in the voices of different species.

The "Voice" manuscripts unfortunately show no approach towards the final stage of working out a complete phylogeny of the group; but this whole volume on behavior is replete with details of likenesses and differences in species, showing here and there species relationships. Many passages, unused elsewhere, but bearing especially on this problem are here gathered together. A considerable body of data on voice and instinct in hybrids contains facts relevant to the subject of species relationships; these data offer, moreover, a contribution to our knowledge of voice and instinct when these are subjected to hybridization.

Admittedly fragmentary as is some of the material at hand, it is certainly desirable to give, in this volume, as much as is possible of the presentable results of the author's studies on the topics indicated under the title of this chapter. It is not practicable to isolate the author's statements on species relationships and present them under the topic placed immediately below in this chapter. The editors have therefore diagrammatically represented the lines of descent in a very condensed form; to these figures little other material is added; the specific statements of the author must be sought in other parts of the chapter and in other chapters. The diagrams will perhaps assist the reader in visualizing those statements. It is thought that these figures,[2] representing as they do the lines of descent of those species most referred to in the present volume, may also prove otherwise helpful to an understanding of some of the statements of this and of other chapters. In their present form these diagrams are indeed largely reconstructions by the editors, but the manuscripts for this and other volumes leave no doubt that they approximate to an accurate representation of the author's conclusions; in most cases, however, the conclusion was not based upon voice and behavior alone, but on other evidence, wholly or in part. The second and third sections of the chapter include data on the modification of voice and instinct in hybrids; these have been divided by us on the basis of closer and wider crosses. In a final section are placed some of the more complete studies on the voice (and behavior) of some pure wild species.

---

[1] This chapter was compiled and edited by Dr. Wallace Craig and Dr. Oscar Riddle.
[2] In figure 2 the parts A and B were drawn by Wallace Craig, C by Oscar Riddle.

ON SPECIES RELATIONSHIPS IN PIGEONS.

The main stem of the pigeon branch, if I read correctly the testimony of color-patterns, is represented most nearly by the turtle-doves (*Turtur orientalis* and *Turtur turtur*) of the Old World. The original turtle-dove pattern, in which all or most of the feathers were similarly differentiated into a "dark center" and a "light edge," seems to have been a very general if not a universal avian pattern. This pattern certainly preceded the chequered type of the rock-pigeon (*C. affinis*), and it is possible still to find connecting types—types in which the turtle pattern coexists with the chequered pattern, the latter coming in to replace or supersede the former. Examples are to be seen in the bronze-winged pigeon (*Phaps chalcoptera*) of Australia, the Florida ground-dove (*Chamæpelia passerina*), and some others. (EM 1.)

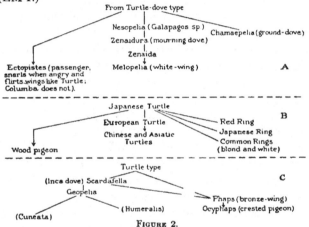

FIGURE 2.

In the above, parts A and B were drawn by Wallace Craig, part C by Oscar Riddle. Of the genus *Columba*, *C. palumbus* seems nearest to the turtle-dove. *C. fasciata* seems separate from the others. *C. rufina* is probably close to *flavirostris*. *C. squamosa* is probably higher than *C. leucocephala*. The stock-dove (*C. œna*) and the rock-dove (*C. livia*) are more closely related to each other than to the wood-pigeon (*C. palumbus*); the stock-dove probably came, not from the rock-dove, but from the same ancestor. *C. gymnopthalma* is related to *C. squamosa* and *C. leucocephala*.

One of us (W. C.) often asked the author to state his conclusions as to species relationships; he never replied at great length. The following notes, made at the time, present some of his conclusions and are worthy of record:

"The Japanese turtle-dove (*T. orientalis*) is the most nearly ancestral. From the Japanese to the Indian and thence to the European species there is a continuous transition toward smaller size. There is a similar transition in ring-doves from Japan to Europe.

"The Inca-dove is probably related to the geopelias; it lifts and spreads the tail the same way in cooing. The geopelias show in their juvenal plumage their relation to the turtle-dove. The Inca-dove is probably the lowest; *G. cuneata* is the highest; *G. humeralis* is probably a branch off by itself, but standing nearly as high as *cuneata*.

"The bronze-wings are somewhat related to the geopelias, as is shown by their behavior, but they have retained most of the turtle-dove pattern.

"There are wild species so much alike that an unpracticed observer could see no difference in appearance. Yet the voice and general behavior are very different. The specificity seems to permeate to every element of the bird's constitution.

VOICE AND INSTINCTS IN HYBRIDS FROM CROSSES OF SPECIES AND GENERA.

"I think the kind of study of instinct that is much needed now is what I might call the morphogenesis of instinct. Instincts certainly did not arise suddenly; they are traceable back to simple beginnings in the lower ancestors." (Conv. '08–'10, W. C.)

VOICE AND INSTINCTS IN HYBRIDS FROM CROSSES OF SPECIES AND GENERA.

In hybrids one finds *intermediate behavior* very well marked. Voice affords a most striking illustration of the same thing. From a hybrid between two distinct species one invariably obtains notes that are intermediates of those of both parents. Sometimes the hybrid will begin with notes that are more nearly those of one parent and then break off into those more nearly those of the other parent; in other words, it will exhibit a sort of lack of coördination, a lack of equilibrium, if the term may be used there. The bird has not complete control of its organs. (SS 10.)

HYBRID BETWEEN A MALE ST. ALBA-RISORIA AND FEMALE SPIL. SURATENSIS.

The "display coo" which is given in courting, or in threatening opponents, is delivered in the manner and time of *suratensis*—i.e., in the manner of both parent species—and in a time that is quicker than that of the ring-dove and possibly a little slower than that of *suratensis*. It has a marked element of the rattling, rapid vibration which is so characteristic of the Surate turtle; but in this it stands midway between the two parent species. The male ring-dove occupies about $2\frac{1}{2}$ seconds in delivery of one display coo and passes continuously from one coo into the next.

The "nest-call" of this hybrid was timed with the following result:

Repeated the call 19 times in one minute.
Repeated the call 18 times in one minute.
Repeated the call 14 times in one-half minute.
Repeated the call 10 times in one-fourth minute.
Repeated the call 10 times in one-half minute.

The call is three-fourths to one second in length; the interval between calls varies. Ten times in 15 seconds is the more rapid rate, with intervals averaging about one-half second. It varies all the way from one-half second to 2 seconds in the above observations, which were continued during 20 minutes.

The call is of two syllables, but these flow together; the first is about one-half the length of the second. The second syllable is a swell, but hardly rises in pitch above the first. The sound is rather loud and harsh, having the vibrations of *suratensis* roughened so as to merit the term harsh. The mode of delivery of this call is that of either parent; the bird getting into the nest-box, raising the tail, and lowering the head close to the bottom of the box.

In dropping one of the first two syllables, the hybrid makes an approach to the ring-dove. The hybrid's call varies not only, as above stated, in length and rate of repetition, but also in the quality of the tones, the relative measure of the syllables, in loudness, degree of roughness, etc. In short, the call is far less even or regular than in a pure-bred species. The nest-call of *St. risoria* is $2\frac{1}{2}$ seconds long as a rule; it may be shortened to 2 seconds.

This ring-*suratensis* hybrid mated, at the age of 22 weeks, with a female ring-dove and gave opportunity to study its "note of sexual pleasure." The ring dove has a "laughing" note after sexual union. The *Spil. suratensis* arches its neck and gives a peculiar, short note, somewhat like the danger note, but expressive of intense pleasure. The same note is given by *Spil. chinensis*, *T. turtur*, *T. orientalis*, and by my fertile hybrid from the common pigeon and the Japanese turtle-dove. The ring-*suratensis* hybrid also gives this note in a modified form.

The mother of this hybrid is now (Mar. 19) mated with a male *Spil. chinensis*. Just now I heard the sexual call of both. It is repeated several times by both—the male standing

114 BEHAVIOR OF PIGEONS.

still, the female often walking around him, back and forth, two or three times, while repeating the call. The first repetition is quite loud and fairly rings out; the later ones gradually diminish in force. This call is given with beak closed and is an orgastic grunt, similar to the danger-note, but with far greater emphasis and delivered with great gusto.

The "perch-call" is the call in which this bird best displays the lack of fixed adjustment in its vocal organs. So much does the bird's voice vary in pitch, rhythm, quality, loudness, etc., that he often appears like a bird practicing—trying to use his organs—but unable to make two calls precisely alike. His voice-machinery seems to wobble up and down, from side to side. The voice is now hoarse, now relatively smooth, now monotone, now dissyllabic, with a strong swell on the second syllable.

The greatest variation seems to be in passing from one syllable to the next, the voice fairly rattling or gurgling at times. In all this variation, the departures are never very wide. There are two syllables, generally suggesting *coo-ooo*, in which the second is a swell more or less strong, and marked with a vibration that reminds one of that of the mother species; but the vibration here is weaker, *i.e.*, it is less marked. Sometimes the call comes nearer *caw-aw*.

In delivering the call the bird swells out the neck so as to show its neck-spots best on the swell. It opens its mouth slightly at the beginning (inhaling), holds the head nearly still, but throws it forward and upward about one-fourth inch when it begins the call. In repeating, the head may move a little or not at all, according to the vigor of the call. If the call is loud, then the one-fourth inch movement is seen. The call is three-fourths to 1 second long. The swell is somewhat the longer part.

The "warning or fighting note" of this hybrid is given when he drives his mate or threatens another dove through the wire. The male ring-dove has a peculiar laughing note for this, to which the hybrid's note seems related. (R 14.)

MALE HYBRID BETWEEN A MALE BLOND RING AND A FEMALE JAPANESE RING.

The "nest-call" is repeated three to four times in the course of 10 seconds; each call occupies $1\frac{1}{2}$ to 2 seconds, the interval (shorter ones) is 1 second or a fraction less. The call is of two syllables or three. If not answered it may rise to four, the same as in the "perch-call." In the nest-call the first syllable is short; the second is prolonged with swell and a slight rattle or rolling sound of *r;* the third syllable is cut quite short and abrupt. The call is low in pitch, rather hoarse and growl-like.

A male *St. douraca* (Japanese ring) was kept alone in a pen in the house for a month or two so that I could compare his cooing with that of the hybrid. The pure ring gave his call at intervals of a few minutes—loud, full, clear, smooth. The hybrid's call had the same number of syllables, delivered in about the same time and inflections, but his voice was decidedly harsh and far less pleasant to hear. It was not so loud and far-going as that of the pure bird.[1]

After counting and timing many instances of the perch-call or song of *St. douraca* and of the hybrid, the author came to the conclusion that the "hybrid keeps up his calls for a longer time." That is, the hybrid gives an average of 10 calls in each continuous series; *St. douraca* gives only about 8.

THE VOICE OF RING DOVES.

The "nest-call" of female blond rings is a short *coo* followed by a trill. Indicated thus: *Coo-r-r-r-r-r-oo.* The whole occupies about $1\frac{1}{2}$ seconds. The *coo* and the final *oo* are of about the same duration, and each occupies not over one-tenth of a second, the remainder of the time being used in the trill.

---

[1] That is to say, the voice of the hybrid is more hoarse than that of either parent species.—EDITOR.

VOICE AND INSTINCT IN PIGEON HYBRIDIZATION AND PHYLOGENY. 115

When the blond ring gets frightened and is pursued it utters a "cry of terror"—a painful shriek or groan on being caught in the hand—often repeating it convulsively. Sometimes it sounds like a sobbing cry, especially if given when the bird is exhausted and is struggling to escape, but sees no escape from the hand closed upon it.

The voice of blond rings is shown in several kinds of crowing. There is the ordinary "crow" (song) which the bird makes when sitting on a perch. This crow is not accompanied by any strutting, bowing, or display of any kind. It may have served in a state of nature as a means of calling the mate when separated. It is made on the nest by both the male and female, and also on the perch during the evening, if the birds are awakened from sleep. In the latter case the crow may have the same meaning that the crow of a rooster does at night. It is an assertion of personal rights, rights of perch, nest-mate, etc. The male very often gives this crow in the daytime. Parents in this way call the young to eat.

Then there is the crow performed before the female (often before males too), which is accompanied by strutting, bowing, and display of form and plumage. This is designed to charm the female and is used in wooing a mate.

The first efforts with the voice have been noted in blond rings. I noticed that one of a pair of young—a bird 10 weeks and 4 days old—made two attempts to crow. His voice has changed enough to permit of a rude crow, which an inexperienced person would hardly recognize as such. It is the first time I have noticed such an effort. I take it as a good sign of the male sex. Another blond-ring young, only a day more than 7 weeks old, was seen to crow—with bows and display—to its mate. The voice was quite imperfect, but the manner was the same as that of the adult.

A sort of "stammering" was noted in some ring-doves. A white ring (*St. alba*) male often wakes up in the evening in my study and begins to call, but stammers for a few moments before being able to give the regular call. One of the young of this white ring stutters just like its father. A blond ring (male) in my possession also stutters in the same way. (R 27.)

VOICE AND INSTINCTS IN HYBRIDS FROM CROSSES OF FAMILIES AND SUBFAMILIES.

A MALE HYBRID BETWEEN A MALE COMMON PIGEON AND A FEMALE JAPANESE TURTLE.

When this male was 5 months old its voice was studied and the following noted: The "danger-note" is precisely like that of the common pigeon. I think both parents agree in this. The bird also solicits the female by billing the wing, as do common doves and Japanese turtles.

The voice is deep, strong, and smoother than in hybrids between the common dove and ring-dove. The "call-note" is peculiar, unlike that of any other dove, although it approaches in form that of the common dove; it differs chiefly in its rapid repetition during 15 to 20 or more seconds at a time. The call is repeated slowly at first (for 4 to 5 seconds), then quickened to about two every second. In the course of an hour I several times counted 27 to 28 calls in 15 seconds; and once 41 calls in 25 seconds.

The "nest-call," differs strongly from the call-note and is distinguished from the nest-call of common doves in being hoarse. In the "coo" the motion is up and down, somewhat like *St. risoria*. The wings are often dropped below the tail, with the quills falling apart, a little as in the ring-dove. The coo resembles that of the common pigeon, while differing strongly. When the hybrid was 6 months old it was noted that the "perch-call" was rather low and hoarse.

The "display coo" is accompanied by the up-and-down movement given somewhat as in the ring-dove. The tail is dropped down as the head rises, but I have not seen it spread and dragged on the ground, as is the case with the common pigeon. It inclines to lift the feet in cooing, sometimes alternating—one foot with one call and the other with the next.

116 BEHAVIOR OF PIGEONS.

Sometimes only one foot beats time, sometimes neither is lifted. This lifting of feet is characteristic of the mother species and turtle-doves in general (also crested pigeon and geopelias). The voice is a deep bass, very strong.

This bird is especially fond of ring-doves, and I have only to bring one to him to get him to coo at any time.[1] He is so tame that within a foot of my head he pays scarcely any attention to me, behaving just as if I were not present.

A brother to the above described hybrid has a "danger-note"—a short grunt or growl—like that of the two parent species. To-day the hybrid "cooed" three times to a ring-dove. The voice is unlike that of any other hybrid, and in quality certainly has something of the mother.

The only female[2] hybrid I have thus far obtained of this kind—one between a homer and a Japanese turtle-dove—was heard to give, after copulation, the peculiar note which is common to the maternal species, the Asiatic turtle, and the mourning-dove. (R 14.)

The following cases of *mixed instincts* in hybrids may be given here, though other cases have been given in previous chapters:

A hybrid between a common pigeon and a ring-dove, when first set free from a pen or when it escapes, is quite as likely *to alight in a tree*,[3] if one is near, as on the roof of a house. This has often been tested in Woods Hole and in Chicago. The hybrid takes to a tree like a ring-dove; the latter shows a decided preference for the tree, and generally at mid-day seeks one in which to rest, even though it must go farther for the tree than for a house.

The ring-dove prefers "night quarters" on the outside, even in the rain, to going in. The same is true of the crested pigeon and others. The dove-cote pigeon seeks shelter early—by sunset or before. This hybrid prefers to go inside at night, but is slower to retire. I have four hybrids free, and some dozen dove-cote pigeons also free; the hybrids are always the last to retire. In other words, these hybrids are less strongly inclined to seek shelter at night. The same is seen in stormy weather, when the hybrids, like the ring-doves, usually remain outside, while the dove-cote pigeons prefer shelter and usually go in.

Why does one prefer shelter from rain and for the night, while the other prefers to remain in the open, refusing to remain inside, however many times it may be driven in? Probably the dove-cote pigeon actually "feels" safer in a cot at night, and finds the shelter from wind agreeable, while the ring-dove is so constituted that it "feels" more comfortable in the open than in the cot. It certainly shows repugnance to the cot or a shed. How is this difference brought about? Originally all prefer the open; the dove-cote pigeon has been trained to "dove-cot," and individuals that keep to cot are safest and therefore protected.[4] (R 14.)

HYBRID BETWEEN A MALE ZENAIDURA CAROLINENSIS AND A FEMALE ST. RISORIA.

This male hybrid calls in the nest-box to a female *Zenaidura* which has just been placed in the adjoining pen. The tail is raised about the same as in either parent species; but it is not spread at all with the call, at least not in this specimen. It is usually, though not always, spread in the mourning-dove. The tails of both are vibrated about the same as in the ring-dove.

The "nest-call" is repeated quite regularly once in 5 seconds, now and then a little short of 5 seconds, so that 1 or 2 seconds may be gained in the course of 6 or 7 calls; at

---

[1] The records show that this hybrid was hatched and reared by ring-doves. (O. R.)

[2] The hybrids obtained from *family* crosses were practically all males. (O. R.)

[3] This refers to the well-known fact that the dove-cote pigeon and the rock-dove shun trees, alighting on the ground, on rocks, or on houses. (W. C.)

[4] *Cf.* Darwin's view that the dove-cote pigeon must have come from a wild ancestor, such as *C. livia*, which lived in caves and not in trees. (Animals and Plants under Domest., Vol. I.)

VOICE AND INSTINCT IN PIGEON HYBRIDIZATION AND PHYLOGENY. 117

other times, in a little over 5 seconds. Each call is a full second long; it consists of two syllables, which flow together so evenly that they seem like one monotone at a distance of a few yards. The first syllable is a short *coo*, and the second is most nearly the sound of *oo* in *coo*, but prolonged in a swell that rises slightly in pitch above the initial sound, falling at the end. The two syllables flow together without any break. The tone is a little rough, but is fairly smooth in some individuals. It is a rather loud call—louder than that of the mourning-dove, and not so pleasant. Heard in the house, at a distance of one floor (below), it sounds like a moan of some one in distress. It is something more mournful than the notes of the mourning-dove.

The nest-call of *Zenaidura* is the same dissyllable, in which the two syllables are plainly distinct, even at any distance in the house. The first part is longer proportionately than in the hybrid, and the second part is a smoother and more marked swell.

In one count, the "perch-call" was repeated 17 times in 20 seconds, and in quite even time. Frequently the call is repeated about once per second. This prolonged repetition (which occurs also in the *Ectopistes* × *risoria* hybrid) does not come from the father (see perch-call of *Zenaidura* below). It is probable that it comes mostly or wholly from the mother, since *St. risoria* repeats its perch-call in rapid succession. The call is more distinctly of two syllables, and a little higher in pitch as well as smoother and more agreeable, than the nest-call. The same letters, *coo-oo*, may be used to express this call, although it is quite different in quality of tone and manner of delivery from the nest-call. The bird stands in normal pose—head up and tail drooping naturally.

Another of these male hybrids exercises his perch-call very freely. His voice is quite full and smooth and far-reaching, telephonic. He repeats the call sometimes as many as 15 times in about 15 seconds; sometimes only 5, 7, or more times, averaging nearly 1 call a second, the calls following one another in continuous strain. The pause between the strains may be only a few seconds, or 15, 30, or longer. But the strains are heard frequently in the morning hours, between dawn and 9 to 10 o'clock, and then again towards evening.

One of these hybrids gives the call in a loud monotone in which two syllables are hardly recognizable. It sounds like blowing over the lip of a bottle-neck, and reminds me of the call I have heard from the Wonga Wonga pigeon (*Leucosarcia*). But the call of the latter is very much less loud and is softer.

In sexual union the male hybrid shakes his feathers—like the male *Zenaidura*, but not so persistently or so vigorously—as a means of getting the attention of his mate when he is about to offer his bill. He opens his bill to receive that of his mate, and seems prone to repeat this several times before mounting. In case the female offers herself he frequently declines, again offering his bill, so as to excite her more before mounting. When he mounts he hurries, executes the act very quickly, in the manner so characteristic of *Zenaidura*. *St. risoria* acts decidedly slower.

After copulation, when the male has resumed his place beside his mate, he arches his neck and gives a short grunt, the "note of sexual pleasure," which is not quite so loud as in *Zenaidura*. It is the note so characteristic of the turtle-doves, and the note which is also given by the wood-pigeon (*C. palumbus*). This bird has refused to mate with ring-doves, either white or blond; but he is very eager to mate with a female *Zenaidura* as soon as I put her near him. Other of these hybrids prefer ring-doves.

Both mourning-doves and these hybrids, when walking about on the floor of their pen, or when on the perch, give the tail an upward toss now and then. I noticed that this motion is not made when flying up and alighting, as it is in *Spil. tigrina*, but always (?) in correlation with a head-movement; *i.e.*, if the bird is looking at you—and from fear, excitement, or what not, gives its head the peculiar back-and-forward motion—it is almost sure to follow it with a toss of the tail, this toss carrying the tail 1, 2, or 2.5 inches high.

9

118   BEHAVIOR OF PIGEONS.

One of these hybrids escaped from its pen early one morning, before feeding. It flew into a large willow close by, where it remained, flying about occasionally from branch to branch, until about $9^h 30^m$ a. m., when it came down into the yard. Finding its own pen, it tried to get in. I opened one of the pens, and soon it went in and was captured. The early return was prompted by need of food and by the semidomestic instincts of its ring-dove mother. Its flight was rapid, and the movement of the wings and the marking of the tail made it look like a true mourning-dove.[1] (R 14.)

HYBRID BETWEEN A MALE ECTOPISTES AND A FEMALE RING-DOVE.

The "nest-call" is a sort of "caw" resembling that of the male parent, but very much weaker. The tail is held up and slightly spread, and the head bowed, as he looks at the female. In the "note of attack" the bird bristles, drops the head, shortens the neck, and gives a scolding or snarling note. This is given when he flies at another dove, or when he jumps to peck through the wire netting of his pen. He often flies up to the side of his pen against another bird, and while the other bird merely tries to peck, making no noise, this male always emits his snarl. This snarl is like that of the male parent, but the hybrid gives it with markedly less vigor and shrillness than it is given by the parent.

This hybrid has the up-and-down motion of a ring-dove, to accompany its "coo," but not so pronounced as in the latter. Its "coo" is the same "caw" repeated several times with the up-and-down motion. It solicits the female by offering the open beak, as a ring-dove does (I have never seen *Ectopistes* do this); but it slurs this part and more often omits it entirely. Often before offering the beak the hybrid bills his wing as the rings and common doves nearly always do, and as *Ectopistes* occasionally does.

These hybrids have thus far shown a decided mating preference for female ring-doves over every other species. They give little attention to female passengers. A hybrid brought into the house in January at once became amorous at sight of a female ring-dove. So eager was he that he pursued her in spite of her strokes—not offering to resist, but simply facing the blows, spreading his tail, and jumping like a male ring-dove.

The "call-note" is a "caw" emitted from 5 to 10 or more times in slow succession. The bird sits fairly erect on the perch, with the body, head, and tail inclined a little. The beak is very slightly nodded at each caw. This call-note in *Ectopistes* is usually emitted *once* at a time, and it differs very much from the shriller and louder note of attack or threat. I do not now understand how it comes to pass that the hybrid emits its call so many times in succession. Possibly this is a peculiarity from the ring-dove mother. The ring-dove repeats its coo or call (5 to 15 times) when calling on the perch, and takes the same position. This would be a curious mixture of instincts. The ring-dove often repeats the call 15 or more times.

Two of my passenger hybrids have *weak voices;* they are barely able to make the call-note audible. They make the same call in the same way, or attempt to do so, but their vocal organs are too weak or ill-constructed to enable them to vocalize strongly. (R 14).

INSTINCTS IN ECTOPISTES RING-DOVE HYBRIDS.

I placed a pan with earth and earthworms in a pen containing 4 hybrids and 2 adult ring-doves. The four hybrids with their ages and designations, were as follows: *D 2,* 8 weeks less 1 day old; *F 2,* 5 weeks less 2 days old; *G 1,* 4 weeks plus 2 days old; *G 2,* 4 weeks plus 2 days old.

---

[1] See voice of mourning-dove in the following section. If the reader will also further compare this account of the voice and behavior of the hybrid with my account of the behavior of the two parent species, he will be able to form a better idea of the relation between the behavior of the hybrid and that of its parents. (W. C.) (See Craig, W., 1909. The Expressions of Emotion in the Pigeons. 1. The Blond Ring-dove, Journ. Comp. Neurol. and Psychol., vol. 19, pp. 29–80, and 1911. The Expressions of Emotion in the Pigeons. II. The Mourning-Dove, The Auk, vol. 28, pp. 398–407.)

VOICE AND INSTINCT IN PIGEON HYBRIDIZATION AND PHYLOGENY. 119

The oldest hybrid (*D 2*) pecked at some worms lying in sight and tried them several times in his beak as if to test them. Coming to a worm which was nearly buried, and which contracted quickly on being seized, the bird became more eager, and with one or two pulls drew it from its burrow. The bird picked it up several times, dropping it after testing it in end of the beak; it then picked up the worm, taking it farther into its beak as if to swallow it, but again dropped it. At the next trial the worm was swallowed. The same bird soon after swallowed two other worms, and without many trials. *F 2* tried the worms over and over, but did not swallow them. *G 2* swallowed one, after many trials with its beak. *G 1* was in a nest-box at the time, and so did not participate.

The male ring-dove walked back and forth over the pan, but never once stopped to touch a worm. (I later saw a worm eaten by one of my ring-doves.)

Here, then, is a case where the instinct, received from the father, acts independently of imitation. The bird's instinct led it to be attracted by the worm at first sight, and the wriggling of the worm stimulated the bird to snatch it quickly from its burrow, just as the adult *Ectopistes* does.[1] The birds had never before tasted of worms, having been bred under ring-doves and having received only seed and bread.

One of these hybrids escaped from a pen and was not seen for 4 days. At the end of 4 days it came back, and after staying about all the afternoon, it tried to get back into its own pen. I opened the door a few inches and it walked in at once. The wild parent would never have returned; its ring-dove parent would probably have returned. The hybrid has the "home instinct" from its mother, and has it certainly in a higher degree than the father.

The passenger-pigeon, when captured, emits a cry of distress or terror, and struggles hard to escape. If it finds its struggles of no avail, it will soon stop and often *lie motionless* in the hand, *feigning dead*, for some moments after the hand is open. It will lie for nearly a minute on a shelf if left undisturbed. It is a mode of playing dead. The passenger hybrid also emits a shriek on being caught, struggles, and at length remains motionless, as if dead. Its action is therefore like that of the paternal species. This trick may be played by almost any dove, but is more marked in the passenger and its hybrid. (R 14.)

VOICE AND BEHAVIOR IN CERTAIN WILD SPECIES.

VOICE AND SEXUAL BEHAVIOR OF ECTOPISTES.[2]

An adult male ring-dove (*C*) and an *Ectopistes* (*I A*) young, a little over 3 weeks old, were allowed to go free in my library. Both were sitting on top of the pens. *C* began to walk towards *I A*, with a view to driving him off. The latter seeing him coming, emitted at intervals a simple sound, much like a low, mild cluck of a sitting hen. This note is quite different from the scolding note when the bird threatens to attack.

A few minutes later *C* again approached rather slowly and without show of hostility. *I A* gave one cluck, lowering his head, and then emitted the single call which the male gives when calling his mate to nest. This cluck is the "danger-note," or at any rate indistinguishable from it. A little later this same day I heard the danger-note emitted when a bird was seen flying in the distance. Another passenger (*I B*) only 4 weeks old, while sitting on his perch, was approached by a ring-dove. The young pecked at the intruder, and in doing so gave an audible puff of air from its beak, quite the same as one hears in the young domestic pigeon when it is approached by anything strange to it (*e.g.*, a hand). The young *Ectopistes* (*I B*) has not been heard to squeal for some time, but it has not yet,

---

[1] A case of a young passenger (4 weeks, 4 days old) eating earthworms is cited under "Food Instincts," Chapter XII. It is stated that ring-doves eat earthworms "when they have young to feed."—EDITOR.

[2] For more than one reason it seems desirable to preserve these records on the voice and behavior of the now extinct passenger-pigeon. —EDITOR.

BEHAVIOR OF PIGEONS.

at 7 weeks old, given the squawk or cluck, although daily under provocation at feeding and roosting. At the age of 8 weeks I heard it give the danger-note or cluck, but it was not the finished note.

A male passenger (*I A*), 2 years and 7 months old, is in a large pen with a female *Ectopistes*. This male has just been separated for two days from a white ring-dove.[1] He does not court the female of his species, but sits at a corner of his pen, where he can see some ring-doves in cages about 10 feet away, and calls to them. He sets his feathers in best order, and puts on a most charming expression as he eyes them. His "call" consists of two very distinct parts: (1) A loud, shrill, piercing squawk,[2] in uttering which the bird draws back its head and as its beak opens expels all its breath in one effort. Just as the cry is made the wings are flirted upward and forward. The whole performance is precisely the same as the threatening-note. The movements of the wings in this case are a means of attracting attention; while in the threatening mood it appears to be a threat to strike or to fly at the intruder. This loud cry, with wing-flirting, is adopted in calling a bird at some distance, and it is usually followed after a few seconds with a second note. (2) This second part is a single guttural sound, or a sort of awkward "coo," in the making of which the bird raises its head, lengthens its neck, and swells the upper part of it, as if the air were forced into this part without being allowed to escape. Until this morning I never quite caught the manner of the calling. Everything to-day was favorable to seeing and understanding the sequence.

The "behavior in uniting" in the passenger-pigeon is as follows: The female, if disposed, often takes the initiative, giving the call and then hugging the male while she presses with her body against him. He returns the call and the hugging and the billing. He reaches over, so that the front of his neck bears on the back of her neck or the top of her head, and often jerks or pulls her head towards him by means of his beak, which is held like a hook over her head. He may often mount several times before the female is ready. When she is ready she stoops and raises both wings to support him. Sometimes she begins to stoop only after he has mounted, gradually and slowly lowering her body to a horizontal position. The male expects her to raise her tail to contact with his; if she does not at once do this he touches her head with his beak, with a single stroke first on one side then on the other, or touches her beak near the base, as if to make her lower her head and raise her tail. It is more probable, however, that he does this to excite her to the point of responding to his movements. The pressure of the body and neck against the female is to induce her to active participation in the act. The pull with the beak hooked over the head and the side stroke of the beak, as well as the fondling of the head feathers, all tend to excitement, and they are the expression of the sexual impulse.

I have never seen the female put her beak within that of the male, an act so common to other pigeons. The male crested pigeon, as well as the passenger, has often been seen to peck gently the head of the female after mounting, to induce her to raise the tail and lower the head.

A male *Ectopistes*, when standing at a distance of a foot or two from the female, will often emit a loud squawk and rush towards her, and hug her with surprising vigor. When he practices this on another species to whom it is unfamiliar he frightens the bird he would court. I have had a female *Ectopistes* mated with a satinette (*C. domestica* var.) all winter and spring. She had often offered herself in the usual way for her species, but the satinette took the passenger's action to be an attack, and though he usually retreated, he sometimes seized her and shook her. It does not seem as if they would ever understand each other. He is always too gallant to press against her. (R 25.)

---

[1] Since a fledgling he had spent various periods with ring-doves.—EDITOR.

[2] This "squawk" is what I have named the "keck." (See Craig, W., 1911. The Expressions of Emotion in the Pigeons. III. The Passenger Pigeon (*Ectopistes migratorius* Linn.) The Auk, vol. 28, 1900. 408–427). (W. C.)

VOICE AND INSTINCT IN PIGEON HYBRIDIZATION AND PHYLOGENY. 121

VOICE OF THE MOURNING-DOVE (ZENAIDURA CAROLINENSIS).

The male has a low "love-grunt," which he gives when he comes up to the female, or flies to her, in the breeding-season. It is a little greeting given as he struts up to or around his mate.[1]

The author gives a record of the time occupied by 144 "perch-calls" (song or coo) of the mourning-dove, in order to show the contrast with other species and with *Zenaidura* hybrids. This record shows that the perch-calls were given in "strains" or series, varying in length from a series of two calls lasting a fraction of a minute to a series of 34 calls lasting 10 minutes. The interval of time from the beginning of one call to the beginning of the next averages about 15 seconds and is never less than about 12 seconds. This rate is strikingly unlike that of the *Zenaidura* × *risoria* hybrid.

The mourning-dove loses its voice towards the end of August and never tries to coo; or if it is sometimes moved to try, it gives a most ridiculous note, as if its organs of voice were out of tune or as if it had forgotten how to do it. If these doves are kept in the house during October they will, after molting is over, reacquire the full voice in the course of a few weeks. Some males mated with ring-doves were placed in pens in my library on Oct. 1. After a week or two I noticed that they began to try their voices. At first the efforts were feeble and repeated only once or a few times a day. The efforts gradually increased until the bird had a full and penetrating voice, and their calls were then repeated so often and with so much vigor that it often became annoying. This loss and return of voice with the breeding-season is of general occurrence among wild migratory birds that breed only in the summer season; for example, in the cuckoo.[2] (R 34.).

VOICE OF ZENAIDA.

A *Z. vinaceo-rufa*, which had recently lost his mate, gave his "perch-song," or "distance call." This call consists of four coos, as does also the "driving-call" given in $3\frac{1}{2}$ seconds. I have never heard it repeated in long strains, as happens in some other pigeons. The syllables (coos) are of nearly equal length, pitch, volume, quality, etc. The call is very low, as compared with that of the mourning-dove, and is delivered so quietly that it frequently escapes attention, even at a distance of only a few yards. The male's "nest-call" is a low, single, abrupt, hoarse muffled note—a *cuh* cut short and barely audible.

In calling a female to the nest a male lowered his head, raised his tail and rump feathers, spread the tail somewhat with each call, and gently vibrated one or both wings, according to occasion. He was very slow in his movements and took great care not to approach the female, as if he wished to avoid giving her the least alarm. He would jump into the nest-box when she alighted on it and quietly try to win her to his side. His eyes then beamed with delight; he would very quietly change his position and move his wings to invite her closer. If she hesitated he would quietly walk away, fly to the perch, and upon alighting would strike the perch or nest-box two or three times quickly with his feet. This striking, done mostly when the female is at a distance on the floor, seems to be a quiet way of attracting attention. The same is done by the mourning-dove.

The call to the young to be fed (call to feed, or "feed-call," as it may be named) is, so far as I can see, exactly the same as the perch-song. The voice of *Zenaida* is, then, a simpler form than that of *Zenaidura;* but it is easy to see that the mourning-dove has a

---

[1] This is evidently the homologue of the "kah" used as a greeting by *Turtur* and *Streptopelia*. In *Zenaidura* it is so greatly reduced that I never heard it myself.—W. C.)

[2] It is much to be regretted that the circumstances of the preparation of this volume have precluded references to Prof. F. H. Herrick's studies on instinct and behavior in birds; included in those studies is a very able presentation of the behavior of the cuckoo. (O. R.)

122 BEHAVIOR OF PIGEONS.

voice modified from the *Zenaida* type of four similar, smooth, even syllables.[1] The first two syllables in *Zenaidura* are together equal to the first in *Zenaida* and they are continuous. I think, therefore, they should be counted as one from the point of view of their origin.

A female *Zenaida amabilis* (?) seems to give a "nest-call" (heard twice so far) that resembles the first syllable (a short initial note followed by a slurred rise in pitch) of the perch-call or song of the male mourning-dove, although it is not so strong. The sound is decidedly similar to that of the mourning-dove in quality and inflection. This bird is higher then in voice and in white bar of wing than *Z. vinaceo-rufa*. (R 2.)

VOICE AND BEHAVIOR OF THE WHITE-WINGED PIGEON (MELOPELIA LEUCOPTERA).

A dozen of the white-wings were kept in the house during the winter. Matings began about the first of January, but with no very serious efforts to nest. About the middle of January 2 or 3 pairs were mated, and these pairs became pugnacious and savage towards the others, almost killing one of them. I then removed from the pen all except 2 pairs; these can probably remain in the same pen, as they have already claimed nest-boxes in opposite corners of the pen. It is interesting to see ownership of nest-territory develop and the disposition to drive away every intruder. The behavior is rather remarkable in this species, as the bird makes demonstrations of its temper with voice, bristling feathers, and especially by peculiar jerks of its tail. To its mate it turns with the utmost fondness and gentleness, even while showing its spiteful scolding and threatening twitches of the tail to an outsider.

When another bird approaches, both sexes manifest their displeasure by jerking the tail up and down—spreading it more or less—and with spiteful quickness with each upward toss. At the same time the bird "bristles up" so to speak, erecting especially the mid-dorsal (interscapular) feathers, so as to give itself a larger and more formidable appearance. It seems to be consciously striving to look as big and fierce as possible, in order to strike terror into the transgressor. The warlike attitude, the fierce look, the erect feathers, the vicious flashy jerks of the tail are reinforced by a spiteful "note of warning." This note I am unable to describe satisfactorily. It is a querulous, fretful snarl, designed to warn off the intruder. If the threat is not heeded, the bird follows it up with a jump toward the offender—a bluff to try its courage. If it retreats the bird dashes boldly after it; if it stands its ground the wings are raised and the birds approach and settle the matter by blows.

When this warning-note or snarl is emitted the beak is slightly opened, so that one can see between the mandibles. I am not sure that the note is to warn. If other birds are in the neighborhood it is uttered frequently as the bird moves about. It may be merely an expression of the fretful state of mind excited by the sight of an intruder. The note is certainly an element in the behavior of the bird, and it fits well with all the other elements which are plainly of a warning nature. The note may be of a similar nature to the note of the Japanese turtle, which is given as the bird strikes at another with its beak. The white-faced pigeon (*Leucosarcia*) raises its tail, lowers the head, and gives a peculiar sound when it threatens to attack. The bleeding-heart pigeon (*Phlogœnas*) takes a similar attitude and gives a similar warning noise before attacking, from which I conclude as to the relationship of these genera.

The "general call" or "coo" is often heard after dark in the early evening, as I learned when these birds were in a large outdoor pen. Both sexes give this call, but the females

---

[1] The attitude of *Zenaida* in uttering this call is essentially the same as that of *Zenaidura*. The bird stands stiffly still with the neck somewhat arched; there is no movement, except that with each coo the crop swells out greatly and the feathers all round the neck are somewhat raised. The general behavior, the attitudes, and gestures of *Zenaida* are much as in *Zenaidura*; for example, the habit of jerking the head, the "nod," consisting of a backward jerk of the head followed by an upward jerk of the tail, with the tail coming slowly down again. (W. C.)

VOICE AND INSTINCT IN PIGEON HYBRIDIZATION AND PHYLOGENY. 123

coo with less fullness, more awkwardly, and more as if it were a lost art with them. The coo of the male is often quite melodious and flute-like in timbre.

The "nest-call" of the male is of 5 syllables—3 in the first half and 2 in the second half. It is very hard to describe this. It often sounds like a low barking—an individual growl (first syllable) followed by the first two barks (second and third syllables), emitted in connection with rising emphasis on the second bark; then follows a closing part—two barks in close connection and with falling inflection, with the final bark somewhat prolonged. The whole call is accurately measured in each syllable, so that there is a certain kind of melody, or at least rhythmic regularity, in the call. The first syllable is really the initial vocalization—a sort of start necessary to the emission of the succeeding notes—flowing directly into the two dissyllables, into which the call proper is divided. The call proper, then, can be said to consist of two distinct parts, each of which is composed of two syllables, and these are preceded by an initial note which serves to set up the regular rhythm.[1]

With the first half of the nest-call the male commonly momentarily raises both wings, slightly spreading them as he spreads his upraised tail. The effect of his white wing-marks and of the white bar of the tail is thus made quite striking. I notice that when the female is out of sight this lifting of the wings is often omitted, and that when the female approaches the nest the male at once shows all his colors. *There is then an evident desire to display to the female.* (R 31.)

SUMMARY.

The turtle-doves of the Old World (*T. orientalis* and *T. turtur*) are considered the nearest of the living species to the ancestral dove or pigeon. Pigeons belonging to families different from the turtle-doves are noted as having one or another degree of the elements of the voice and the behavior of the turtle-dove. It is only in these comparisons, however, that any considerable description of the voice or behavior of the Japanese and European turtle-doves is given. The degree or order of relationship to the turtle-doves, of the species most referred to in this volume, is figured in condensed form at the beginning of the chapter.

In hybridization, the voice and instincts of the parents are blended in the hybrid, the latter possessing voice and behavior intermediate to those of the parental species. Numerous examples are given. They are to be found in the descriptions of all the hybrids, from the close and from the wide crosses. The data of the manuscripts do not, however, consider the second generation of hybrids. It is an open question, therefore, whether the elements of voice and behavior blend or segregate there. It seems to be a rule that the voices of hybrids are less smooth—more hoarse and less coördinated than those of pure-breds. The description of nearly every hybrid considered refers to this fact.

Various features of the pigeon voice and behavior, as exhibited in the different species or groups, are homologized; in some cases conclusions are drawn as to the lower and higher members of a group; and additional descriptions of the voice and behavior of a number of species are given.

---

[1] The "voice" of the bronze-wing (*Phaps*) is given in considerable detail in Chapters II, V, and VI. The material was thus divided and used because of its relation to topics in those chapters.—EDITOR.

CHAPTER XI.

THE HOMING INSTINCT.

Besides the material given in this chapter, several of the author's manuscripts contain quotations and digests, with running comments thereon, from the writings of Reynaud, Wood, Moore, Mills, Wallace, Kobelt, Gatke, Weismann, Gourand, Jacobi, and Palmen, on the migration, orientation, and homing instinct of birds. These comments are hardly of such a nature as to warrant their utilization. In addition there are a few rough outline notes of the author's, and the following list of animals under the title of "cases of migration": (1) herring, shad, whitefish, salmon, eels; (2) fishes, toads, *Amblystoma*, turtles, seals (Lemming); (3) *a*, Stork; *b*, swallow, robin, flicker, larger woodpecker of Europe; *c*, homer-carriers, turtle-dove, wood-pigeon, *Ectopistes*, mourning-dove; *d*, ducks, geese, terns, gulls, eider-duck (Weismann); (4) Grasshopper (locusts), ants, caterpillars (Loeb), *Nereis*. It is apparent from this list, and the accompanying notes and comment, that the author contemplated an extended study of the phylogeny of migration and homing, similar to his phylogenetic treatment of the incubation instinct as given in Chapter VIII. For a further study of this subject the above list is helpfully suggestive.

GENERAL PRINCIPLES.

A discussion of the "homing instinct" is perhaps not without its value.[1] People are inclined to believe that there is something mysterious in regard to the homing instinct in the birds, perhaps a "sixth sense," a "sense of direction," or something of that sort. The way to find out whether a homer pigeon has any unusual instinct or unusual sense, is, of course, to make a test of the case, and this is very easily done.

In considering such tests, let us suppose that some homers have been kept in a pen, with no opportunity to fly about and see the country, and that this lack of opportunity has extended from the time they were hatched up to an age of a few months or a year; and that these homers were then let out into a small yard—a yard as extensive as a large room. One would think that a bird might find its way in a yard of that size, even if it had not been there before, particularly if it had always been looking out into such a yard from its smaller pen. I have repeatedly made experiments of this kind, and have found that the behavior of the birds is, in all cases, practically the same. They never seem to know what to do when they get out into this small yard. They are in a new world. The only world they know anything about is the small pen on the side of the yard. They had looked out upon this main yard daily, for months, but they have never traveled around it nor used their wings in getting from one pen to another; they have used their wings only in the small cage. The moment you let them out they smooth down their feathers and act as though they were afraid. Every step is taken with caution. They look around to see what everything means before they venture to feel that it is safe to go over it; they step around on the ground very, very cautiously indeed, and act as though they were in a new world.

---

[1] Stenographic notes (corrected and edited) on a lecture delivered at Woods Hole, Aug. 10, 1906. The questions of the audience and their answers have been, in so far as this was possible, incorporated into the text.—EDITOR.

BEHAVIOR OF PIGEONS.

If the birds thus released happen to be an old pair, with young or eggs to look after, they naturally want to attend to these at the regular times. Let us suppose that we now deal with a bird that wants to get back to its cage—a male at 10 o'clock, the time the male usually goes to the nest. At that time he will show an uneasiness and will try to find his nest; he will try by flying up to get to it, but will not know the right way to go. So he will fly hither and thither to many places, and it will sometimes seem a matter of accident if he happens to get to the right door. As soon as he gets to the right door, where he can readily see what he has been familiar with, he will go to his nest as quickly as possible and take his position.

My conclusion, from all that I have seen in the case of pigeons, is that they have no means of finding their homes excepting their *wings* and *eyesight* and *experience*. Eyesight and experience are the principal things. Pigeons have very, very sharp eyesight. Anyone who has watched pigeons in the yard has noticed how quickly they see a hawk in the air. They are always far quicker than I am in that respect, and even I can always tell when a hawk is around by the behavior of the pigeons; they are looking in the direction of the hawk, and I often find that the hawk is so high up that it is difficult to see; in fact, I may have to hunt around for it. The pigeons see it immediately, and if there are many of them about, they all seem to see it at the same time. There is no hesitation in the matter.

We may consider for a moment the method used in training homing pigeons. As you know, they are allowed their freedom and they are birds that like to fly about. They take high flights and long flights, they become acquainted with the country round about. They evidently recognize the mountains and the houses and know these houses one from another, just as well as we know individuals. Then, for training, such birds are taken a certain number of miles from home and have no difficulty in finding their way back. The next time they are taken in the *same direction* a number of miles farther. They have had a good deal of experience on the first trip, having circled round and round and taken in everything. They have good memories, and when you take them 10 miles farther they really catch the landmarks that they have seen before, and also become acquainted with landmarks in other directions; so that in this way their acquaintance with the country, far and near, is extended. The next time they are taken farther away in the same direction, and the birds are thus gradually trained, trained in the country, directions, etc. It is evidently this sort of experience that they depend upon in finding the way home.

I may give you an instance of a bird's memory. I had a pair of homers that I took from Chicago to Woods Hole, Massachusetts, and left them there during the winter. The next year I took them back. In the year of their absence I had moved my residence some 7 or 8 blocks from the home where these birds had spent several years. In taking them back to Chicago I took them to the new home. I kept them for some time in the basement of my home, since the pens were not ready to receive them; a little later, probably some time in January, I finally put them in a cot in the barn. Here they went to work and made a nest, laid their eggs, and started incubation. I thought it would then be quite safe to let them out; so I opened the cot and the birds were permitted to come out. The two birds stayed on the cot stand for a few seconds, took a few looks in different directions, and then, of a sudden, they both started and went straight down to the old home, 7 or 8 blocks away; and they did not return. They left their eggs, although they wanted to take care of those eggs as much as any parent birds would care for that. I went down to the old home and found them on the top of the house. The pens that they used to live in had all been destroyed and there was nothing except the house for them to recognize as their home. A few days later I managed to get the male bird down and into a cage. I may note that I left these birds for two or three days before I undertook to capture them again. The female was lost, was perhaps killed by a cat. But I succeeded, as noted above, in getting the male down into the cage. I put some seed into his cage, and after some time gave him

THE HOMING INSTINCT.   127

another female that was ready to mate. He accepted her and they went to work. He was then put into the same dove-cote as before. This time he apparently decided it was best to stay and he did not go back to his old home again.

On several different summers I have taken my birds from Chicago to Woods Hole, and I find those that have been to the latter place before have no trouble whatever in remembering where they were previously located; that is, whether on the west side of the barn or on the east side, or the south or north. The dove-cote holes are in different places and it is very curious to watch a bird and see him go straight back to his old home; even the manner of flying down from the roof of the house to his cot is simply a repetition of what he has done hundreds of times before. He takes the proper precaution, if his mate is out of sight, comes down and alights on the dove-stand, just as perfectly as he did it a year before. I am inclined to think these birds have as good a memory as we have.

The question of the relation of inheritance to behavior may next be briefly considered. In the first place, it may be said that the behavior of pigeons is inherited just as much as anything else is inherited; and, with the proper qualifications, the same may be said for the behavior of the homing pigeons. I should not, of course, claim that the pigeon inherits "the want to find its way"; it inherits "the way to learn." The young bird in the nest is a homer from the beginning. He sits in the nest and has a home-like air. Let him be taken away, only a little away, and he is frightened and wants to get back. As soon as he gets into the nest he feels at home. Very soon after they get their feathers the young birds begin to get out of the nest. First of all, they get to the ends of the cot where they live—just experimenting; but if any noise is made, anything that startles them, you see them hustling back to the boxes in which they have lived. In the same way they learn their way out of the dove-cote. They look out of the window first and then they venture to step out on the platform and sit there a second or two the first time; the second time they are less fearful, sit longer, shake their wings, etc., and then get back. Perhaps the next day they sit longer, and after 2 or 3 days they venture to fly down. They see the old birds and recognize them on the stand, and are afforded a pretty good chance of finding their way back in that way. Usually they are pretty careful not to get more than a few feet away. They really learn every step of their way. The homing instinct is something that is perfectly natural to them. (SS 10.)

On this topic the editor appends the following quotation from Fulton (*op. cit.* pp. 438-40):

"It has been frequently and vigorously contended that the birds "home"—as it is termed—by instinct pure and simple; also, that instinct has nothing to do with their power of homing at all, but that the sight alone enables them to reach their lofts. Various other theories have been started, as that they will only fly to the north; but the true theory doubtless is that it is partly instinct and, partly sight, intelligence, and memory. I say *partly* instinct advisedly, though probably many on reading thus far only would be ready to combat the idea. The mainspring of the resolute action of the homing bird in endeavoring to reach its home is, no doubt, the natural love of home, which is shared in by all the homing pigeons, and this I term instinct. As far as one can tell by careful observation, *every* homing bird, when thrown, endeavors to find its home at first. It stretches its neck as it flies round—or even if it pitches on some neighboring roof—in its apparent endeavor to ascertain which direction it ought to make for. This, which is developed in every bird, surely may properly be called instinct.

"It is the same with dogs, cats, horses, cattle. It is, in fact on record that a race was once carried out with cats, which were taken away from their homes and let loose; with dogs it is an everyday occurrence. And it is well known that cattle, when escaped from a field—at a distance from home—will often beat about, until at last they walk into the homestead. But though this instinct may cause all the birds thrown at one time and place to endeavor to reach their respective homes, it does not enable them all to attain success. When they have started—and done their best to find out which way to go—instinct seems to have run its course.

128   BEHAVIOR OF PIGEONS.

"All these birds, then, having probably—as I contend—the same instinct, have used it for the same purpose, and to the same end. But now come upon the scene other forces, namely, memory, intelligence, and observation. These enable a bird to remember the localities in which it has been flown before, to recognize landmarks it has noticed previously, and which are now pointed out to it by an intelligent observation of the country beneath it. Thus it is seen that though all may start fair, as it were, at first, still those endowed with the more retentive memory, the greatest intelligence, and the most accurate power of observation will, *cæteris paribus*, come home first. The instinct, then—being naturally present to a certain given extent—forms a basis upon which man can work; and the materials to be used in the work are the memory, intelligence, and power of observation. These must be educated, improved, perfected by man's labour and toil, in order to obtain a first-class bird. What one has to do, then, in training, is to give the birds a good knowledge of locality by repeated and ever-increasing trials, which will try the endurance of the bird as well as bring its gifts to perfection, and in doing so the greatest care is needed. . . . .

"Having selected the birds one wishes to train, they must be taken out in a box or basket to be thrown the first time. The distance should not be more than 500 or 600 yards, and the time morning, as early as you like. The birds should be hungry, not voracious, but just nicely hungry, so that when home they may come into the loft to feed at once. A nice, clear, tolerably still day should be selected for each throw when commencing to train, if possible, in order to give the young birds every advantage. They may then be taken the next day, or as soon as convenient, but the sooner the better, to the same distance, in another direction, and so on until they have been sent in four, or at least three, directions around their home. This done, the distance may be doubled, and again sent to the four points of the compass. They will next be taken a mile or a mile and half in each direction, and by this time will have a pretty general acquaintance with the country immediately adjacent to their home in all directions. . . . .

"The Belgian method of training is pretty much the same as described above, except that the stages are, after fifty miles, exceedingly severe, the birds being sent fifty, a hundred, and even more miles at a single stage, but the losses among these birds are likewise proportionately heavy in bad weather. Some of the best lofts in Belgium have been fearfully depopulated at a single stage."

ILLUSTRATIVE MATERIAL.

MEMORY.

Under the title of "Memory," the editor finds an account of seven pairs of birds that had lived at Woods Hole, Massachusetts, and at the author's former home in Chicago. On returning from Woods Hole in the autumn of 1901, these birds were taken to a new Chicago home, at a distance of several blocks from their former home. In the following spring they were allowed to nest, and they were given their freedom while incubating eggs. The account describes their behavior in these novel surroundings. These records constitute in large part the basis for the preceding discussion of the homing instinct.

By way of further introduction, the editor may note that memory for home was shown by pairs which were carried back and forth between Chicago and Woods Hole. The oldest pair of common pigeons knew their cots, both at Woods Hole and in Chicago, and never got lost or confused. They seemed quite at home when let out in either place, although, for a few minutes, they showed that they had not forgotten the place from which they were last moved. Other pairs, let out for the first time, got lost, confused, and were often unable to find their nest within a small yard.

(1) A pair of homers was taken from my former home in Chicago to Woods Hole, in June 1900, and left there until October 1901. They were returned to my new home in Chicago, and kept in a pen in the back yard, where they nested. They had young about 10 days old when I removed them to a cot newly prepared in the barn. After keeping them and their young shut up in the cot for two days, I opened the cot and let them out on the morning of the third day. I saw both birds come out soon; within one-half of a

THE HOMING INSTINCT. 129

minute they started off in the direction of their former home (during winters), which was about 5 blocks away. They did not return, but went off for good, not even coming back to the young. The next day I found the male sitting contentedly on the barn of a neighbor, close to our (former) back yard, where he formerly had his pen. The pens had all been removed, so he had only the buildings with which to locate his home. I did not see his mate, but think she may have been near by. This pair had then been away from their old winter home for fully 1 year and 7 months. Nevertheless they (or he) still knew his home, after all the dove-cotes and pens had been removed. This is a decided proof of memory of home and its environment. This homer is at least 6 years old, possibly 7 years.

On Jan. 14, 1902, I took two cages to our former home. In one of these cages was a female homer; in the other I placed a dish of seed. The cages were placed in the back yard, and the escaped male soon came down and went into the open cage for the seed, and was easily captured and returned. There is no mistake about identity; the bird could be recognized among a hundred, by his size, shape, and evident age, as well as by his behavior. When returned to his deserted cot he felt at once at home and began to coo. This male was placed in the same cot from which it had flown away, and shut in.

Five days later this male homer was placed with a young female homer (hatched in 1901) that was ready to mate. The mating was immediate, and two eggs were laid on Feb. 6 and 8. On Feb. 10, at noon, when the male was sitting, I opened the cot. The female had never been free and she came out only very cautiously, first stretching out the neck and putting her head out just enough to see the other birds flying about. Finally, she came out trembling, and stepping as if possessed with fear. She saw other doves above her on the stands, and soon ventured to fly up to one of the stands. *She did not once look back into her own hole before she left her stand,* so she is not likely to recognize it easily. She is now ($1^h 40^m$ p.m.) on the roof of the barn, and has taken no flight. At 3 p.m. she found her way to her own stand and her mate came out, and then she followed him in. She took the nest and he came out again. The male went out and in three times within 2 minutes. The fourth time he flew to another stand, went in and fought with its inmates, claiming it as his own, until I drove him out. He flew to the roof of the barn, to the top of the court, to the top of the pens beneath his stand, walked about, and took one short circle around the barn and pens. His behavior is quite different from what it was when let out with his former mate. Now he has a new mate, a new cot, and a new nest of eggs, and he is wholly intent in caring for them, having no desire to fly away. At $3^h 30^m$, seeking for his cot, he flew to a stand above him and rushed in the hole as if it were his own, and battled with the owners until I parted them and put him back in his own cot, where he remained without coming out. The two cots are exactly alike, so that it is not strange that he made the mistake of claiming the wrong place. He remained in the rest of the day, not coming out. At this season of the year all the dove-cote pigeons return to the cot by 4 p.m., or even earlier if they are not hungry or thirsty.

On the second day (Feb. 11) both birds were out and in their cot and perfectly contented. The male tried once during the morning to take possession of the cot above him, and had to be taken out and replaced in his own place. Since then he has remained at home.

(2) A second pair of homers were hatched on Apr. 26 and Mar. 26, 1900, at our former home. They are the offspring of the pair whose conduct has already been described. They were placed in a cot in the barn (Jan. 6, 1902), and here laid an egg on Jan. 13. Just before the second egg was expected, on the 15th at about $12^h 30^m$ p. m., I opened the door of the cot. Both birds soon came out on the stand and looked cautiously about; soon the male flew down to the roof of the pens, about 4 feet below, and the female soon followed, flying *heavily,* as birds do when carrying an egg soon to be laid. The birds then soon flew up to the roof of the barn, and after running about as if to find their nest—but shyly, as if realizing that they were not on familiar ground—they flew off, the female behind the male, across the street to the house on the south. The male soon started back with the female

130   BEHAVIOR OF PIGEONS.

after him; they stopped on my house, where they saw my male frill-back. They took three flights away, the second time about 2 blocks away, and the third time they escaped from sight, but returned after about 30 minutes. It was then 4 p.m. They searched about to find their nest, but in vain. The female sat down on the roof of the pens, and I caught her without difficulty and placed her in a cage on the ground. The male came to her, was caught, and both were replaced in the cot; the female at once took the nest. I left the cot open, and the next morning the male came out about 7 o'clock and after a few minutes went in. He did this three times in the course of a half hour, and then seemed to be content, remaining inside on the nest; meanwhile the female walked about, or sat still on the perch in the cot, not once coming out, although she once came to the door and looked out. At 10^h 30^m a. m., both were inside the cot, and apparently contented.

Evidently this pair (kept at our former home, during the winter of 1901) did not discover their old winter home, and were not so keenly oriented as the older birds. Still, had the female been unimpeded by the egg she carried, the birds might have discovered the old home. The return to my present home was insured by their having walked about and seen the premises before they first flew away, and probably by their seeing my frill-back. One return made the next more probable. The birds have not yet learned to find their cot; but will probably do so in the course of to-day, the third day after their first egg was laid.

(3) A third pair, which consisted of two frill-backs, hatched in the spring of 1901, had been kept in pens from the time they could fly, in Chicago and in Woods Hole. I placed them in a cot in the barn at my later Chicago home on Jan. 14, 1902. Two days later, at about 1 p.m., I opened the door of the cot. The birds soon came out, but did not act as shy or as keenly sensitive to strangeness of the place as did the homers. They were awkward in flight, somewhat like young birds that have just begun to fly. The important point is that they appeared to have no memory of a home elsewhere, and they made *no sign of a desire to find a lost home*, not making a single attempt to fly away or to circle about in search. After being out for a couple of hours *they did try to find a cot*, and the male succeeded, after looking for some time on the wrong side of the barn, by seeing another frill-back with a cot next to his fly to his stand. He merely followed, but was driven off by the other frill-back, and so did not really discover the way to his cot, although he recognized it after landing on the stand. After being driven off, he went back to his mate on the south side of the barn. Both birds soon flew to the stands on the south side of the barn, and I caught the female and returned her to her cot (about 3^h 30^m p.m.), where she remained without venturing out again for the day. The male, in his search for her, soon flew to his own stand, after trying several others, and once there, he saw his mate through the window, and then soon found his way through the hole into his cot. He then began cooing and strutting and appeared fully satisfied and even delighted with his home. Since the first day they have held possession.

Here we see an absence of any *memory* of home. The birds know no home but a pen. Coming near a pen, they seemed to regard it as a place they know, but they did not try to reach it. This species is a fully domesticated one, and probably they would never have a liking for a particular home equal to that of homers.

(4) A pair of red-chequered homers, bought in the spring of 1901, were kept confined in a pen at our former home, until I took them to Woods Hole, at the end of June. They were returned to Chicago to our new home in October 1901. They were kept in a pen in the basement until Jan. 8, 1902, when I placed them in a cot, in the barn, on the "south side." On Jan. 14 the female laid the first egg; the second was laid 2 days later. Two days still later, at 3 p.m., I opened the cot; the female was sitting, and the male was off the nest. He soon took the nest without coming out. She came out to the stand at 3^h 30^m, paused a minute or two, looking, and stretching once, and then went in without flying. She came out on the stand again at 3^h 35^m, went in again without flying, after looking for a moment,

THE HOMING INSTINCT.

but at once came out again, and soon flew down to the roof of the pens (2 feet below). At 3^h 49^m she flew up to the top of the barn. A male homer—of another pair—was the only dove out at the time. At 3^h 50^m, she flew down to the court, just as her mate was driving the other homer off his stand. Her mate went to his nest at 3^h 55^m, the female having flown to the stand above him. At 3^h 56^m she came down again on the roof of the pens. At 3^h 58^m she flew to the highest stand on the "east side" of the barn. At 4 she again flew to the roof of the barn, and in a moment came down to the court on the south side. At 4^h 01^m she was on the stand above her own. At 4^h 11^m, she went to the rear shed, thence to her own stand, and in at once.

These birds have no memory of a home in Chicago, and their memory of their home in Woods Hole does not suffice to send them flying at any distance. The nest is now a strong attraction, and perhaps they are themselves more like highly domesticated pigeons, which have less love for a particular home.

(5) I allowed a pair of black barbs to go free at our former home, took them to Woods Hole at the end of June, and brought the male and two young back to our new home in October. The female died at Woods Hole. One young was black, the other was gray with two black bars. The black one turned out to be a female, and she mated with her sire. I placed the pair in a cot on the south side of the barn on Jan. 16, 1902. Three days later I opened the cot at 10^h 30^m a.m. *The birds had no eggs.* The female came out on the stand at 10^h 40^m. She looked shy, stretched her neck, but went back in a few moments, the male remaining within. She came out again at 10^h 44^m, but went back after one or two looks. Then the male came out at 10^h 44^m, but went back after one or two looks. Then the male came out at 10^h 45^m, and was soon followed by the female. He went in at 10^h 46^m and immediately came out again and flew down to the roof of the rear pens at 10^h 47^m, and then to the roof of the barn, flapping his wings for exercise. He then came down to the court and the female flew to him. At 10^h 48^m both were on the roof of the barn, the female following the male; at 10^h 50^m both were on the court and walked to the rear roof of the pens, the male leading. At 10^h 51^m he flew to his stand, and was followed by the female after a moment. He went in, came out, then went in, and was followed this time by the female. Both came out again at 10^h 54^m, the male flying down to the roof of the pens, being followed by the female.

Both seem contented, but the female, never before free, seems very timid, while the male walks with assurance, but as if examining his new environment. At 10^h 57^m, both flew to an adjoining barn, and came back to the north-side roof of my barn. The female always hesitates to alight on a new place, stopping a moment or two before venturing to touch her feet. At 11^h 30^m they flew away, but soon came back to the barn, where they sat for the remainder of the forenoon. I found them both on their own stand at 1 p.m. and apparently fully contented.

(6) A pair of homers was allowed their freedom at our former home during the years 1900 and 1901, and at Woods Hole during July and August 1901. The pair was returned to our new home at the end of August 1901, and kept in an outside pen until Jan. 8, 1902. Eggs were laid in a cot on Jan. 18 and 20. This was opened at 10^h 30^m a. m., on Jan. 22. The male remained on the nest. The female came out again, and in course of an hour flew from the barn to the house and back in company with the other birds. At 11^h 30^m she is on a stand on the east end of the barn and shows every sign of contentment. Evidently, if birds have a nest with eggs and only one comes out at a time, there is little danger of their going away.

(7) Another pair of homers had been free, both at Woods Hole and at our former Chicago home. They were placed in a cot in a barn at our new home on Jan. 19, 1902. Eggs were laid on Feb. 3 and 5. The cot was opened at 3^h 15^m p. m. on Feb. 12, on the ninth day of incubation. The male was on the nest and the female came out and flew around and went back to the cot at 3^h 40^m p. m. The male then came out and twice got into the wrong

132 BEHAVIOR OF PIGEONS.

cot and had to be returned to his own home. On the day following he failed to find his cot and was thus prevented from sitting during the middle of the day. Again, on the next day, he became lost and did not return until 4 p. m. (R 9.)

ORIENTATION.

A pair of black common pigeons were put in a cot in the barn on May 1, 1907. They were fastened in until they made a nest and laid eggs (May 5). About 10 days later I put up a small wire cage (2 feet by 15 inches by 18 inches high) on the shelf to their cot, and so placed that its open door was close to the cot-hole. The birds could go in and out of this wire cage at pleasure. Of course, when out of this cage, they could become acquainted with the yard, the rear of the house, the dove-pens, and their neighbors in the adjoining cots to right and left, above and below. Their cot was in the second tier from below. On the evening of June 3, after dark, I removed the cage, leaving free egress from their cot.

At 5 o'clock the next morning it was dark and rainy, and these common pigeons had not left the cot. The male was on the young; the female soon came out and walked inquisitively about, as if missing the cage. Soon she came down and fed on the ground with the other pigeons, to which I had thrown seed. After a time she felt like returning, but flew to the roof of the barn, and appeared wholly at sea, although her cot was but 10 or 12 feet below. She tried several shelves, and in the course of 30 minutes reached her own shelf, by mere accident. She was not then sure of her place, but, peering into the hole, she saw her mate and went in. Soon afterward the male came out and, after behaving as if in a strange place, flew to the roof. Later the female came out and flew to the yard for food; the mate recognized her and followed. After eating and walking about the yard, she flew up and tried to find her cot. She succeeded only after blundering a little less than in the first instance. The male followed her up, but went to the roof, and found his way back about 11 a. m. Then both birds came out together, spent a half hour in the yard, and then flew to the roof of the house and to the barn. About 4 p. m. I found both in the cot above them and to the north. They fought for this cot, but at length were beaten off. After some more searching they found their cot and remained with it. At $5^h 35^m$ p. m. the female came out and flew down to feed. After 10 or 15 minutes she returned, going straight to her shelf. The cage made these birds somewhat at home in the yard, so that they *did not start off on long flights;* but they still could not steer to a cot, and were as if in a world from which no lines to their cot had ever been impressed upon their brains. The essentials for finding home were not there, and they were slowly and blunderingly discovered by accidental hits, which they were impelled to make by the need of relief from their stock of food for their young. (R 10.)

HOME INSTINCT.

The following records are found in several manuscripts under the title of "Home Instinct." They refer to the conduct of birds in confinement that were given their freedom or that had succeeded in escaping from their pens.

All my geopelias seem to be fairly sure not to go away when they escape singly. What they would do if two got out at the same time I do not know. But when one alone escapes, it always returns in search of its companions, and I have succeeded in recapturing them in every case. The social instinct is strong with them, and I believe this instinct is the foundation of the home instinct; that is, given the social instinct, the home instinct would inevitably follow, natural selection aiding its development.

One of my crested pigeons got away at Woods Hole and never returned. Whether the social instinct in this species would enable one to let the bird have its freedom safely I do not know. I think it might in case the bird was very tame.

One of my mourning-doves, which was mated with a ring-dove, got out of its cage; it stayed near for a short time, cooing for its mate. Soon it flew off and did not return. I

THE HOMING INSTINCT. 133

believe this dove could easily be trained to come home. I have a very tame one which escaped and flew back to my hand. Another escaped and could not be found for some hours, but was then discovered trying to get back into its pen.

A beautiful hybrid between a male homer and a Japanese turtle (*Turtur orientalis*) escaped and was gone for two whole days before it returned. When it came back I was standing in the yard. It flew down to the pens and at once recognized its own pen from others and tried to get in. It was evidently hungry. I opened a pen door and soon drove it in and captured it.

A hybrid between a male passenger and a ring-dove escaped from its pen. It flew at once into a *tree*. Soon after, it started on a straight, swift flight away from home and was quickly out of sight. I never expected to see it again. About noon of the same day it was found sitting over one of the pens and was captured. This return could not have been due to the instincts of the *paternal* species, for the wild pigeon would never return. Another similar hybrid returned after an absence of 4 days.[1]

A male mourning-dove from California, which had been kept in confinement for two years, escaped from the pen in Woods Hole on July 2. He stayed about the pens and roosted near his own pen. Some one tried to capture him after dark and failed. It flew off and was not seen for 5 days. On July 8 he came into the yard and fed with the other doves on the ground. I allowed him his freedom for two days, during which time he remained about the yard, and then again captured him and put him in a pen. I think the bird would have remained with me, if nothing had happened to drive him away. The same bird escaped again on July 24. I caught him at night when he was on the ground beside a pen, and put him in the shed, leaving him to go free when the door was opened the next morning. He loitered about a pen in which another male mourning-dove was kept and fancied he had found a mate. Probably he might fly away were there no other mourning-doves about to coo and thus attract him. As it is, he stays by all day.

One of my white-winged pigeons (*Melopelia leucoptera*) escaped and flew into the willow behind the house. It was about 4 o'clock. She sat there in the same place until $5^h 30^m$, then flew over the pen to a tree behind a neighbor's house. About 6 o'clock she again flew, but passed over the pens and up over the roof of a large house a block away. I never expected to see the bird again. In about 5 minutes the bird was found trying to get into the pen from which it escaped. She tried in vain, and finally took a position for the night in the outer door, where a pane of glass had been broken. There was an inner door which prevented her going further. After dark I went up and captured her. The bird had been kept in the house all winter and had been in the outside pen only about 2 weeks.

Four *Zenaida vinaceo-rufa* escaped on Sept. 9. One of these was an old bird, and 3 were birds hatched during the summer and had finished or nearly finished the first molt. They escaped from a pen in which I had 17 zenaidas and hybrids. The rest of the flock was isolated in an adjoining pen, and the feed-door of their own pen was left open in the hope they would enter. One was caught on Sept. 11, after it had entered a small cage to get seed left there to entice it. One was caught in a small cage on Sept. 15, after being out for 6 days. Two Japanese turtle × European turtle hybrids escaped at the same time. One of these was seen the next day, but up until Sept. 17, I have not seen either again. One naked-eyed pigeon (*Columba guinea?*) escaped at the same time. It returned the same day, walked into the barn, and was easily captured.

A female ring-dove which had just left its nest—about 8 a. m.—to the male was allowed to come out of its pen in the back yard. I opened wide the door, thinking that as the bird had a nest and as she was due to lay a second egg that morning she would not go away. She flew to the ground, and after a minute or so up into the large willow; after a few minutes she flew to an adjoining house, soon returned to the willow, but a few minutes later flew over the same adjoining house and was not seen again. This same pair had had their free-

10   [1] This case was described in Chapter X.

dom during all of the summer at Woods Hole and had never lost their home. In the present case it was evident that the female lost her bearings and did not know how to find her nest. This seems strange, as the other doves were cooing loud. She was in haste to get back to her nest when she flew out of sight. This shows that one must proceed very carefully in liberating these birds in a city, where all the houses are so much alike that the bird can not distinguish. Once out of sight of the nest the bird is lost. If she is let out when she is young she will be more cautious, and if the male is with her he will help her to find her way back. Had I taken care to teach this bird to find her nest once or twice, she would then have got on all right.

It is an interesting fact that these ring-doves, though they may become extremely tame, yet do not seem to have any decided "home instinct." If a blond ring is let out of its cage it is very likely to fly off at random, taking no note of the place it has left, and it is unable to find its way back, though it tries to do so. As partly indicated above, however, the situation can be so arranged that it will return. If its cage is opened near the ground, and there are not many buildings which would mislead it, it will walk around and come back, especially if it has young or eggs. At Woods Hole I have mated these with dove-cote pigeons, have allowed them to go entirely free, and have not lost one of them.

I have found, however, that though many adult ring-doves, let loose for the first time, fly away and are unable to return, yet this is not true of all of them. The young birds certainly can be managed better. I have allowed 3 young rings to go free during a whole summer, and they stayed around the house and at night even went into the shed where their parents were kept in cages. Perhaps they would not have thus gone inside if their parents had been outside. The young of the domestic pigeon sticks close to his home when allowed its freedom. In its first flights it keeps its home in sight, and returns to, or near to, the spot it left. (R 6, A 1/1, R 17.)

LACK OF INTELLIGENCE.

It is astonishing how easily the common pigeon may fail to find its home (cot) even under favorable circumstances, and when the field of search is limited to a space not over 20 by 30 feet. I placed a pair of pigeons in a cot about 10 feet from the ground, behind the house, keeping them there for several days until they had built a nest and the female was about ready to lay. Yesterday, at about 4 p. m., I allowed the male to come out while the female sat on the nest. He flew out upon the pens, which were about 15 feet distant and on a level with his cot. He was very restless, as he at once discovered that his mate was not with him; he eagerly searched for her and did not seem to have the slightest idea of her precise location. He walked back and forth hurriedly over the pens, looking now and then anxiously down toward the inclosed pigeons to see if his mate was among them. Not finding her in the yard, and becoming greatly agitated at her absence, he at length started to fly out of the yard. At that moment another dove, from a cot higher up, started to fly with him. He was alarmed and flew as if a hawk was behind him, but circled round, flying across the yard and over into the back stairway of a house about 50 feet away; here I caught him and then returned him to his cot. The next day I allowed both doves to come out in the middle of the day. It soon began to shower. The two birds remained in the yard on the top of the pens until about 3 p. m., when they began a search for shelter. The female was the first to begin this search. She limited her efforts to different parts of the yard (20 by 30 feet), and herein showed that *she knew that her home was near by.* There her cot was— in open plain sight—just below, on the outside of the porch. She had no idea where to look for it. She ran about looking everywhere except in the right direction. Once only did she even fly over to it, alighting, not on the stand, but on the roof of the cot. She soon flew back to the top of the pens. After about an hour's search she flew to the stand and immediately went in to her nest. The male saw her go in and motioned as if to follow, but hesitated to fly and soon settled down as if forgetting her. Soon after (4 o'clock) he began

THE HOMING INSTINCT. 135

searching for his cot, for it was time to be on his perch. Several times he stopped, looked towards the cot, but then renewed his aimless and stupid search around the pens of the yard. This time he did not venture to fly out of the yard. After a half-hour spent in vain, he finally flew to the stand and at once recognized his home and went in.

I think old doves are, in some respects, worse off than young doves in the matter of finding home. The young are afraid to fly much, and hence go out on the stand for several days before venturing to leave it. When they do fly from it they alight in the nearest place, and seldom get out of sight of the old ones. Moreover, the old birds fly back and forth to the cot, and thus teach the young just what to do to find home.[1] The young follow the parents to their home. When this has been done once or twice, they have learned the lesson and can depend upon themselves. Old doves, on the contrary, when set free for the first time in a new place—which they know only as seen from a window of the cot—are liable to fly more freely and then be utterly unable to find their way back. I have lost several doves in this way. (R 7.)

SUMMARY.

True to his phylogenetic conception of instinct, the author regards the capacity of homing pigeons as but an unusual development of tendencies and power possessed by all pigeons. In the subsequent chapter this view is more explicitly stated as to the instincts of tumbling and pouting.[2] As a consequence, the observations are not limited to homers, but concern the attempts of any pigeon to return to its cot or nest. In a sense, homing is also an aspect of migration, a phenomenon which is rather widely distributed throughout the animal world, and the author was evidently considering a study of homing in the light of its wider genetic relations. This discussion is not to be regarded as a final treatment of the phenomenon; it is to be considered as the formulation of a tentative hypothesis useful for further study.

One must distinguish between the motivating "impulses" in homing and the "means" by which these impulses are gratified. There is no unique and single homing impulse. The return to home may be motivated by any one of several impulses. A home is particular only as a definite place or position; the concept is complex from the side of satisfaction obtained. A home may mean food, safety, companions, mate, nest and young, or a place to roost. An impulse or motive is a tendency to act in response to a present sensory stimulus. An act is not motivated by its sensory consequences. A bird removed from home does not respond to a home stimulus, nor does it seek a return because of the resultant satisfaction. The bird reacts negatively to the present situation rather than

---

[1] In the matter of leading the young, the common pigeon is a good bird to watch. When the young first comes out of the cot, its first trip to the ground is often made by falling off the edge of the shelf. But however it gets to the ground, it of course knows very little about the way back again. The parent flies down to the young one and no doubt helps it to find the way. This is especially true of the male, because the female is likely to be in the cot laying or about to lay; the female, however, also helps the young sometimes. When the male is trying to get the young one up to the cot, the young bird is of course much confused by the new situation and the strange birds around it; but the father feeds it a little and thus keeps up acquaintance with it, and then flies up to the cot. When it is time for the young to go to roost the father will fly back and forth, back and forth, between it and the cot, perhaps feeding it a little each time. He shows great solicitude until the young are safely inside. The parents show this solicitude especially the first time the young are out of the cot. (Conv. 7/10, W. C.)

[2] In this connection it is well to note that all fancy pigeons, such as homers, tumblers, and pouters, are not *true species*, but are strains or varieties developed by the breeding art of the pigeon fancier. This would indicate that these special characters are but improvements on traits and tendencies already present. The wild species *Columba livia* is commonly supposed to be the progenitor of all domestic varieties. *Columba livia* is a gregarious species, a fact which is interesting in connection with the author's suggestion that the "social instinct is the foundation of the home instinct."

136   BEHAVIOR OF PIGEONS.

positively to the home environment. The motivating stimulus is hunger, not food; loneliness, not companionship; fear, not safety, etc. Most of these motives are suggested by the author.

The social or gregarious instinct is considered of prime importance. The author indicates that a bird with gregarious habits is more likely to return than one in whom the social instinct is less well developed; a single bird will return when a pair or group will not.

Hunger is also a motive. Homers are trained when hungry, according to Fulton; and Whitman asserts that hunger was responsible for the return of some of his escaped birds. Obviously hunger could not operate with wild birds capable of finding sustenance in the open. It would apply only to domestic and semi-domestic breeds which have been accustomed to obtain their food in a certain locality and which find difficulty in living a life of freedom.

Wildness is a factor. Wild pigeons rarely return to the cot when they escape. Semi-domesticated birds may return if they have been tamed. In a sense, the failure of wild pigeons to return is a case of homing, for these birds seek and return to an environment which they instinctively prefer. They react against confinement and too close proximity to man.

Fear of unfamiliar surroundings induces return to a familiar environment where experience has justified a reasonable degree of safety. Homers manifest fear and caution when first released. A young bird taken a short distance from the nest is frightened and seeks to get back. The parents assist the young in making its first returns. When exploring, the young hustle for the nest whenever startled.

The impulse to incubate or to feed the young may instigate returns. These impulses arise at definite times, and a free bird may manifest perfect contentment away from the nest until the onset of these internal stimuli. The reader will recognize that in many cases the notes offer insufficient proof of the efficacy of these motives.

Since these impulses are avoiding reactions toward the environment, and not positive responses to the home situation, they do not furnish the means or mechanism of homing. The motive may be present and yet the bird may fail dismally in the attempt. The mechanism, according to the author, is "eyesight" and "experience." The bird can "home" because it has learned a system of positive responses toward the visual aspects of the environment. Placed in a new situation, the bird must wander aimlessly until by accident a familiar situation is reached. The influence of experience in this capacity is rather well attested by the observations on the young in leaving the nest, by the experiments on adult homers when freed for the first time, and by the methods of training homing pigeons. The influence of vision in the reaction is an assumption without adequate factual support so far as the notes are concerned. If this view is correct, two facts are significant—the readiness and ease with which these position habits are acquired and the strength with which they are retained for considerable periods of time. However, it is well to note that all behavior studies reveal the fundamental importance of position habits in the life of animals.

CHAPTER XII.

OTHER INSTINCTS.

This chapter for the most part consists of miscellaneous observations of various traits and behavior tendencies of pigeons, with some account of specific differences. The significance and genetic relations of these characters are not discussed as a rule. The topics are those of the author, but similar observations from various manuscripts have been brought together by the editor. Unity and coherence of treatment has proved difficult of attainment with some of these materials. The topics have been grouped by the editor under the general heading of "Instinct" for the sake of convenience; one may well question the applicability of this term to some of the acts described. The first part of the first topic treated is a reprint of a paper by the author, published in 1899 in Woods Hole Biological Lectures.[1]

TUMBLING AND POUTING.

The evidence adduced to show that habit may pass into instinct can not here be examined in detail. Romanes brings forward two cases—the instincts of *tumbling* and *pouting* in pigeons—which he declares are alone sufficient to demonstrate the theory. We may, therefore, take these as fair examples of the argument generally appealed to.

After quoting Darwin's remarks on this subject, Romanes adds:

"This case of the tumblers and pouters is singularly interesting and very apposite to the proposition before us; for not only are the actions utterly useless to the animals themselves, but they have now become so ingrained into their psychology as to have become severally distinctive of different breeds, and so not distinguishable from true instincts. This extension of an hereditary and useless habit into a distinction of race or type is most important in the present connection. *If these cases stood alone, they would be enough to show that useless habits may become hereditary,* and this to an extent which renders them indistinguishable from true instincts." [2]

Granting that we have here true instincts—and I do not doubt that—what proof have we that they originated in habits? Did there pre-exist in the ancestors of these breeds organized instinct bases, which, through the fancier's art of selective breeding, were gradually strengthened until they attained the development which now characterizes the tumblers and pouters? Or was there no such basis to start with, but only a new mode of behavior, accidentally acquired by some one or more individuals, and then perpetuated by transmission to their offspring and further developed by artificial selection? The original action in either species is called a "habit," and this so-called habit must have been inherited; *ergo*, habit can become instinct. Obviously, argument of that kind can have weight only with those who overlook the test-point, namely, the real nature and origin of the initial action.

If the instinct had its inception in a true habit, *i.e.*, in an action reduced to habit by repetition in the individual, and not determined in any already existing hereditary activity, is it at all credible that it could have been transmitted from parent to progeny? Does not our general experience contradict such an assumption in the most positive manner? But may not the habit have originated a great many times, and by repetition in successive generations, gradually have become "stereotyped into a permanent instinct"? To suppose

---

[1] Republished by courtesy of Messrs. Ginn & Co., Boston.   [2] Mental Evolution in Animals, p. 189.

138   BEHAVIOR OF PIGEONS.

that such *utterly useless* action originated a great many times without compelling conditions or any organic predisposition is not at all admissible.

Darwin saw at once from the nature of the actions that they could not have been taught, but "*must have appeared naturally*, though probably afterwards vastly improved by the continued selection of those birds which showed the strongest *propensity.*" Darwin, then, postulates as to the foundation of each instinct a "propensity"—something given in the constitution. That view of the matter is in entire accord with the theory adopted in the case of "neuter insects" and quite incompatible with the habit theory.

THE INSTINCT OF POUTING.

I believe the case is much stronger than Darwin suspected, and that it shows, not the genesis of instinct from habit, but from a preëxisting congenital basis. Such a basis of the pouting instinct exists in every dove-cote pigeon, and is already an organized instinct, differing from the instinct displayed in the typical pouter only in degree. I could show that the instinct is widely spread, if not universal, among pigeons. It will suffice here to call attention to the instinct as exhibited in the common pigeon. Observe a male pigeon while cooing to his mate or his neighbors. Notice that he inflates his throat and crop, and that this feature is an invariable feature in the act, often continued for some moments after the cooing ceases. Compare the pouter and notice how he increases the inflation whenever he begins cooing. The pouter's behavior is nothing but the universal instinct enormously exaggerated, as any attentive observer may readily see under favorable circumstances.

THE INSTINCT OF TUMBLING.

The origin of the tumbling instinct can not be fixed by the same direct mode of identification; but I believe that here also it is possible to point to a more general action, instinctively performed by the dove-cote pigeons as the probable source of origin. I have noticed a great many times that common pigeons, when on the point of being overtaken and seized by a hawk, suddenly flirt themselves directly downward in a manner suggestive of tumbling, and thus elude the hawk's swoop. The hawk is carried on by its momentum, and often gives up the chase on the first failure. In one case I saw the chase renewed three times and eluded with success each time. The pigeon was a white dove-cote pigeon with a trace of fantail blood. I saw this same pigeon repeatedly pursued by a swift hawk during one winter and invariably escaping in the same way. I have seen the same performance in other dove-cote pigeons under similar circumstances.

But this is not all. It is well known that dove-cote pigeons delight in quite extended flights, circling about their home. I once raised two pairs of these birds by hand in a place several miles from any other pigeons. Soon after they were able to fly about they began these flights, usually in the morning. I frequently saw one or more of the flock while in the middle of a high flight, and, sweeping along swiftly, suddenly plunge downwards, often zigzagging with a quick, helter-skelter flirting of the wings. The behavior often looked like play, and probably it was that in most cases. I incline to think, however, that it was sometimes prompted by some degree of alarm. In such flights the birds would frequently get separated, and one thus falling behind would hasten its flight to the utmost speed in order to overtake its companions. Under such circumstances the stray bird coming from the rear might be mistaken for the moment for a hawk in pursuit, and one or more of the birds about to be overtaken would be thus induced to resort to this method of throwing themselves out of reach of danger.

The same act is often performed at the very start, as the pigeon leaves its stand. The movement is so quick and crazy in its aimlessness that the bird often seems to be in danger of dashing against the ground, but it always clears every object.

OTHER INSTINCTS. 139

As this act is performed by young and old alike, and by young that have never learned it by example, it must be regarded as instinctive, and I venture to suggest that it probably represents the foundation of the more highly developed tumbling instinct.

The behavior of the Abyssinian pigeon, which, when "fired at, plunges downwards so as to almost touch the sportsman, and then mounts to an immoderate height," may well be due to the same instinct. The noise of the gun, even if the birds were not hit, would surprise and alarm it, and the impulse to save itself from danger would naturally take the form determined by the instinct, if the instinct existed. This seems to me more probable than Darwin's suggestion of a mere trick or play.

Bearing on the above discussion of the instinct of tumbling, the editor finds a quotation from an article in Nature[1] to the effect that "pigeons have all three semicircular canals well developed." Concerning this statement the author remarked that "possibly the center of balance is so placed in these pigeons as to facilitate the tumbling."

Three letters from correspondents relate to the tumbling phenomenon, and were evidently intended for publication as illustrative of some of the points treated in the quotation that has just been given.

"What you have to say about the 'habit of tumbling' in pigeons prompts me to ask if you have ever heard that scoters, when flying in flocks at a great elevation, will almost invariably descend nearly vertically almost to the ground or water if a gun be fired beneath them. I have often seen them do it. I remember even firing at a flock which was approaching at a height of more than 1,000 feet and then with the second barrel, killing one of them as the flock dashed past me low over the water after their descent. Most of our sea-fowl hunters know this trick and practice it more or less often and successfully. It is the *report* of the gun, not the charge which it contains, which brings the birds down." (William Brewster, of Cambridge, Massachusetts, Nov. 23, 1899.)

"Last summer I observed a common mourning-dove in flight which—twice within a distance of an eighth of a mile—went through the process of tumbling like a common tumbler pigeon. I do not know if this is a common habit of the mourning-dove or whether it is of any interest. If you are interested I would be glad to tell you anything further you may ask so far as I observed. I have not known that wild birds had this habit." (Professor M. M. Metcalf, of Baltimore, Maryland, Jan. 4, 1900.)

In response to a request for further details of this instance of tumbling in the mourning-dove, Dr. Metcalf wrote as follows:

"Mrs. Metcalf and I were driving one evening last July in the Fox River Valley, north of Elgin, Illinois, when we saw the tumbler mourning-dove. It was about sun-down. I remember thinking the birds were probably bound for their roost, which I thought might be near the river some 2 miles east of us. There were three birds about 800 feet apart, flying fast in a direction almost due east. The middle one showed the peculiarity in flight. I have seen tumbler pigeons but few times, and could never tell what were the exact evolutions of the birds. The impression from this mourning-dove was the same as from tumbler pigeons I have seen—a sudden cessation of onward flight, a peculiar fluttering, the bird dropping backwards, then recovering its balance, and going on as swiftly as before. The drop was, I should say, about 12 feet, Mrs. Metcalf thinks more. The bird tumbled (?) twice in about an eighth of a mile. I watched them about as far beyond the point of second tumbling and saw nothing of the sort again.

"It was wholly different from a stopping in flight such as one often sees. The bird evidently lost its balance and recovered again. The three were flying swiftly, one behind the other, over prairie pastures. They flew low, within easy gunshot from the ground. When the first tumbling occurred the bird was about 400 feet from me. It did not pass quite over the carriage. No other birds were seen by me at the time, nor did I observe anything of interest in this connection. The first tumbling occurred in the middle of a pasture west of the road. The bird tumbled a second time after flying over a fence one field west of the road. There was a single tree about 150 feet from the bird toward myself which the bird had just passed when it tumbled a second time. The appearance of the evolution seemed to me to correspond to that of tumbling. There was the same startling fluttering effect.

---

[1] The Origin of Tumbling of Pigeons, Nature, 1901, p. 395.

140 BEHAVIOR OF PIGEONS.

The observation, however, to be of real value should have been made by one more familiar with tumblers than I am. Mrs. Metcalf confirms these estimates of distances." (Professor M. M. Metcalf, Baltimore, Maryland, Jan. 12, 1900.)

SOCIABILITY.

Two pairs of crested pigeons, when resting during the day, are often seen sitting "in close order" on the perch. When "roosting" at night they get as close as possible to one another, and the two pairs brought up in separate pens until Oct. 1st have never shown hostility to one another. The two older ones, as soon as they were attacked by the male of a pair of ring-doves, began to retaliate and soon made themselves masters of the pen. Their swiftness of motion and skill in striking terrific blows generally caused the male ring-dove to retreat. But the ring first claimed the nest-boxes and yielded his position there only occasionally, and then only for the moment. He too is no unskillful fighter. Although inferior in striking, he is quick to take advantage by flying upon the back of his antagonist, where he can scratch, peck, and strike with impunity. In this way he drives the much larger and stronger *Ectopistes*, and often puts to rout even the crested pigeons. The crested pigeons, while perfectly friendly to one another, regard the young *Ectopistes* as enemies on the perch at night (not while eating). This is due to the fact that the latter insist on free roosting-space and peck at intruders that come within reach. The crested pigeons therefore take care on their part not to let the passengers or the ring-doves come too near their section of the perch. If these do not keep at a safe distance, at least 6 to 12 inches away, one of the crested pigeons will attack furiously and return to his place only after having put the enemy at a longer distance than he would have claimed unmolested. The point seems to be to make it understood that there can be no trespassing on roosting quarters.

Two young *Ectopistes* never sleep side by side. They always claim free space on both sides—6 or more inches. The mourning-doves do the same. This is interesting in relation to the fact that the passenger pigeons are well known to prefer company in nesting and in feeding, keeping together in large flocks. Mourning-doves, on the other hand, seek a place apart for a nest, and only later in feeding or migrating are found in flocks.

The zebra-doves (certain geopelias) as well as the ground-doves of Florida (*Chamœpelia*) sit in close order at night, often struggling to get the inside place as the warmest. The same is true of *Geopelia humeralis*.

I have seen for a week or two that the second of a young pair, of crested pigeons, 74 days old, insists on roosting with its foster parents (ring-doves). This pair of ring-doves and two young passengers are all in the same pen in my library. The ring-doves are hostile to the older crested pigeons and often so to the younger, mistaking them for enemies. But these submit to being pecked rather roughly and snuggle down beside their foster-parents. The first of the pair has now finally deserted its foster-parents and prefers to roost with the older pair of its kind. The second young still insists on sitting beside its ring-dove parents.

A male crested pigeon mated with a ring-dove (*GF 1*) roosts on the nest-box close beside his mate. For the first two nights he sat on one side of the box and she on one end. To-night he took his place beside her, and so close that she several times withdrew to another side. He followed her each time and insisted on sitting as close as possible. At last she submitted and went to sleep beside him. Here we see the female cross her own instincts— of roosting apart. In the case of another pair, common-pigeon male and ring-dove female, the female learned to follow the male into the cot every night, while other ring-doves steadily preferred to sit outside.

It is possible that the "home instinct" might be developed in ring-doves mated with domestic doves and then allowed to go free. The male domestic would follow his mate and lead her back to the cot. A female ring-dove mated with an archangel follows him into the cot and nests there. The same is true for female ring-doves mated with white fantails and black tumblers. In the reversed cross—*i.e.*, where the male is a ring-dove and the female a homer—the pair nest in the cot, but the male sits out at night and she sits with him if she has no young or eggs to care for.

In a cross between a satinette male and a crested-pigeon female, both sit out of doors rather than in the cot. The male prefers to roost inside, but she persists in staying outside, and he finally, after several nights, concluded to stay out with her.

The young of *G. humeralis* are not weaned—or rather are not driven off by the parents—as early as in other species. A 7-weeks-old young has been treated kindly, and when I took him away the old male seemed to be quite disturbed; when night came the young called and the male answered and was long uneasy. Even the next day the young kept up its call and the male parent responded. The sociability of this species is evinced from the start by the young. They are extremely attractive in their fondness for their parents, in their sweet, almost musical notes, in their loving head-movements, in their roosting between the old birds, etc.

A young speckled-neck (*Sp. suratensis*) about 6 weeks old likes the company of his foster-father (a ring-dove), and seeks to sit close beside him at night. It is very interesting to notice its behavior as it approaches the old bird. It comes up in a very inoffensive, affectionate way, and before snuggling down beside the old bird puts up its beak and fondly caresses the head and beak of the old bird, as if to make sure of his good will and to win favor. It reminds one of the dog that crouches and wags its tail as it approaches its master in some doubt of a friendly reception. The same kind of behavior is very common with young pigeons of all kinds, and even with mates. The young of crested pigeons and of *G. humeralis* are peculiarly demonstrative in their social manners.

A 6-months-old crested pigeon was placed in a cage with an 8-weeks-old hybrid between a black tumbler and a ring-dove. The hybrid showed some affection for his companion, although he had been brought up with his parents and never before had seen a crested pigeon. This crested pigeon is very gentle and inoffensive, never attacking or showing the slightest disposition to quarrel. The hybrid soon learned that the crested was harmless and trustworthy, and "confidence" is a condition of friendly relations. Let a dove strike or peck and it may expect the same in return or to be feared and shunned. (B 2C, R 7.)

FIGHTING.

The young of the ring-dove show the instinct to fight at the sight of individuals of their own species and of other birds which are more or less strangers to them. The instinct is first shown in the nest at the approach of any strange object, such as the hand. The mode of fight is to swell up the breast and raise the feathers, or pin-feathers, so as to look "large." The eye looks fierce and the mandibles are snapped, and with each snap a puff of air is expelled, much as a kitten "spits" in the face of an antagonist—a dog. If the hand is moved rather quickly, the young may strike with the beak and with the wing. All these movements are purely instinctive, or, shall we say, reflex acts?

After the young get out of the nest they are generally very inoffensive and seldom attack a companion. But when night comes and the roost is taken they become tenacious of their place and are quick to warn intruders not to come near. This is true especially of the domestic dove and of passengers, which do not sit in close order at night, as do the crested pigeons.

At first the instinct to fight may not appear at all during eating, although it is called out from the start on the roost. In the course of time they begin to claim food and to drive away those coming second. *Ectopistes* begins this quite early. The disposition to fight and drive other doves away from the neighborhood of the nest becomes strong as soon as nest-building begins, and is still stronger when the eggs are laid and after hatching. A

142 BEHAVIOR OF PIGEONS.

young passenger bristled up, raised his wings, and scolded fiercely at the crested pigeons in an adjoining pen as soon as the first egg was laid.

The disposition to fight is periodic and comes on in all pigeons at the time of mating and choosing a nesting-place. In a pair of homers, while fixing on a nesting-place, the male was pugnacious, fighting off other males whenever they came near. Just as soon, however, as the nest-place was settled and the two birds began to spend some time on the nest every day and copulations became frequent—about a week before laying—the male began to follow his mate jealously and closely, if other males were about. This male is now so anxious to guard his mate that he will not in many cases stop to fight off a strange male even from his own stand, but will keep his eye constantly on her, paying no heed to another male, except to drive his mate out of reach of the latter.

When a strange pigeon, *e.g.*, a homer, approaches on the floor of the pen, the Nicobar pigeon (*Cal. nicobarica*) raises its neck and back feathers, reaches forward with its head with beak open, threatening to bite (not to peck). It opens the beak and "grunts" as it "throws" its head towards the intruder with beak open. The head keeps moving as if the bird was trying to reach the opponent, but the purpose served is to frighten off the other bird. If the intruder comes quite near there will probably be no actual biting, but there may be a retreat or a defense by striking with the wing. The grunt sounds much like that of a pig that comes up to be fed or scratched.

I saw two bleeding-heart pigeons (*Phlogœnas luzonica*) threatening each other while taking their breakfast. The method was peculiar. The birds walked around each other at a distance of about $1\frac{1}{2}$ feet, each watching his opponent for an opportunity to get in a blow. One would dart on top of the other and give a blow with the wing and a peck, and then off, again walking around for another chance.

My Florida ground-doves (*Chamœpelia*), which are very timid and frightened at the least motion, have learned to trust me far enough to fly often upon my hand to get seed. But in doing so they usually raise one or both wings almost vertically, evidently with the design of protecting themselves from attacks or approach while eating. This practice of raising the wings in a fight, or in the presence of an antagonist, is widespread among pigeons, as is attested by the several instances next to be described.

The ring-doves, and pigeons generally, involuntarily raise the wings when suddenly surprised by a strange animal or a bird brought into their presence. They not only raise both wings, but nearly all the feathers of the body—especially those of the back—and spread the tail, ready to defend themselves or to escape by flight. Common pigeons in fighting often raise the wings to guard against the blows of their opponents. A ring-dove learned to raise his wings and lower his head when a crested pigeon approached to strike him. He finally learned that he could drive the crested pigeon by flying upon his back. In this way the ring-dove claimed and held his nest-box, although at first he had to surrender it.

My bronze doves or green-wings (*Chalcophaps*) and my *Geopelia humeralis* both raise the wings high when threatened by another dove. The bronze doves always raise both wings as high as they can reach when attacked and during a fight. I have noticed too that these birds, on getting a hold on the feathers of an antagonist, jump, helping themselves with their wings and legs much as common fowls do. *G. humeralis* raises the wings in precisely the same way. This bird is decidedly courageous, a fact made evident by the following paragraphs:

My small *G. humeralis* do not hesitate to attack the large white-wing pigeon (*Leucosarcia picata*), and the latter allows itself to be driven about. It is like a pigmy driving a giant. The white-faced pigeon appears to have no spirit for fighting and not wit enough to defend itself against *G. humeralis*. Most doves are quick to understand that they can whip doves of smaller size. But the *G. humeralis* continually lords it over the *Leucosarcia*. One little fellow drove both of the large birds into a corner, where they tried to hide their

OTHER INSTINCTS.

heads from him. There they stood in abject submission to the little bully. Twice I saw a *G. humeralis*, after driving them to the corner, coo before them with a bowing and raising of the wings and tail, in the manner so characteristic of the crested pigeon. In this case it was a crow of superiority.

I received by express in the same shipment, 4 specimens of *G. humeralis* and 2 of *L. picata*. I was astonished to see that at the outset one of the little geopelia was actually driving the large leucosarcia and catching hold of the neck-feathers and twitching them with all its power. The white-faced pigeon stood and took it all without returning a blow, merely raising one wing to shield itself. The geopelia quickly discovered that they could bulldoze their larger cousins, and they had sense enough to take advantage of the stupid impotence of their big companions. It is hard to define, but it is evident that *Geopelia* has a higher *grade of intelligence* than the white-faced pigeon. It was ludicrous to see so large a bird imposed upon by a mere pigmy. Courage in birds often means intelligence.

In the struggle of two common-dove cocks for mastery of a roost or nesting-place we see strong determination and an appreciation of any "advantage of position," such as the inside position on a shelf. Any advantage of "hold" is maintained as long as possible and made the most of, as when one gets the other by the feathers on the side of head and holds him so that he can not return any blows. Once I saw a fantail take a homer by one of his primaries and run him around a yard without once giving up the hold.

I placed a young domestic, full-fledged, in a cage with a passenger. This fellow would eat from my hand and would peck at the wild passenger when it came to eat with it. If the wild pigeon went off his courage was of course good; but if the wild pigeon retaliated he at once lost all courage to fight and would try to hold his place by lovingly fondling the feathers of the head of the former. I saw this done several times, and I take it to indicate almost human intelligence in dealing with opponents.

A male domestic dove, which is mated to a female ring-dove, is wild and afraid to eat from my hand. I pretend to be afraid of him, putting my hand slowly towards him, and then withdrawing it as if in fear of him. He at once took courage and came to attack me. As long as I kept up the play he was brave and seemed to think he had mastered. In the course of a few days he became bold enough to fight vigorously. The dove is thus quick to take advantage of fear in its antagonist, as is the case in so many of the higher animals. I have a male blond ring-dove that is fearless and easily induced to fight, although ordinarily he treats me as a friend and never thinks of pecking at me even when I lift him from his nest.

Doves frequently make a show of courage just to intimidate. If they succeed in this way they follow it up and practice it on every occasion. They remember that it works well. This was well illustrated in my mourning-doves. The smallest of the flock of 10 found that a sudden jump was enough usually to frighten off his large companions, and in this way he drove every bird in the pen. I have known a mourning-dove to frighten the much larger ring-dove in this way, and so drive it about. Sometimes the wings are thrown outward with a quick jerk, as if threatening to strike. *Ectopistes* does this when it scolds.

If pecked at by old birds, the young squeal and beg with their wings. If abused they *hang their heads low* and submit without an effort to defend. Often they will endure very rough treatment without moving; often they will turn and run in search of a place of safety, generally to the nest. If pursued and there is no escape, they will stand and be scalped— let the feathers be stripped from the head and back, flayed alive, but bearing it with the heroism of religious martyrs. This endurance of severe pain without resistance or attempt to flee is sometimes exhibited by adult pigeons; *e.g.*, an adult geopelia, attacked by a fellow, hung its head and stood motionless until the other tired of the attack. In a case where the old birds wanted the nest for a new set of eggs they began to drive their young of $3\frac{1}{2}$ weeks. These, wonderful to say, bore it for a while, and then began to resist and fought with such desperation that the old ones left them. I saw this repeated several times. (R 7, R 17.)

144 BEHAVIOR OF PIGEONS.

FEAR.

If one or more doves become frightened *at night* and flutter in the attempt to go through the window or wire netting of the pen, the fright is thereby communicated to other doves in the same room or within hearing. One night, at 1 or 2 o'clock, a young mourning-dove, about 4 weeks old, got startled and flew against the window, fluttering vigorously. The fright became general, and two quite tame mourning-doves at the opposite side of the room were so alarmed that both dashed violently against the wire, the female leaving her eggs. A pair of tiger turtles were sitting at the same time; the male left his perch and was found on the floor; the female of this pair was badly frightened, but did not leave her eggs. I have several times seen a whole room full of ring-doves fearfully frightened by the fluttering of a wild passenger-pigeon, though the ring-doves were perfectly tame. Fright by night, when the bird can not see the cause of the disturbance, is often extreme and easily communicated. *Wildness* also is often communicated by example. A single wild dove among a dozen tame ones will often turn them all wild, just as a tame dove will often help in taming wild ones.

Four of my passenger pigeons have never had their freedom, having been raised by Mr. Whittaker, and although only 3 or 4 years old, they have behaved as if terror-stricken, and their fear has disappeared only very gradually and so slowly that I can but wonder at it. A mourning-dove which I obtained from Florida was far less timid and learned to eat from my hand with confidence in a few days. But the passenger-pigeons, although I have compelled them to accept all their food from the hand, were very difficult to manage at first, and to this day they have not lost their fear of me. They were taught to eat quite readily from the hand, but they watched every movement of my person and often tried to get through the wire screen of the coop. At first, in order to break them in, I kept them in a large cage near my writing desk and spent much time in trying to get them accustomed to me. For weeks I could not go to the cage without alarming them; they would dash against the wire so recklessly in trying to get away that they broke off the ends of their wing-quills and tail-feathers, and made their wings bleed from the wounds caused by flapping against the wire. I have lately allowed them to eat from the shelf and they have grown wilder, so that they now refuse to eat from my hand.

A young *G. humeralis* (7 weeks old) had been separated from its nest-mate soon after hatching and placed under the care of ring-doves. To-day I brought the two together. The one that had been under the care of the ring-doves was terrified at the sight of its own mate and raised its wings and bristled up for defense. This occurred toward night. I left the two together in a pen by themselves. The two still kept apart the next morning, or rather the one brought up under its own parents seemed not to fear the other much, but the other continued to manifest great fear. This fact shows two things: The one brought up under its parents, and familiar with its own species, saw no cause for alarm in its mate; but the latter, brought up with ring-doves, recognized its mate of its own species as a *stranger* and an *enemy*. These two birds were kept by themselves in a cage and after 4 days they finally got acquainted and roosted together side by side.[1] (R 23, SS 4, R 7.)

FOOD.

I have noticed that the *Ectopistes* parents, especially the female, searches the ground over and over, looking under the plants and along the edge of the boards. Is she hunting for worms or insects? Whatever the object may be, I have seen both male and female on the ground searching and working in the grass with the beak, as if to find worms. On a later occasion I placed a handful of earthworms in the food-dish of a cage containing an

---

[1] That the alarmed white-faced pigeon (*Leucosarcia*) attempts to "hide" by lowering the breast and head to the ground—standing still, with tail raised toward the source of danger—has already been mentioned (Chapter V, topic, Hiding on Nest). In the case there cited a young bird of only 18 days displayed this behavior.—EDITOR.

OTHER INSTINCTS. 145

Ectopistes young only 32 days old. This bird was hatched under ring-doves, had been reared under them, and had never before seen a worm. After a glance or two the young passenger descended from his perch, took up a worm, tried it at the end of his beak, and then dropped it. After repeating the act three times he at length swallowed the worm and then ate several others, generally testing them a little first.[1] I have noticed that the green-winged pigeons (*Chalcophaps*) eat earthworms, and occasionally the ring-dove will do so. The large white-faced doves of Australia were seen to eat several earthworms which were thrown to them.

I find further that stock doves (*C. œnas*), the guinea-pigeon (*C. guinea*), and its hybrids (by homer), Japanese turtle-doves (*T. orientalis*), ring-doves, and hybrids between Japanese turtles and ring, all eat earthworms when they have young to feed. I am inclined to think that pigeons very generally eat earthworms.

Grass is much liked by wood-pigeons (*C. palumbus*) as well as by other pigeons. They also like the plantain leaves growing in the yard. Lettuce is eaten quite freely by pigeons generally. Salt (rock) is very necessary, as is cuttlefish-bone[2] and ground oyster-shell. (SS 4, B 2a.)

BATHING.

I watched a young ectopistes, a little more than 2 months old, take its bath in a shallow glass basin. After trying the water by immersing its beak and shaking it, it plunged in and gave itself a vigorous shaking several times. After each shaking it would lie over on one side and lift up the wing of the other side, stretching it vertically or a little inclined and as far as it could reach. I have often noticed this habit of lifting the wing during a bath in other pigeons. They frequently perform these same motions when it rains, especially if they are disposed to a bath. The wing is raised so as to expose its under surface to the falling rain. The same movements are also often employed in "sunning" themselves.

A 3-weeks-old hybrid between a white fantail and a ring-dove, which was just about ready to fly a little, discovered the water that was kept in a basin about 3 inches deep. The bird felt the desire to bathe, but, not knowing how to get into the water, simply ducked its head and squatted outside the dish and shook its feathers as if in the water. Soon afterward it found its way to the edge of the dish and then jumped in and took a good bath in the approved style. This was certainly the first bath. (R 17, R 7.)

INSTINCTIVE PREFERENCES.[3]

Ring-doves do not seek the coop to escape the rain, but sit out in the heaviest showers, even when a coop is near at hand. The young and old behave alike, even when accustomed to spending the night inside. The domestic dove usually goes in out of the rain. Domestic pigeons prefer the coop to the open at night. Ring-doves have to be forced to go in. In time they learn to roost inside, but only after being repeatedly driven in. A particular ring-dove female which I have mated with a common pigeon follows her mate into the coop without any assistance.

A male common pigeon and a Japanese turtle had a nest and eggs in a pen on the east side of the house. The nest was on a shelf and was covered by a box about 2 feet long. One-half of one side of this box was open. The female laid her first egg in that end of the box having the aperture. When the male took the nest the next day he moved the nest and the egg along to the other end of the box, away from the aperture. The female in

---

[1] See Chapter X.

[2] I do not quite know why the birds eat so much cuttlefish-bone. It seems in some way to promote their digestion and general health. It probably contains a good deal of salts, which may have a beneficial effect. Some of them do not eat it; some have never learned to do so. Those which do eat it usually grow passionately fond of it. When they see me bring some in and break it up for them, they understand and make a great commotion. (Conv. 7/2/10, W. C.)

[3] Other illustrations are given in Chapter X.

146 BEHAVIOR OF PIGEONS.

turn moved them back before the opening, when she took her turn at incubation. This behavior was repeated by each on the two following days. The male thus preferred to nest under cover, under that part of the box which was entirely covered, while the female preferred an open space for the nest, *i.e.*, she preferred that part of the box having one open side. (R 17.)

APPRECIATION OF HEIGHT.

A young white ring-dove, which had been kept on the floor of the cage in a box 3 inches high, jumped out of the box for the first time. This bird was unable to fly and yet ventured out of the nest, which it would not have done if the nest had been placed at a greater height from the floor. This shows an instinctive (?) appreciation of distance and safety. Similarly a young hybrid between a white fantail and a ring-dove, when just 2 weeks old— a full week before it would venture to fly from its nest—stepped out of the nest-box, which was kept on the floor of the pen, to the floor and walked around with the foster-parents, which were eating their breakfast. The young bird then, without experience, appreciates the conditions which make it safe or unsafe to leave the nest. If this nest had been several feet above the floor the young bird would not have ventured out for at least a week. (R 7, R 6.)

SLEEP.

I notice that pigeons fall asleep very quickly after getting to their accustomed place on the perch at nightfall. But they are easily aroused. Every time I come into my room, and every time I move with some noise after a period of quiet, they are awakened, and they habitually shake their feathers quite vigorously all over when thus aroused from sleep. It is interesting to hear this shaking run through a dozen or more doves all at once. The eyes are closed in sleep and the head and tail are held in nearly the same horizontal plane, so that the dove, especially when roosting in the open air, looks as if it were on the watch for enemies from below. That is the attitude only when they hear something. In the cages the head is held a little higher, but the body is nearly horizontal. The bird supports itself by resting the body on the perch, as they sometimes do in the daytime when they drop the wings beneath as supports and as an aid to balance.

Crested pigeons sit on the perch with the head, body, and tail in a nearly horizontal line, the tail falling but a little beneath this line. The head is so held that the crest is vertical and in line with the beak, which is drawn so close to the breast that it is almost covered with feathers. The eyes are closed, and the appearance is that of sound, restful sleep. Slight noises arouse them to open an eye, but it soon closes. They sit as close together as possible, not for warmth, for they do so in warm weather, but because they are fond of company and feel a satisfaction in close contact. The young cresteds which were reared by a pair of blond rings were accustomed to crowd so close as to push the old birds off the perch; and they would not rest until they succeeded in nestling close to one another.

The passenger-pigeon holds its head in sleep somewhat higher, but drawn back upon the breast, so that the beak is pretty well covered with feathers. The tail droops to an angle of about 45°. In both passengers and cresteds the beak is held straight in the middle line of the breast. (R 17.)

MODIFICATION OF INSTINCT.

I notice that a pair of young mourning-doves, only 1 and 2 days old, are sleeping quite uncovered in front of their parent. The young birds are in the nest and the parent bird seems to have drawn back a little to one side of the nest, so that the young can sit uncovered. The heat is oppressive (June) for the first time this season, and the birds are left uncovered because more comfortable so. In cold weather this would not happen.

OTHER INSTINCTS. **147**

Wildness is often communicated by example. A single wild dove among a dozen tame ones will often turn them all wild, just as a tame dove will often help in taming wild ones.

At Woods Hole I have mated blond rings with dove-cote pigeons, have allowed them to go entirely free, and have not lost one of them. The only difference between them and the common pigeon is that they delight to go into trees, and if they get frightened they go to some tree; the common pigeon avoids trees and alights on the roof of some building. It is extremely interesting to note the behavior of the male domestic pigeons which I had mated with these birds. The male takes a very jealous interest in his mate and follows her wherever she goes. The moment she flies from the perch he is after her. But the ring-dove is swift of wing and sometimes gets out of sight. On such occasions the male is very anxious and flies about in search—calls, and flies and looks. Usually, if the ring flies away some distance, she comes back to the place she has left, and then the mate is ready to meet her. From her mate she "learns" to take up her quarters inside in the dove-cote. If both of the pair are blond rings and they are set free, they prefer to roost outside. It is only when mated with the dove-cote pigeon that they will roost inside. Sometimes they will then go outside; as a rule they will follow their mates. Sometimes I have observed that the dove-cote pigeon has "learned" to fly into trees.

ILLUSTRATIONS OF VARIATION OF HABITS AND INSTINCTS—INDUCED AND SPONTANEOUS.

A female ring-dove learns from a male crested pigeon to sit in close contact on the roost at night. A female ring-dove learns from a male common dove to roost inside the dove-house rather than outside, and to go in for shelter from the rain. A *male* fantail broods the young at night. A *male* white ring-dove sat on the egg the first night after it was laid. A young hybrid fed a companion of the same age. A male passenger-pigeon sat regularly of *nights* on the eggs, while the female sat on the edge of the box. A pair of cresteds repeatedly laid sets of eggs before the previous set hatched, so that they had 4 eggs to sit upon. A female *G. humeralis* mated with a ring-dove does not flee from him after a union, as she does from a mate of her own species. Her difference of action is due to the different behavior on the part of the male. The male ring-dove allows himself at this time to be fondled by the female and she expresses her joy by so doing. The male *Geopelia*, on the contrary, bristles up in a most savage manner, repels her love, and drives her off, acting as if his pleasure had turned to displeasure and nausea.

DOMESTICATION OF AFRICAN GUINEA-PIGEON.

A young guinea-pigeon (*C. guinea*) was hatched under a pair of pouters in April, 1909. It was transferred when 5 days old to a pair of owl pigeons. It came out of its cot when 29 days old, and flew to the ground into the back yard with one of the owls. I allowed him to go free and he continued to return to his cot and to go inside at night. I removed one of the owls on the same day the young guinea came out, in order that the other owl might give full attention to the young guinea; this he did, and all went well. 13 days later the young guinea went into his cot as usual, but he was alone, as I found next morning, the owl having been accidentally shut into the barn and thus prevented from returning to the cot. At 6 o'clock, the next morning I was unable to find the young guinea anywhere. He had probably left his cot early that day in search of the owl, which had continued to feed the young bird in part. Not finding his foster-father, he probably flew off in company with some passing stranger, mistaken for the owl. At any rate, the guinea-pigeon was not to be found, and as he did not return at night I concluded that I should probably never see him again.

All of the following day I kept on watch, but the lost bird did not appear until between 5 and 6 p. m. When I came home at about 6 p. m., however, the young guinea was sit-

148   BEHAVIOR OF PIGEONS.

ting quite composedly on the cot-stand. He soon went inside and I closed the door, inclosing both the owl and the guinea. Three days later, at the age of 9 weeks and 4 days, this bird died, probably of indigestion, after a short illness. Up to the last it continued to remain at home, and to share the cot with the male owl.[1]

Although this bird lived a little less than 10 weeks, I feel sure that it demonstrates the possibility of successful domestication in this species. My experience with other species leads me to think that any of them, of similar nesting and food habits, could be easily domesticated; and still more easily, if one lived fairly isolated in the country, where the birds would have but one home, shelter, and supply of food. (R6, R23, A1/1, R17, X S3.)

SUMMARY.

The naturalistic account of various bits of behavior hardly permits of an adequate summary. Marked specific differences are noted, but no generalizations of species relationship are possible. The phylogenetic conception of the evolution of instinct previously developed for incubation and homing is again asserted of tumbling and pouting. The traits of these two breeds of pigeons are but unusual developments of powers and tendencies common to all pigeons. In addition to those cases noted in connection with the reproductive cycle, several interesting examples of modification of instinct are described. When two birds possessing different tendencies are mated, one bird will modify certain instincts so as to adapt itself to the unusual social situation. A female will roost close to her mate, although her natural inclination prompts her to roost with some degree of isolation. Some species naturally roost in a cot, while others prefer to roost outside. In a mating of two birds with such opposed tendencies, some pairs will roost inside, while other pairs will stay outside for the night. In such circumstances a free bird may nest inside a cot when its natural tendency is otherwise.

By social pressure, dove-cote pigeons may be induced to fly into trees. In the cases cited it was the female bird that adapted herself to the male in the majority of cases, but the rule is not universal. The modification of instinct in the above cases may be considered as due to a conflict with other tendencies, e.g., the instinctive and acquired preference for the mate. The social influence is again evident in such traits as wildness and fear. The capacity to learn is also mentioned. Attitudes of fear or trust toward other birds or man are modified by experience. Courage in fighting is strengthened by success. New modes of attack, occurring accidentally at first, are retained when successful, and ring-doves will acquire the habit of roosting inside after being driven in repeatedly.

---

[1] I had removed the owl mate at the time when she began to lose interest in the care of the young guinea. I did this so that the old owl should not turn against the guinea and drive it out of the cot, as it would do if the female owl had been allowed to remain and renew her nest. In fact, she had already become a little hostile to the young. After I removed her the male owl took more interest in the young guinea and seemed to regard it as a mate. The guinea was a splendid bird, and it is a surprise that it should die. I think, however, that coarse seed may have been responsible.

CHAPTER XIII.

HABIT, INSTINCT, AND INTELLIGENCE.

In this chapter the editor has grouped under appropriate topics all those observations of activities in which the effect of previous experience is evident. The material is thus significant from the standpoint of learning, habit formation, and intelligence. For the final topic we have added a selection from a lecture which states in a very succinct form the author's view of the relation of intelligence to instinct. Intelligence, according to Whitman, is not a power, force, or faculty; it is the capacity to learn, to form habits, to profit from previous experience. Instincts are not always perfect; they have faults or deficiencies, they may conflict or interfere with each other. They are not absolutely stereotyped or invariable in their expression, but are plastic or variable to some degree. Intelligence is the capacity to learn, to adjust to novel or variable conditions, and hence is a result of this plastic and variable aspect of instinctive organization. As to the meaning of "memory," the author follows rather consistently the biological usage of the term. To the biologist, memory is the capacity to form habits, and any act exhibits "memory" in so far as it is the resultant of previous experience. Memory is thus equivalent to intelligence. Some readers may prefer a more restricted usage of the term, but questions of terminology are relatively unimportant in comparison with questions of fact and interpretation.

Pigeons are generally regarded as rather stupid creatures, but every organism is relatively stupid along certain lines and relatively intelligent in other respects. As the author states in a footnote in this chapter, an animal may exhibit a good memory for certain activities and a poor memory for others. Pigeons are unutterably stupid from some standpoints. They may injure their young in feeding them, cast the young bird from the nest along with the shells, and incubate, day after day, an empty nest. Yet pigeons do learn quite a variety of things, and some acts are mastered with a surprising degree of readiness. Besides the material given in this chapter, other illustrations of learning capacity have been noted in the summaries of Chapters IX, XI, and XII. A perusal of this material should convince the reader that the pigeon is not altogether stupid, that intelligent capacity does exist, that certain acts are learned very quickly, but that this intelligence is manifested only in certain situations and for certain types of activity. For convenience these powers may be roughly grouped in several classes:

(1) The capacity to acquire habits of reacting to the position aspect of objects is noteworthy. In this respect pigeons are not different from most other animals, for this power is deeply seated and widely distributed in animal life. For the prevalence and significance of this gift we may offer the following suggestions: Among active animals endowed with strong powers of locomotion their position in reference to the topography of the country is of necessity highly variable. Many animals are so organized that certain fixed positions are essential to many of their

150   BEHAVIOR OF PIGEONS.

activities. Feeding-grounds and breeding-grounds are illustrations. In the pigeon most of these needs center around the nesting-site and its immediate vicinity. Such animals must be able to react to topographical relations. An instinctive organization will hardly suffice for an animal whose relation to the environment is exceedingly complex and variable. Instincts are adaptations to the relatively fixed and constant aspects of environmental conditions. The ability to learn easily and quickly a complex system of topographical habits would thus be one of the fundamental needs of animal organization. Most animals have the degree and kind of intelligence which their life demands. Many illustrations of this capacity of pigeons are given. The preference for a roosting-site may be established in one night. In "pair D" the preference for a new nesting-site in a box filled with dry dung was fixed with one experience of an hour's duration. A male broke one nesting habit and developed a new one in 5 or 6 trials. The nest is not wholly an object, but partly a position in reference to other objects. Freed birds at first are lost, but they learn to locate the nest in a large yard in a couple of trials. The ability of homers is supposed to consist of this capacity to learn quickly and retain tenaciously a complex system of topographical habits. Viewed from this standpoint, one is almost tempted to assert that pigeons possess as much intelligent capacity as humans for these particular lines of activity.

(2) Pigeons are also able to acquire rather readily systems of differential reactions to the individuals of the group. Because a bird can acquire a habit of reacting to another bird as an individual, *e.g.*, a mate, it does not follow that as a matter of fact it does acquire a habit for each individual of the group. The differentiation may be between mate and not mate, species and foreigners, member of flock and stranger, etc., but individual reactions are possible. While certain distinctions such as species, sex, and enemy find a basis in instinct, yet instinct does not provide in advance for all possibilities of individual differentiation. While such species differentiation is partly innate, it is to a large extent acquired.

A novel species reaction was acquired by a young geopelia at the age of 7 weeks. Placed with its own kind, a new reaction was acquired in less than 4 days. The selection of a mate is at first a process of discovery; each bird reacts instinctively to a certain type of behavior. After the mating is established, however, the members of a pair react to each other on a different basis. They react to each other as individuals and recognize each other at a distance. This new mode of reaction is acquired and easily established. A pair of young brought up with each other will have learned at the age of 4 weeks to respond differently to each other than to others of like age and species. Inside of a large group smaller groups are formed and differential habits established. Attitudes of fear, distrust, and confidence toward individual birds are very easily modified with experience.

(3) Many acts are improved through *exercise*. The influence of experience is probably influential upon all of the fundamental activities. Illustrations noted in the manuscripts refer to such activities as egg-laying, flying, drinking and eating, and methods of fighting.

HABIT, INSTINCT, AND INTELLIGENCE.

(4) The emotion of fear exercises a disturbing influence upon all instinctive and acquired activities and attitudes, and these disrupting effects are tenaciously *retained*. Acquired attitudes toward other birds, humans, and other animals can thus be inculcated. Roosting habits will be disrupted with one experience. The incubation activities are likewise permanently affected with a single experience. The ability to be easily affected and permanently *influenced* by fright is very essential for timid animals. Fear alone is hardly sufficient; a further value is contributed by the retention of these effects.

Pigeons thus have a facile intelligence for some things, but the capacity is extremely limited in scope. Intelligence, in the main, supplements instinct and ministers to the more fundamental needs in so far as these can not be completely provided for by an instinctive organization.

HABIT OF PLACE OR POSITION.[1]

(1) On Apr. 25 I placed a nest-box containing a pair of newly-hatched young and the male parent on the floor of the coop. This male is perfectly tame, having not the least fear of being handled. He sat quietly on the nest-box while I placed it on the floor. After remaining on the floor a few minutes he walked off from the nest and flew up to the empty box which had previously contained the nest-box; he went into this box and sat down as if covering the young. I repeated the same experiment several times on this and the following day, and he behaved each time in the same way. The female on two occasions, seeing the young left uncovered, took her place on the nest, although the nest was on the floor and not in its usual place. In the case of the male it is evident that the *habit* of sitting in a box 3 feet above the floor of the coop, at a fixed elevation and position, had become so firmly established during the two preceding weeks of incubation that he felt that he was in the wrong place. He takes and feels contented in *the place to which he was accustomed*, notwithstanding that the nest and young have been removed. The nest-box and young do not satisfy him, except in their usual place.[1] He leaves them without any signs of hesitation, unless the few moments of delay be such. He is apparently *quite blind* to the purpose of his instinct of brooding. The *habit of place* is stronger than the stimuli supplied by nest and young. He would probably leave them to die of cold and hunger. The female in this case displays a higher power of adaptation—a better appreciation of the needs.

On Apr. 28, at $2^h 30^m$ p.m., I fed the female on the floor of the coop; the male, seeing this, left the young and came down to eat. While he was eating I again placed the nest-box on the floor. After a minute or two he turned around, looked at the box with young, and then flew up to the empty box; not finding his young, he turned right-about-face, as if to leave the box, but soon decided to remain, and went in and sat down as if all was right. Meanwhile the female went to the young on the floor and fed them both at once. She certainly understands her business better than the male. But it is also evident that *the male is conscious of not finding the young as he expected to do*, for his turning around as if to leave the box shows that.

On the following morning, at 9 o'clock, after the male had taken the nest, I again raised the nest-box out of the containing-box, holding it a minute or two at the level of the latter; then I lowered it half way to the floor, held it there for about 3 minutes, and then placed it on the floor. The male sat on as if he would remain, but after 5 minutes he got off to attack a male in the adjoining coop, ate a little and drank; he then went up to the

---

[1] Numerous other instances of memory for "position" are given in the chapter on the Homing Instinct.—EDITOR.

152 BEHAVIOR OF PIGEONS.

empty box and quietly sat down as if all was right. At 9ʰ 39ᵐ I took him from the box and placed him on the nest-box. He felt the young and finally covered them, but not without looking up once, as if in doubt whether he should not return to the old place. He settled down, however, and remained. I left the nest-box on the floor overnight, the female remaining contentedly. The next morning, at his usual time to take the nest, the male went to the nest-box while it was still on the floor. He has now become *habituated* to finding his nest on the floor of the coop.

(2) The above experiment was partially repeated with a pair consisting of a white-ring male and a blond-ring female. I took the nest-box from the containing-box and placed it on the floor of the coop. The nest contained one young about 1½ days old. The female soon left the nest and flew back to the empty box, which, in this case, was about 2 feet above the floor. She saw that the young and nest were not there, and immediately returned to the floor and went on the nest. Although she was not satisfied with the nest on the floor, she recognized it and did not blindly desert it to sit in the habitual place. Here intelligence, instinct, and habit all come into play. There is *the instinct to sit on the nest and young, the habit of place, and the intelligence which is sufficient to correct habit.*

(3) I have a black tumbler (common pigeon), which I imported from Japan, mated with a blond ring-dove. These doves have eggs on which they have sat about a week. They are kept in a pen outside of the house. The nest-box is about 10 inches square and 2 inches deep. Wanting to bring the birds into the house to protect them from the cold, and knowing that the female would perhaps desert the nest, I took the precaution to change the egg to a smaller box (one about 8 by 5 inches) which would go into the door of a small wire cage. It was about 4 p.m. when I put the egg in the new box and the new box into the old one. Its surroundings were therefore the same as before, but the box was narrower and deeper (about 4 inches deep). The female, although she noticed the egg and got into the nest, refused to cover it and soon came out, apparently feeling nonplussed. I then returned the egg to the old nest-box, taking away the new one, and she at once went on the nest and covered the egg. After 10 minutes or so I again repeated the experiment with the new box and with like result. Again giving her the old nest-box and egg, she was contented and sat. After 15 minutes I again changed her to the new box. She did not like the new place, jumped several times to the edge of the box, but returned, and examined the nest as if strongly doubting that it was her own. After some time in sitting, turning around, and getting up, she at length decided to occupy the box. Had I brought it into the house or removed it from its place she would have deserted it. At 10 o'clock that night I brought her and her mate inside, keeping them in the dark all night.

The next morning the female came off the nest and remained off, and the male did not take his place. At 10 a.m. I placed the new nest out of doors in the old pen and she went on with hesitation and perplexity, after looking and examining to see if it was really her nest. There is evident, in this female, a mental activity of a very low order. She recognizes the *difference* between her nest and the one offered her, and, although she wants to sit, she declines to do so except on her own nest, and she is only brought to it by sitting overnight on the new nest when she has no sight to disturb her confidence. She *remembers* her old nest in the morning after it was removed, as she still behaves as if puzzled to know what to do, and as if wanting to find what she had known as her nest. ·

On the following night, after dark, the female was found off the nest and the male was on; I then returned the old nest-box again, and strange to say, the female felt it at once to be her nest and took her place over the egg! Several times I tried to get her to cover the egg in the new box, but she could not be induced to do so, and I therefore left her in the old box. As a result of my experiments and the cold weather the female finally deserted the nest.

HABIT, INSTINCT, AND INTELLIGENCE.

153

(4) The female of "pair D" was true to the impulse to sit, but having sat for a short time in an empty box, she felt impelled to repeat the action in the *same place*. The presence of the eggs was of no account to her, and "seeing" them or "feeling" them did not call the bird to her proper business. Even the sight of her sister on the nest, and her departure, had no effect in preventing her from returning to the place she had adopted. She persisted during all of the second day (and the record[1] will show what followed later) in sitting in the empty box after having been driven away many times, and after the box had been covered.

(5) A male ring-dove mated with a common dove had been kept in a cage for 3 or 4 weeks. On opening the door to let them into a pen the female soon walked out; then the male, anxious to follow, started to go through the door, but in passing halted and held his head back with manifest fear of striking it against the wire, which was not there. The head was held back and turned at right angles to the body with just the motions the bird would make to avoid hitting the wire. The bird had become accustomed to avoiding hitting the wire, and acted, *not from a sense of sight nor from feeling*, or any other *external stimulus*, but from memory. It expected to meet the wire where it had always found it before. Such action does not imply that the sense of sight is not used, but that the bird did not act on a sight stimulus, since it has a contrary internal stimulus. When a door is opened the bird usually behaves, in the course of a longer or shorter time, as if it noticed it, but it only gradually comes to trying to pass.

(6) The return of the parents to the nest, to call the young back for feeding after they have wandered out, seems to be by *force of habit* rather than by instinct. From the outset the young have been fed in the nest and the parent comes to associate the nest with feeding, and hence keeps up the habit some time after the young have learned to walk about on the floor of the coop.

(7) Some pigeons show a peculiar tenacity to hold their first chosen spot for roosting. They insist on the identical spot, and sit in the same direction, often fighting for it as for life. It is remarkable how persistently a dove seeks to gain the place it has once roosted on, often taking precisely the same position with the head directed one way. If turned around they immediately resume the old position. If one of a pair has had the right end of the perch, and his mate happens to get this first, then both are *uneasy* and appear to feel that something is wrong. They often work some time to exchange places, and then they settle down contentedly. I have seen the birds of many caged pairs take up precisely the same position and direction night after night. If a position is changed one night, it is usually repeated the next.

(8) A young homer flew from the nest out into the yard and the male parent accompanied it. It was captured and returned. The father seemed to be anxiously looking for the young after I captured it and removed it from his sight. He flew back several times to where he *last* saw the young sitting, and then went to other windows, as if searching for it.

(9) The young of pigeons and doves usually turn so as to sit with the head pointing backward under the parent. This position is the one almost invariably taken by young passengers, ring-doves, crested pigeons, and domestic doves.

(10) A female ring-dove had a rather poor nest and one of her eggs got separated a little from the other; it was lying just outside the space covered by the bird, but quite near enough to be touched by the bird's feathers. She did not even try to cover it, and I found it still outside on the next day. It finally got several inches away, never receiving any attention. A second occurrence of the same kind was noted some time later. (R 17, R 7.)

---

[1] These experiments with pair D are described in detail in Chapter III, under the topic "Pairing of Two Females."—EDITOR.

154 BEHAVIOR OF PIGEONS.

RECOGNITION OF INDIVIDUALS.

Old birds distinguish their own young from other young and from adults in wild species, where marking, color, size, etc., are so nearly alike that we can not distinguish individuals. Birds are able to distinguish their own mates instantly. I think, too, that the parents remember and recognize their young, but not as offspring. They have no more interest in them than they have in any other bird. They seem to know them; they remember things of that sort. They remember individual birds. Every bird in a flock remembers every other bird, but I do not think they know any particular birds as their own offspring.

A young *Geopelia humeralis*, 7 weeks old, had been separated from its mate soon after hatching and placed under the care of ring-doves. Later I brought the two together. The one that had been under the care of ring-doves was terrified at the sight of his own mate, raised his wings, and bristled up for defense. This was toward night. I left the two together in a pen by themselves. The next morning, the two still kept apart, or rather the one brought up under its parents seemed not to have much fear of the other, but the latter continued to have equally great fear. This shows two things: the one brought up under its parents, familiar with its own species, saw no cause for alarm in its mate; but the latter, familiar with ring-doves, recognized its own mate—the same species— as a "stranger" and as an "enemy." These two birds finally got acquainted, when kept by themselves in the same cage, and now after 4 days together they roost together, side by side.

Two pairs of young common pigeons, each pair about 4 weeks old, were reared in nest-boxes on the floor of two adjoining pens in my library; they were reared within 3 to 6 inches of each other, being separated only by a coarse wire netting. Here these two pairs could see each other plainly and were therefore not strangers by sight. To-day I put both pairs together, removing the old birds from the pen in which they were placed.

They did not at first appear quarrelsome at all, and I supposed they were to get on kindly together. But when night came one pair got into a nest-box about 8 feet above the floor and refused to allow the other pair to sit with them. The pair that were masters were very cordial to each other, fondling each others' head, etc., and never making the mistake of attacking each other while battling off the others—a mistake easy to make when four doves are contending for a place less than a foot square. One pair was driven out and, when I put them back, they were hustled out more quickly than before. I then gave them a perch below the box, and here they sat close beside each other, while the victors sat above them. The next night the victors took the place they had won and the conquered took the lower seat. The matter was settled; each knew its place. The mates of each pair were fond of each other, but the two pairs did not like each other.

Sitting side by side in the same box, the mates had evidently acquired a *filial affection for each other*, and they felt differently towards the other pair and always kept up the distinction. Here is *recognition* of partners, *love*; recognition of *non-partners, aversion*; the *union* of the pair owning the roost against the *newcomers*; and *submission* to the results of victory as final on the part of the conquered. Is that not human? Is such behavior conceivable without some intelligence?

That ring-doves remember and recognize each other after a period of separation was illustrated in the case of the two females of "pair *D*".[1] I separated these females, giving the larger one as a mate to a white-ring male and putting the other in a cage alone and out of the sight of the first. Nine days after the separation I brought the caged female back to her sister, who was sitting quietly on her eggs. As soon as the dove from the cage saw the sister on the nest she at once gave a laugh of joy and recognition. She flew to the nest, but was repelled by her sister, who was taken by surprise. But after a moment

---

[1] The complete record is given in Chapter III, under the heading "The Pairing of Two Females."—EDITOR.

HABIT, INSTINCT, AND INTELLIGENCE. 155

the dove left her eggs, went to the perch, and was at once solicited to act as a male, which she did. There can be no question that this extraordinary conduct meant the fullest recognition on the part of both doves and a memory of their former relations. 26 days later I brought the same female (*D 2*) from the coop behind the house to her sister (*D 1*) in the house. *D 2* seemed to behave as if she still remembered the place and recognized her sister mate, but the latter gave no certain indication of recognition. She soon flew at *D 2* and treated her as an intruder to be driven off as speedily as possible.

Two wild mourning-doves (*Zenaidura*) were captured when 14 to 16 days old. The smaller of the two was placed under the female of pair (*G*) of ring-doves, whose young were 1 week old. Here it passed the night. This bird was about the size of the ring-dove young, but was more feathered and much darker in plumage. When the old birds attempted to feed their young the next day they viewed the new-comer with suspicion and alarm, while it exhibited fear of them. It was then placed with another pair (*C*) of ring-doves, whose young were but 2 days old. At the time of feeding I placed this young in position to feed and the mother fed it abundantly.

The larger of the two young mourning-doves was placed in the pen with the ring-doves, "pair *C*," and both birds exhibited fear. It was then placed in the nest at the time of feeding. Both birds fed it and made no objection to its further presence in the nest. Later this young bird jumped out of the nest onto the floor and the old male then attacked it several times. The bird was then placed with "pair *G*," who fed it when it was introduced into the nest at the time of feeding, but manifested hostility as soon as the feeding was finished, although the bird remained in the nest. This young bird also reacted with a show of hostility to both pairs of these ring-doves, although it eagerly accepted food from them. This manifestation of hostility usually occurred when the foster-parents returned to the nest after a short absence. After 17 days the old birds and the young became accustomed to each other. All signs of fear and hostility disappeared and normal relations were established.

There is evidently some difference between pairs in their capacity to distinguish their own offspring from foreigners. "Pair *C*" was able to distinguish out of the nest but made no distinction within the nest. There is some degree of species reaction, but this can be modified in the course of a few weeks.

A hybrid from a common dove and a Japanese turtle-dove was in a cage containing several other young, among which was a crested pigeon. The hybrid and the crested pigeon sit side by side, fondling each others' head most affectionately; but the hybrid refuses to allow either of the other two birds to come near him. If they approach he attacks with his beak vigorously and they retreat to the perch. It may be that this affection is due to his having had a crested pigeon for a foster-mother. I am more inclined to think so, as this hybrid (and all others from the same parents) is rather quarrelsome and little inclined to make friends with strangers.

A pair of young *Spilopelia tigrina*[1] were placed, at the age of 6 weeks, in a pen with numerous other doves (geopelia, green-wing, white-wing, ring-dove, and two hybrids). They were placed in a nest-box on the right side of the pen and about 2 feet above the floor. They snuggled down here, in preference to sleeping on the edge of the box, so as to keep warm. I placed with them a young hybrid from the common dove and Japanese turtle-dove, which was a cripple in one leg. All three made friends and slept together. Ever after these same birds have invariably sought this same nest-box at night, and to-night they are together *inside the box*. The young *tigrina* know their hybrid companion, and he knows them, and all three of them will attack the other hybrids or the ring-doves, if the latter try to roost on their box. Sometimes the hybrid companion attacks the two

---

[1] It is possible that these young were *Spil. suratensis*.—EDITOR.

156 BEHAVIOR OF PIGEONS.

tigrina; these have learned never to resist him, but simply hang their heads and keep still until he stops, which he does after a peck or two. These tiger turtle-doves thus seem: (1) to distinguish between a warm and a cooler place; (2) to distinguish companions from other associates; (3) to know when it is safe to attack and when not. All this points to considerable intelligence. (R 7, SS 10, R 9.)

IMITATION.

It is wonderful how much and how quickly doves learn by imitation. The first young of a pair of ring-doves were placed on the floor of the cage very early and were walking about at the age of 2 weeks. These little fellows had seen their parents "jump" at doves in adjoining cages, on either side, whenever those doves came near and attempted to put their heads through the holes of the wire net. Likewise, these young, before they could walk properly, would perform the same jump and drive away outsiders. It was most amusing to watch them.

My dwarf pigeons (smaller geopelia) for a long time utterly refused to take any notice of bread crumbs. I let them go hungry for a while and then fed them only fine crumbs of bread. One of them tried a bit, tested it several times, and finally swallowed it; then he took several more pieces, and finally decided that it was good. Another one, seeing him pick up the crumbs, *put his head close down to him and looked at him* as he took in the bread, and then tried it himself; and so it went until all learned, and in a day or two they would all eat bread with avidity. If one bird is let out of the cage into my room the other dwarfs see this and at once become very uneasy and try hard to get out also. At 2 weeks of age, the first or second day after the young get out of the nest, they usually learn to pick up seed and bread crumbs if these are placed near them; but they are almost invariably, if not always, led to do this by seeing the parents eat. The parental example is the guiding stimulus.

It is very amusing to see young just out of the nest for the first time undertake police duty, which they do by imitation. One of a pair of young ring-doves, for example, out of the nest yesterday, exhibited himself to-day as a most valiant defender of the camp. He would drop his head a little, look a moment at the intruders from another pen as they put their heads through the wire netting to steal seed; then he would "jump" in the most approved fashion, and rush at them with such an air of authority as to frighten them off. This fellow kept up this exhibition for some 10 minutes, and seemed to enjoy the business. It tried the same method on its own brother and sister, who were a month or so older, and several times jumped so vigorously as to land on the back of the dove aimed at. The parents had been seen to do this often, and no doubt the little fellow was doing what he had seen and remembered. I noticed that it did not try to drive its parents, but when they came around it began to tease them for food.

It is a curious fact that when a dove sees its mate feeding the young it is often moved by sympathy to go through the motions of feeding. This may very often be seen in ring-doves. Moreover, when one dove sees another eating it is often thereby stimulated to go and eat also. The same is true with the act of bathing or sunning. If one young dove begins to play, by flapping its wings and skipping, the others are apt to be incited to join in. Old birds often manifest sympathy if they see their young act as if suffering, or if their young are handled roughly. The cry of terror sets every dove within hearing on edge. (R 17.)

EFFECTS OF EXPERIENCE.

Indisputable evidence of *memory* is shown by pigeons when they forsake a roosting-place which has been found to be liable to danger from cats, men, or other enemies. Pigeons are very constant to their chosen roosting-places, but when once molested in these they do not forget it the next night. Handle a pigeon roughly and it becomes wild; *it remembers that you are dangerous, and tries to keep out of reach.*

HABIT, INSTINCT, AND INTELLIGENCE.   157

In the young dove an act once done seems indelibly stamped into the organization. An interesting illustration recently came under my observation. From seeing the parents eat, one of the first young of a pair of ring-doves had, at about 2 weeks of age, *just learned to pick up little bits of bread*. The movements of the mandibles consisted, of course, of first *opening* and then *closing*. This movement was learned. I presented a dish of water to the bird and it put its beak into it and finding it to be something it wanted, it *tried to drink*. But instead of keeping its beak in the water and drinking continuously as the old ones do, it opened its beak and then closed it, *just exactly as if picking up a piece of bread*, and then lifting its beak out of the water, it raised its head as if to let the water run down its throat as a hen does. This curious behavior occurred several times over, just after the bird had, *for the first time*, picked up crumbs of bread. The act of picking—opening and closing the beak—had already become impressed on the creature so strongly that for the time it determined the *method of drinking*, though the acquired method was *quite unlike the normal*. The next day this bird had learned to drink like its parents.

A young bird, about 4 weeks old, was once taken into the house for hand-care, as the parents did not appear to be feeding it sufficiently. This bird, though unable to fly, learned in a few minutes to pick up seed while with its parents on the ground of the pen. The interesting point is that after being removed from the parents, and while alone and picking up seed for itself, it keeps up squealing and frequent wagging of its wings, as it does when teasing the old birds to feed it. These acts have been so long coördinated with feeding that by force of habit—after the use is passed—the bird continues them.

When adult pigeons (5 to 6 months old) are first turned loose in the open, after having always been kept in a pen, it is curious to see how awkward they are about flying. If they fly up on the roof of a three-story house and then want to get back they look over the roof-edge and seem to shrink from the attempt, as a person would shrink from jumping at a great height. If they get up the courage to try it, after seeing another bird do it, they invariably fly off on the horizontal or near it, not having yet learned to throw themselves downward fearlessly. After they have *learned* that they can do it and not fall or get harmed, they dive down gracefully in perfect confidence.

The relation of lack of experience to the matter of flying in young pigeons is illustrated in the following case: A young homer hybrid, about 5 weeks old, flew for the first time from his cot-opening to a distance of about 25 feet—across to the railing on the back stairs of an adjoining house. The male parent accompanied it. I went up these stairs and, approaching it slowly, keeping one hand in front of it and the other behind it, easily captured it. Why did it not fly before I cornered it? Evidently because it did not feel sure on the wing, and therefore hesitated until I had time to intercept its chances of escape. It had not been handled, and surely wished to escape; and had not my hands been in its way it probably would have flown. The young dove, then, stands like a child, unacquainted with the world and *inexperienced* in the use of its powers. It hesitates to fly from fear and from lack of knowing where it can go for safety.

Doves learn, and learn quickly, to measure their chances against different competitors. For example:

(1) A large dove will generally refuse to budge for a smaller one. The sense of strength is felt by the larger bird. With young birds the case is different, for all young birds are submissive and non-resistant.

(2) The victor often follows up his victory, becomes more domineering, more encroachful. Power is learned by experience.

(3) Some small birds show their superiority by imposing on larger birds; *e.g.*, the case (given elsewhere) of some small geopelias and the large white-faced pigeon. Again, the common mourning-dove is often quite keen in frightening off other doves by sudden jumps or flirts of the wings.

158 BEHAVIOR OF PIGEONS.

(4) A common pigeon mated with a small ring-dove shows great care in mounting its mate, apparently fearing to injure or treat it roughly.

(5) A male dove, when it sees another male in the act of soliciting or mounting its mate, appears to understand instantly what the purpose is, and often makes frantic efforts to intercept this act, giving the danger signal in the loudest and most excited form and flying directly at the offending bird.

An archangel brings straws from the yard and, in reaching his nest, goes in at a door B, which is kept open, and then jumps off the partition C to get to the nest. The first egg was already laid; the door B had been open during all the time of preparing the nest, but the door A, which led directly to the nest, was kept closed. He had learned the indirect way completely. I opened A while he was off after a straw; when he returned he went through A, taking the direct way rather than the indirect. He did this the first time the opportunity was presented, and repeated the same the second time. The third time he entered at B, apparently from habit and not noticing that A was open.

Obedience to impulse, or dependence upon it at all times, conduces to its power; *i. e.*, yielding to its promptings makes its promptings absolute master. These promptings are the voice of instincts. Perhaps the extraordinary *keenness of the sense-organs* is due largely to the *obedient attention given to their messages*. Obedience is practically complete; the connection between ingoing message and outgoing response becomes strong and inviolable. The instinctive act follows the signal given. The signals are literally watched for and the acts are fitted to them. If we continually listened to and depended upon our instincts, they would soon control and exclude judgment or reason. If we followed our senses as animals do we should have keener senses. (R 7, R 17.)

INSTINCT AND INTELLIGENCE.

In order to see how instinctive action may graduate into intelligent action it is well to study closely animals in which the instincts have attained a high degree of complexity and in which there can be no doubt about the automatic character of the activities. These conditions are perfectly fulfilled in the pigeons, a group in which we have the further advantage that wild and domestic species can be studied comparatively.

It is quite certain that pigeons are totally blind to the meanings which we discover in incubation. They follow the impulse to sit without a thought of consequences; and no matter how many times the act has been performed, no idea of young pigeons ever enters into the act.[1] They sit because they feel like it, begin when they feel impelled to do so, and stop when the feeling is satisfied. Their time is generally correct, but they measure it as blindly as a child measures its hours of sleep. A bird that sits after failing to lay an egg, or after its eggs have been removed, is not acting from "expectation," but because she finds it agreeable to do so and disagreeable not to do so. The same holds true of the feeding instinct. The young are not fed from any desire to do them any good, but solely for the relief of the parent. The evidence on this point can not be given here,[2] but I believe it is conclusive.

But if all this be true, where does the graduation towards intelligence manifest itself? Certainly not in a comprehension of utilities which are discoverable only by human intelligence. Whatever the pigeon instinct-mind contains, it is safe to say that the intelligence is hardly more than a grain hidden in bushels of instinct, and one may search more than a day and not find it.

---

[1] Professor James (Psychology, II, p. 390) thinks such an idea may arise and that it may encourage the bird to sit. "*Every instinctive act in an animal with memory,*" says James, "*must cease to be 'blind' after being once repeated.*" That must depend on the kind of memory the animal has. It is possible to have memory of a certain kind in some things, while having absolutely none of any kind on other things. That is the case in pigeons, as I feel very sure.

[2] See Chapter VI.—EDITOR.

HABIT, INSTINCT, AND INTELLIGENCE.

EXPERIMENT WITH PIGEONS.

Among many tests, take the simple one of removing the eggs to one side of the nest, leaving them in full sight and within a few inches of the bird on the nest. The bird sees the uncovered eggs, but shows no interest in them; she keeps her position, if she is a tame bird, and after some moments begins to act as if the current of her feelings had been slightly disturbed. At the most she only acts as if a little puzzled, as if she realized dimly a change in feeling. She is accustomed to the eggs and now misses something, she knows not what. Although she does not know or show any care for the eggs out of the nest, she does appear to sense a difference between having and not having.

There is, then, something akin to memory and discrimination, and little as this implies, it can not mean less than some faint adumbration of intelligence. Now this inkling of intelligence, or, if you prefer, this nadir of stupidity, so remote from the zenith of intelligence, is not something independent of and foreign to instinct. It is instinct itself just moved by a ripple of change in the environment. The usual adjustment is slightly disturbed, and a little confusion in the currents of feeling arises which manifests itself in quasi-mental perplexity. That is about as near as I can get to the contents of the pigeon mind without being able, by a sort of metempsychosis suggested by Bonnet, to live some time in the head of the bird.

In this feeble perplexity of the pigeon's instinct-mind, in this "nethermost abyss" of stupidity, there is a glimmer of light, and nature's least is always suggestive of more. The pigeon has no hope of graduating into a *homo sapiens*, but her little light may flicker a little higher, and all we need to know is, how instinct behavior can take one step toward mind behavior. This is the dark point on which I have nothing really new to offer, although I hope not to make it darker.

THE STEP FROM INSTINCT TO INTELLIGENCE.

Some notion of what is involved in the step may be gathered by comparing wild with semi-domesticated and fully domesticated species. These grades differ from each other in respects that are highly suggestive. In the wild species the instincts are kept up to the higher degrees of rigid invariability, while in species under domestication they are reduced to various degrees of flexibility, and there is a correspondingly greater freedom of action, with, of course, greater liability to irregularities and so-called "faults." These faults of instinct, so far from indicating physical retrogression, are, I believe, the first signs of greater plasticity in the congenital coördinations and, consequently, of greater facility in forming those new combinations implied in choice of action.

If we place the three grades of pigeons under the same conditions and test each in turn in precisely the same way, we can best see how domestication lets down the bars to choice and at the same time gives more opportunities for free action. The simplest experiment is always the best. Let us take three species at the time of incubation and repeat with each the experiment of removing the eggs to a distance of 2 inches outside the edge of the nest. The three grades are well represented in the wild passenger-pigeon (*Ectopistes*), the little ring-dove (*Streptopelia risoria*), and the common dove-cote pigeon (*Columba livia domestica*). The results will not, of course, always be the same, but the average will be about as follows:

(1) *The passenger-pigeon.*—The passenger-pigeon leaves the nest when approached, but returns soon after you leave. On returning she looks at the nest, steps into it, and sits down as if nothing had happened. She soon finds out, not by sight, but by feeling, that something is missing. Her instinct is keenly attuned and she acts quite promptly, leaving the nest after a few minutes without heeding the egg. The conduct varies relatively little in different individuals.

(2) *The ring-dove.*—The ring-dove is tame and sits on while you remove the eggs. After a few moments she moves a little and perhaps puts her head down, as if to feel the missing

160 BEHAVIOR OF PIGEONS.

eggs with her beak. Then she may glance at the eggs and appear as if half consciously recognizing them, but makes no move to replace them, and after 10 to 20 minutes or more leaves the nest with a contented air, as if her duty were done; or, she may stretch her neck toward the eggs and try to roll one back into the nest. If she succeeds in recovering *one* she is satisfied and again sinks into her usual restful state, with no further concern for the second egg. The conduct varies considerably with different individuals.

(3) *The dove-cote pigeon*—The dove-cote pigeon behaves in a similar way, but will generally try to get *both* eggs back and, failing in this, she resigns the nest with more hesitation than does the ring-dove.

(4) *Results considered*—The passenger-pigeon's instinct is wound up to a high point of uniformity and promptness, and her conduct is almost too blindly regular to be credited even with that stupidity which implies a grain of intelligence. The ring-dove's stupidity is satisfied with one egg. The dove-cote pigeon's stupidity may claim both eggs, but it is not always up to that mark.

In these three grades the advance is from extreme blind uniformity of action, with little or no choice, to a stage of less rigid uniformity, with the least bit of perplexity and a very feeble, uncertain, dreamy sense of sameness between eggs *in* and eggs *out* of the nest, which prompts the action of rolling the eggs back into the nest. That is the instinctive way of placing the eggs when in the nest, and the neck is only a little further extended in drawing the eggs in from the outside. How very narrow is the difference between the ordinary and the extraordinary act! How little does the pendulum of normal action have to swing beyond its usual limit![1]

But this little is in a forward direction, and we are in no doubt as to the general character of the changes and the modifying influences through which it has been made possible. Under conditions of domestication the action of natural selection has been relaxed, with the result that the rigor of instinctive coördinations which bars alternative action is more or less reduced. Not only is the door to choice thus unlocked, but more varied opportunities and provocations arise, and thus the internal mechanism and the external conditions and stimuli work both in the same direction to favor greater freedom of action.

When choice thus enters no new factor is introduced. There is greater plasticity within and more provocation without, and hence the same bird, without the addition or loss of a single nerve-cell, becomes capable of higher action and is encouraged and even constrained by circumstances to *learn* to use its privilege of choice.

Choice, as I conceive, is not introduced as a little deity, encapsuled in the brain. Instinct has supplied the teleological mechanism, and stimulus must continue to set it in motion. But increased plasticity invites greater interaction of stimuli and gives more even chances for conflicting impulses. Choice runs on blindly at first, and ceases to be blind only in proportion as the animal learns through nature's system of compulsory education. The teleological alternatives are organically provided; one is taken and fails to give satisfaction; another is tried and gives contentment. This little freedom is the dawning grace of a new dispensation, in which education by experience comes in as an amelioration of the law of elimination. This slight amenability to natural educational influences can not, of course, work any great miracles of transformation in a pigeon's brain; but it shows the way to the open door of a freer commerce with the eternal world, through which a brain with richer instinctive endowments might rise to higher achievement.

---

[1] We come to equally surprising results in many different ways. Change the position of the nest box of the ring-dove, without otherwise disturbing bird, nest, or contents, and the birds will have great difficulty in recognizing their nest, for they know it only as something in a definite position in a fixed environment. If a pair of these birds have a nest in a cage, and the cage be moved from one room to another, or even a few feet from its original position in the same room, the nest ceases to be the same thing to them, and they walk over the eggs or young as if completely devoid of any acquaintance with or interest in them. Return the cage to its original place and the birds know the nest and return to it at once.

HABIT, INSTINCT, AND INTELLIGENCE. 161

The conditions of amelioration under domestication do not differ in kind from those presented in nature. Domestication merely bunches nature's opportunities and thus concentrates results in forms accessible to observation. Natural conditions are certainly working in the same direction, only more slowly. The direction and the method of progress must, in the nature of things, remain essentially the same.

Nature works to the same ends as intelligence, and to the natural course of events I should look for just such results as Lloyd Morgan[1] so clearly pictures and ascribes to intelligence: He says

"Suppose the modifications are of various kinds and in various directions, and that, associated with the instinctive activity, a tendency to modify it *indefinitely* be inherited. Under such circumstances *intelligence would have a tendency to break up and render plastic a previously stereotyped instinct;* for the instinctive character of the activities is maintained through the constancy and uniformity of their performance. But if the normal activities were thus caused to vary in different directions in different individuals, the offspring arising from the union of these differing individuals would be imperfect, and there would be an inherited tendency to vary. *And this, if continued, would tend to convert what had been a stereotyped instinct into innate capacity; that is, a general tendency to certain activities (mental or bodily), the exact form and direction of which are not fixed, until by training, from imitation or through the guidance of individual intelligence, it became habitual. Thus it may be that it has come about that man, with his enormous store of innate capacity, has so small a number of stereotyped instincts.*"

The following from Professor James[2] is suggestive:

"Nature implants contrary impulses to act on many classes of things, and leaves it to slight alterations in the conditions of the individual case to decide which impulse shall carry the day. Thus, greediness and suspicion, curiosity and timidity, coyness and desire, bashfulness and vanity, sociability and pugnacity seem to shoot over into each other as quickly, and to remain in as unstable equilibrium, in the higher birds and mammals as in man. They are all impulses, congenital, blind at first, and productive of motor reactions of a rigorously determinate sort. Each one of them, then, is an instinct, as instinct is commonly defined. *But they contradict each other; experience, in each particular opportunity of application, usually deciding the issue. The animal that exhibits them loses the "instinctive" demeanor and appears to lead a life of hesitation and choice, an intellectual life; not, however, because he has no instincts—rather because he has so many that they block each other's path.*"

Looking only to the more salient points of direction and method in nature's advance towards intelligence, the general course of events may be briefly adumbrated. Organic mechanisms capable of doing teleological work through blindly determined adjustments, reproduced congenitally and carried to various degrees of complexity and inflexibility of action, were first evolved. With the organization of instinctive propensities, liable to antagonistic stimulation, came both the possibility and the provocation to choice. In the absence of intelligent motive, choice would stand for the outcome of conflicting impulses. The power of blind choice could be transmitted, and that is what man himself begins with.

Superiority in instinct endowments and concurring advantages of environment would tend to liberate the possessors from the severities of natural selection; and thus nature, like domestication, would furnish conditions inviting to greater freedom of action, and with the same result, namely, that the instincts would become more plastic and tractable. Plasticity of instinct is not intelligence, but it is the open door through which the great educator, experience, comes in and works every wonder of intelligence.

Spencer[3] has shown clearly that this plasticity must inevitably result from the progressive complication of the instincts. He says:

That progressive complication of the instincts which, as we have found, involves a progressive diminution of their purely automatic character, likewise involves a simultaneous commencement of memory and reason.

---

[1] Animal Life and Intelligence, pp. 452, 453.   [2] Psychology, II, pp. 392, 393.   [3] Psychology, I, pp. 443 and 454, 455.

Made in the USA
Coppell, TX
23 October 2022

85193495R00103